BEST of the BEST
from
OHIO

Selected Recipes from Ohio's
FAVORITE COOKBOOKS

BEST of the BEST
from
OHIO

Selected Recipes from Ohio's
FAVORITE COOKBOOKS

Edited by
GWEN MCKEE
and
Barbara Moseley

Illustrated by Tupper England

QUAIL RIDGE PRESS

Library of Congress Cataloging-in-Publication Data

Best of the best from Ohio: selected recipes from Ohio's favorite
cookbooks / edited by Gwen McKee and Barbara Moseley;
illustrated by Tupper England.
    p. cm.
    Includes index.
    ISBN 0-937552-68-2
    1. Cookery. 2. Cookery--Ohio.   I. McKee, Gwen.
II. Moseley, Barbara.
TX714.B446   1996
641.59771--dc20   96-33095
                                                    CIP

First printing, September 1996 • Second, November 1997
Third, September 1998 • Fourth, September 2000 • Fifth, July 2001
Sixth, November 2002 • Seventh, September 2004

Manufactured in the United States of America.

Cover photo: Shawnee State Park golf course, West Portsmouth,
courtesy of Ohio Department of Tourism.

Chapter opening photos courtesy of Ohio Department of Tourism, Warren County
Convention & Visitors Bureau, Dan Feicht, Erie County Visitors & Convention Bureau,
Greater Cincinnati Convention & Visitors Bureau, Greater Logan County Area Convention &
Tourist Bureau, Youngstown/Mahoning County Convention & Visitors Bureau,
Canton/Stark County Convention & Visitors Bureau.

QUAIL RIDGE PRESS • 1-800-343-1583
P. O. Box 123 • Brandon, MS 39043
info@quailridge.com • www.quailridge.com

The Santa Maria is a full-scale replica of Christopher Columbus' famous flagship. Columbus.

CONTENTS

PREFACE

Ohio...The Gateway to the Midwest.... From the beginning, Ohio has been both urban and rural, and remains so to this day. Major cities, small towns, industries, mountains, cliffs, waterfalls, caves, beautiful lakes and rolling fields all make up the land known as "The Buckeye State." We are told that Ohio was settled primarily by New Englanders who came to live and till the soil and fish the waters in Northern Ohio. Soon thereafter the Hungarians, Polish, Czechs, Germans, Swiss, and Italians came and formed their own communities throughout the state, all bringing their proven recipes for sauerkraut, pork, tomatoes, potatoes, breads, fish, wine, beer... from fancy to homemade fare, the food has always been fabulous!

Ohio can be proud of the achievements of her native sons and daughters: Ohio has given the nation more Presidents than any other state; Harriet Beecher Stowe drew from stories of escaped slaves to pen her famous *Uncle Tom's Cabin;* Annie Oakley learned to shoot in the woods of Darke County; Jack Nicklaus learned to play a "fair game of golf" in Columbus; and the list goes on and on.

Ohio can also be proud of her culinary achievements; making the use of what's at hand has never been accomplished more deliciously. The likes of Sweet and Sauerkraut, Apple-Pumpkin Streusel Muffins, Pork Roast with Mustard Sauce and Honey Apples, or Chocolate Raspberry Torte, and of course Buckeyes, all set the table in the kitchens of Ohio's finest "home chefs." We are delighted to present for your enjoyment some of the most popular recipes available from favorite Ohio cookbooks. These recipes give insight to the homelife and eating style of the fine cooks throughout the state. The book includes recipes handed down for generations, as well as new fat-free, diabetic, herbs and spices recipes, and some geared toward children, seniors, mothers of twins, and "real men." The contributing cookbooks come from a variety of service organizations, churches, families, restaurants, and very talented individuals. Something for everyone must surely be the cook's motto in the Buckeye State.

We want to say thank you to all these wonderful Ohio cooks who created and cooked and gratiously shared their recipes; and that includes all the authors, editors, chairpersons, and publishers for their cooperation in making this book possible. Their books may be ordered directly from them by using the catalog listing that begins on page 319. Also we wish to say a special thanks to our office staff: to Sheila and Annette, who have dug deep and constant to help us find these ninety-one contributing cookbooks and photographs and fascinating Ohio facts; to Shawn whose new and innovative ideas, as well as wizardry with the computer, keep us jumping; and, to Madonna who fills in any and everywhere she is needed. Tupper England always comes up with the perfect illustrations to accompany the recipes and reflect the essence of the state. Thanks to all the chambers of commerce, tourist and convention offices, and food editors across the state who have helped us with this great undertaking. And as always, we beg forgiveness from any cookbook that might have been inadvertently overlooked.

Reading, sampling, and collecting cookbooks is pure enjoyment to so many people; we appreciate the input these people give us in our quest to find the "best" recipes available. Hearing from our "Best" friends is always a happy experience. We hope this collection of recipes from Ohio's finest cookbooks will find a special place on your cookbook shelf.

Enjoy, as we did, exploring Ohio through her culinary highways.

Gwen McKee and Barbara Moseley

Contributing Cookbooks

Affolter Heritage Reunion Cookbook and More...
The Amish Way Cookbook
Angels and Friends Favorite Recipes I
Angels and Friends Favorite Recipes I I
Appletizers
Aren't You Going to Taste It, Honey?
Best Recipes of Ohio Inns and Restaurant
Bountiful Ohio
By Our Cookstove
Cincinnati Recipe Treasury: The Queen City's Culinary Heritage
A Cleveland Collection
Cook, Line and Sinker
Cooking GRACEfully
Cooking on the Wild Side
Cooking with Class
Cooking with Hope Ridge Families
Cooking with Marilyn
Cooking with TLC
Czech Dancers Polka Club Cook Book
Dining in Historic Ohio
Down Home Cookin' Without the Down Home Fat
Down Home Cooking from Hocking County
Easy Cooking with Herbs & Spices
The Fat-Free Real Food Cookbook
Favorite Recipes
Favorite Recipes from Poland Women's Club
Favorite Recipes from the Heart of Amish Country
The Fifth Generation Cookbook
Firebelles Cookbook
500 Recipes Using Zucchini
Five Star Sensations

Contributing Cookbooks

Gardner's Delight
Generation to Generation
Hats Off to "Real Men Cook"
Heartland: The Best of the Old and the New from Midwest Kitchens
Heartline Cookbook
Heavenly Dishes
Heavenly Food II
Heirloom Recipes and By Gone Days
Herbs: From Cultivation to Cooking
The Heritage Tradition
Home Cookin' with 4-H
Incredible Edibles
The Kettle Cookbook: Second Helpings
Kinder Kuisine
Lifetime Warranty
Light Kitchen Choreography
Mary Yoder's Amish Kitchen
A Matter of Taste
MDA Favorite Recipes
More Cooking with Marilyn Harris
Now That Mom's Not Around Cookbook
Oeder Family & Friends Cookbook
The Ohio State Grange Cookbook
175th Anniversary Quilt Cookbook
One Nation Under Sauerkraut
Onions, Onions, Onions
Ottoville Sesquicentennial Cookbook
Our Collection of Heavenly Recipes
Plain & Fancy Favorites
The PTA Pantry
Recipe Rehab

Contributing Cookbooks

Recipes and Remembrances
Recipes from "The Little Switzerland of Ohio"
Robert Rothschild Recipes
Salem Mennonite Church 100th Anniversary Cookbook
Saturday Night Suppers
Seasoned With Love
The Shaker Cookbook
Share with Love Something Olde and Something New
Sharing Our Best
Sharing Our Best: The Elizabeth House for Assisted Living
Simply Sensational
A Sprinkling of Favorite Recipes
St. Gerard's 75th Jubilee Cookbook
A Taste of Columbus, Volume III
A Taste of Columbus, Volume IV
A Taste of Toronto - Ohio, that is
Tasty Recipes
Touches of the Hands and Heart
Treasured Recipes
Treasured Recipes from Mason, Ohio
Treasures and Pleasures
Tried & True by Mothers of 2's
Tried & True Volume II: Diabetic Cookbook
Tumm Yummies
25th Anniversary Cookbook
Viva Italia
Wadsworth-Rittman Hospital Cookbook: 75th Anniversary Edition
What's Cooking at Holden School
Women's Centennial Cookbook

Appetizers and Beverages

Canoeing on the Little Miami. Warren County.

Hot Peppermint Chocolate

Refreshing and warm on a cold Ohio winter night.

3 cups hot milk
8 chocolate peppermint
   patties (the small ones)

$^1/_8$ teaspoon salt
1 cup cream

Combine $^1/_2$ cup hot milk with chocolate peppermint patties. Add salt and $2^1/_2$ cups hot milk; heat to simmering. Add cream.

Touches of the Hands & Heart

Eggnog

A real treat at Christmas. Buy enough ingredients for several batches. You'll need them!

1$^1/_2$ cups fat-free egg
   substitute
2 cups skim milk
$^1/_3$ cup sugar
1 teaspoon vanilla extract

1 cup nonfat vanilla frozen
   yogurt
$^1/_2$ teaspoon nutmeg
$^1/_4$ cup light rum (optional)
$^1/_4$ cup bourbon (optional)

Combine all ingredients in blender. Mix well. Chill at least 4 hours before serving. Sprinkle with additional nutmeg if desired. Yield: 5 cups /10 ($^1/_2$-cup) servings.

Nutrients per serving: Cal 82; Fat <1g (1%); Carb 15g; Chol 1mg; Sod 84mg; Pro 5g.

Recipe Rehab

Plain People's Lemonade

Lemonade is a favorite beverage among Amish and Mennonite families. The Amish traditionally prepare lemonade by pressing sliced lemons to release the flavorful oils. However, this easy recipe with grated lemon rind seems to impart a similar flavor.

1 ½ cups sugar
1 tablespoon grated lemon
 rind
½ cup boiling water

1 ½ cups freshly squeezed
 lemon juice (from about 6
 large lemons)
6 cups cold water
Ice cubes

In jar with tight-fitting lid, combine sugar, rind and boiling water; shake until sugar dissolves. Add lemon juice; shake well. Chill. Before serving, add water and ice cubes. Makes 2 quarts.

Bountiful Ohio

Fruit Daiquiri Slush

A wonderful blend of flavors that's sure to be a summertime hit!

1 (6-ounce) can limeade
6 ounces rum
1 small ripe banana

½ cup sweetened, frozen
 strawberries
1 tray of ice cubes

Place ingredients in blender and blend on grate speed until slushy. Serve in a chilled daiquiri glass. Yield: 8 servings.

Cooking on the Wild Side

Orange Sherbet Punch

2 packages orange Kool-Aid
2 cups sugar
1 (12-ounce) can frozen
 orange juice concentrate

1 gallon water
1 quart 7-Up
½ gallon orange sherbet

Mix all ingredients except sherbet and 7-Up. Add 7-Up and sherbet just before serving. Drop sherbet in punch with ice cream scoop.

Favorite Recipes from the Heart of Amish Country

Punch

2 cups sugar
2 cups water
12 tea bags
3 cups boiling water
4 lemons, squeezed

4 oranges, squeezed
1 package cherry Kool-Aid,
  make as directed
1 cup crushed pineapple
2 quarts ginger ale

Boil together sugar and 2 cups water. Make tea by putting all ingredients (except ale) into a gallon jug. When ready to serve, remove tea bags and add ginger ale.

Favorite Recipes

Angel Frost

1 (6-ounce) pink lemonade
  concentrate, thawed
1 cup milk
1 (10-ounce) carton frozen
  strawberries, partially thawed

1 pint French vanilla ice
  cream

Place in blender in order given. Blend until smooth. Pour into glasses. Top with fresh strawberries.

Sharing Our Best (Ashland Church of God)

Orange Wassail

1 cup water
1 cup sugar
12 whole cloves (place in tea
  ball)

2-4 cinnamon sticks
3 quarts orange juice
32 ounces cranberry juice

Combine first 4 ingredients in a large Dutch oven and simmer for 10 minutes. Add juices and heat through. Allow to remain on low heat to serve warm. Yields 4 quarts.

What's Cooking at Holden School

Orange Smoothie

Like a Creamsicle in a glass.

1 cup nonfat vanilla frozen
  yogurt
³/₄ cup lowfat (1%) milk

¹/₄ cup frozen orange juice
  concentrate

Combine ingredients in a blender and blend until smooth. Serves 1.

Per Serving: Cal 165; Prot 7g; Fat 2g; Carb 0g; Sod 94mg; Chol 75mg.

Cooking with Hope Ridge Families

Sauerkraut Balls

1 pound sausage
¹/₂ cup onion
1 (8-ounce) package cream
  cheese
4 tablespoons bread crumbs
4 tablespoons parsley
2 tablespoons garlic salt

2 teaspoons mustard
¹/₄ teaspoon pepper
1 quart sauerkraut, drained
  and chopped
Flour
3 eggs
Bread crumbs

Fry sausage and onion; let drain. Cool. Add cooled sausage and onion to next 7 ingredients. Mix well. Make balls. Roll in flour, then in 3 eggs, beaten, then in bread crumbs. French-fry until brown.

Recipes & Remembrances

Sauerkraut Balls

A favorite at New Year's Eve parties in this German settlement.

1 pound ground chuck,
   browned
2¹/₂ cups sauerkraut, drained
1 medium onion
4¹/₂ tablespoons flour
2 eggs, beaten

1 cup instant potatoes
¹/₄ teaspoon each of salt,
   pepper, and garlic salt
1 beef bouillon cube dissolved
   in ¹/₄ cup hot water
Cracker crumbs

Drain sauerkraut well. In food processor place sauerkraut and onion and pulsate until onion and sauerkraut are chopped fine. Place above mixture in a bowl and add browned meat, flour, eggs, instant potatoes, seasonings and beef bouillon mixture.

Blend well and roll into 1-inch balls, then roll in cracker crumbs. Deep fry until brown. Drain on paper towels. Serve hot or cold.

Touches of the Hands & Heart

Sauerkraut Balls

1 (32-ounce) bag sauerkraut
2 pounds fresh ground pork
1 cup fine bread crumbs
2 eggs
¹/₂ teaspoon salt

Pepper, to taste
1 tablespoon minced onion
1 tablespoon sugar
1¹/₂ tablespoons
   Worcestershire sauce

Squeeze juice from kraut. Then chop very fine. Combine with remaining ingredients and shape into 2-inch diameter balls. Put in oblong baking dish and cover with foil. Bake at 350° for 1 - 1¹/₂ hours until cooked through. Remove foil during last 15 minutes of baking. Makes 32-36 balls. Preparation time: 15-20 minutes.

Cooking with TLC

Sausage Meatballs

1 pound turkey breakfast
sausage (85% lean or better),
thawed
1/4 cup egg substitute
1/2 cup seasoned bread
crumbs

3/4 cup chili sauce
1/4 teaspoon garlic powder
6 tablespoons brown sugar
2 tablespoons vinegar
2 tablespoons soy sauce
1 tablespoon margarine

In a mixing bowl, combine turkey breakfast sausage, egg substitute, and bread crumbs; mix well. Shape into 1 - 1 1/2-inch meatballs and place on the rack of a broiler pan. Put in a 400° oven and bake for 4 minutes. Turn the oven to Broil (500°) and broil the meatballs for 2-4 minutes. This eliminates the need to turn the meatballs during cooking. Remove the meatballs from the oven and put them on several layers of paper towels; blot with several more layers. In a saucepan, combine the remaining ingredients and simmer 5 minutes. Add the drained meatballs and simmer for 15 minutes. Serve hot. Yield: 36-40 turkey meatballs.

Lifetime Warranty

Sweet & Sour Meatballs

1 1/2 pounds hamburger
2 beaten eggs
1 cup bread crumbs
1 medium chopped onion

1 bottle chili sauce
3/4 cup brown sugar
1/4 cup vinegar
1/4 cup water

Mix hamburger, eggs, bread crumbs, and onion in a bowl. Make into meatballs. Place in a 13x9-inch pan. Combine chili sauce, brown sugar, vinegar, and water. Pour over uncooked meatballs. Bake uncovered for one hour at 300°.

Favorite Recipes

 German Village is famous for its architecture, shops and restaurants. Its narrow brick streets are lined with houses that hug the curbs, and window boxes overflowing with flowers. The smell of homemade sausage and freshly baked breads combine to make it a popular and enjoyable place to visit.

Cranberry Meatballs

SAUCE:

1 pound fresh cranberries
1 (12-ounce) bottle chili sauce
2 tablespoons dark brown
　　sugar

1 tablespoon lemon juice

MEATBALLS:

1 pound ground turkey (90%
　　lean)
1 pound ground round (90%
　　lean)
1 cup cornflake crumbs
1/3 cup dried parsley flakes
1/2 cup egg substitute

2 tablespoons soy sauce
1/4 teaspoon pepper
1/2 teaspoon garlic powder
2 tablespoons dehydrated
　　minced onion
1/3 cup ketchup

Put cranberries in medium saucepan and cover with water. Over medium heat, cook until cranberries pop. Add chili sauce, brown sugar and lemon juice, heat through, stirring occasionally. In a large bowl, combine ground turkey, ground round, corn flake crumbs, parsley, egg subsititute, soy sauce, pepper, garlic powder, onion, and ketchup; mix thoroughly. Shape into walnut-sized balls. Place in a shallow roasting pan. Bake in 350° oven for 20 minutes; pour off any grease. Bake for 10-15 minutes longer; pour off any grease and blot the meatballs with paper towels. Cover with heated sauce. These can be made ahead and frozen. As an appetizer: place in a crock pot or chafing dish to keep warm; serve with toothpicks. As an entrée: serve over cooked rice. Yield: 60 meatballs.

Lifetime Warranty

Sausage Stars

Won-Ton wrappers
1 pound sausage, cook and
   drain well
1¹/₂ cups Monterey Jack
   cheese, shredded
1¹/₂ cups sharp Cheddar
   cheese, shredded

1 cup Hidden Valley Original
   Ranch Dressing Mix
   (prepared as directed)
¹/₂ cup sliced ripe olives
¹/₂ cup red pepper, chopped

Form Won-Ton wrappers into lightly greased muffin tins, brush lightly with oil. Bake in 350° oven for 5-7 minutes or until golden. Take out of tins, put onto a cookie sheet, fill with mixture of remaining ingredients. Bake at 350° about 7-10 minutes, until hot and bubbly. Makes 3-4 dozen.

Note: You can find Won-Ton wrappers in the produce section of your grocery store.

Tried and True by Mothers of 2's

Sausage and Rye

1 pound ground beef
1 pound ground sausage (hot
   if you prefer)
1 teaspoon oregano
¹/₂ teaspoon garlic salt

1 pound Velveeta cheese, cut
   in small pieces
1¹/₂ - 2 loaves rye bread
   (about 48 slices)

Brown and drain meat. Add oregano, garlic salt, and cheese. Stir until cheese is melted. Spread on rye slices and freeze on cookie sheets. Place in plastic bag when frozen. When ready to use, put under broiler until lightly browned. A yummy snack!

By Our Cookstove

 Golf is bound to be king in Ohio since the master himself, Jack Nicklaus, is from Columbus.

Little Ham Sandwiches

1 package (24) small dinner rolls
2 sticks butter or margarine
3 tablespoons mustard
1 teaspoon Worcestershire
  sauce
3 tablespoons poppy seeds

1 medium onion, chopped
1/2 pound Swiss or Mozzarella
  cheese, grated
1 pound ham, chopped or
  grated

Slice whole package of rolls in half horizontally. Place lower half in a pan. Melt butter in a small saucepan, add mustard, and next 3 ingredients. Simmer 5 minutes. Spread on both halves of rolls. Put ham and cheese on bottom halves of rolls in the pan. Put other half on top. Cover with foil and heat for 30 minutes, or until hot, in a 350° oven. Cut before serving.

Tried and True by Mothers of 2's

Crab Strudel

1/2 pound crabmeat
1 tablespoon lemon juice
1 tablespoon butter
2 tablespoons minced green
  onions
2 tablespoons parsley,
  chopped
2 drops Tabasco sauce

Dash salt
Dash pepper
1/2 pound Brie cheese, cut
  into small, thin pieces
6 sheets frozen phyllo dough,
  thawed
2 tablespoons of melted
  butter

Preheat oven to 375°. Sprinkle lemon juice over crabmeat. Sauté green onions in 1 tablespoon butter. Add crabmeat and heat through. Add parsley, Tabasco sauce, salt and pepper. Mix well. Place Brie slices over top of crabmeat mixture; allow to melt. Gently mix together. Stack 2 sheets of phyllo dough; brush with melted butter. Spread 1/3 of crab mixture along short end. Roll, tucking ends under; brush with butter. Place on cookie sheet. Repeat for remaining dough. Bake at 375° for 20-25 minutes. To serve, slice each roll into 12 pieces. Serves 15.

Variation: Use Feta cheese and spinach in place of Brie and crab.

A Cleveland Collection

Hot Crabmeat Puffs

MINIATURE CREAM PUFFS:

1 cup water
1/2 cup margarine or butter
1 cup all-purpose flour

Salt to taste
4 eggs

Preheat oven to 400°. Bring water and margarine to a boil. Add flour and salt. Stir vigorously over low heat until mixture forms a ball. Add eggs, one at a time, beating until smooth. Drop teaspoonfuls of batter onto ungreased baking sheet. Bake for 30-35 minutes and remove from baking sheet.

CRABMEAT FILLING:

1 (8-ounce) package cream
   cheese, softened
1 tablespoon milk
1/2 teaspoon horseradish
   sauce
Pepper to taste

1 (61/2-ounce) can crabmeat,
   drained
1/2 cup slivered almonds,
   toasted
2 tablespoons finely chopped
   onion

Lower the oven temperature to 375°. Combine softened cream cheese, milk, horseradish sauce, and pepper. Mix until well blended. Stir in crabmeat, almonds, and onion.

To assemble cream puffs, cut tops from cream puffs and fill with crab mixture. Replace tops. Bake for 10 minutes and serve. Yield: 36 appetizers.

Note: Easier than it looks. Be sure to make cream puffs small.

Five Star Sensations

Hot Crab Puffs

36 (2-inch) toast rounds
7¹/₂ ounces crab meat
6 ounces water chestnuts,
  finely chopped
1 cup Swiss cheese, shredded
¹/₂ cup margarine, softened

¹/₂ teaspoon dillweed
2 teaspoons green onions, tops
  and bottoms, minced
1 teaspoon lemon juice
Salt and pepper to taste

Cut bread in rounds and toast on one side. Mix remaining ingredients together. Spread on untoasted side of bread rounds. Place on cookie sheet and bake at 350° for 10-15 minutes until hot. Yield: 3 dozen.

Angels and Friends Cookbook II

Special Crab Spread

1 (8-ounce) package cream
  cheese at room temperature

1 (8-ounce) bottle chili sauce
1 can crabmeat or shrimp

Spread cream cheese over serving plate. Top with chili sauce; sprinkle with crabmeat or shrimp. Serve with crackers.

Sharing Our Best (Elizabeth House)

Devilicious Ham Spread

A kids' favorite for toast or crackers.

1 (8-ounce) container cream
  cheese, softened
1 (2¹/₂-ounce) can deviled
  ham
1 tablespoon sweet pickle
  relish

1 teaspoon prepared mustard
¹/₄ teaspoon salt
Dash of pepper

Combine cream cheese and deviled ham until well blended. Add remaining ingredients; mix thoroughly. Chill. Serve with party rye bread or small wheat crackers. Yield: 1¹/₂ cups.

Cooking with Hope Ridge Families

Chicken Liver Spread

"This is delicious! What is it?" they ask.

1 container chicken livers
  sautéed in butter
1 tablespoon finely chopped
  onion
3 tablespoons mayonnaise
2 tablespoons lemon juice

2 tablespoons butter, softened
8-10 drops hot pepper
$1/2$ teaspoon salt
$1/2$ teaspoon dry mustard
Dash of pepper

Grind the cooked chicken livers and blend in the remaining ingredients. Spread on your favorite crackers or party breads.

A Taste of Toronto—Ohio, that is

Quick Liver Pâté

Children may like this because the "liver" flavor is lightened by the cream cheese.

1 (8-ounce) package
  Neufchatel cream cheese,
  softened
8 ounces gooseliver or
  braunschweiger, mashed

2 ounces plain yogurt
1 teaspoon Dijon mustard
1 tablespoon finely chopped
  parsley (optional)

In bowl, blend cream cheese and gooseliver or braunschweiger with electric mixer. Add remaining ingredients and beat until smooth. Place in covered container and refrigerate. Allow to stand for several minutes before serving with bread sticks and rye or sesame crackers.

Kinder Kuisine

Pumpkin Cheese Spread

²/₃ cup pumpkin, solid pack
4 teaspoons margarine,
  softened
2 (8-ounce) packages cream
  cheese, softened
1 teaspoon cinnamon
¹/₂ teaspoon allspice

¹/₄ teaspoon nutmeg
5 teaspoons confectioners'
  sugar
5 teaspoons orange juice
  concentrate
¹/₄ cup pecans, chopped

Cream together margarine and cream cheese. Beat with electric mixer until smooth. Add pumpkin, spices, and confectioners' sugar and beat well. Add orange juice which has been thawed. Beat once again to blend.

Chill in refrigerator at least overnight to allow flavors to blend. When ready to serve, place in desired serving bowl and garnish with pecans. Serve with crackers or bread such as zucchini bread.

Now That Mom's Not Around

Hummus Spread

¹/₂ cup chopped parsley
1 garlic clove, minced
3 tablespoons sesame seed
  paste

3-4 tablespoons lemon juice
1 (15¹/₂-ounce) can garbanzo
  beans, drained
¹/₂ teaspoon salt

Place all ingredients in a blender or food processor fitted with the metal blade. Process until smooth. Refrigerate several hours before serving. May be stored in refrigerator up to 1 month. Serve cold as a dip or spread. Makes 1 cup.

Note: Sesame seed paste, or sesame tahini, can be purchased from gourmet shops or some grocery stores.

Generation to Generation

Un-Mexican Haystack

A surprise of ham and chopped walnuts make this a uniquely attractive presentation.

2 (8-ounce) packages cream
  cheese, softened
3 tablespoons mayonnaise
8 green onions, chopped
1 green pepper, chopped
1 tablespoon Worcestershire
  sauce

1 teaspoon garlic powder
1 dash Tabasco sauce
Salt and pepper to taste
2 cups ham, shredded
12 medium-size flour tortillas
1/2 cup walnuts, chopped
Fresh parsley, chopped

In a large mixing bowl or food processor, combine cream cheese, mayonnaise, onions, green pepper, Worcestershire sauce, garlic powder, Tabasco sauce, salt, and pepper. Mix well. Stir in ham.

Place a tortilla on a large round plate. Spread a thin layer of ham mixture over tortilla. Repeat layers, ending with ham mixture on top of entire stack. Sprinkle chopped nuts and chopped parsley on the top layer of the stack. Cover and refrigerate at least one hour. Cut into wedges or small cubes and serve with a decorative toothpick inserted in each piece. May be prepared one day ahead and refrigerated. Yield: 16-20.

Simply Sensational

Pizza Crackers

HiHo or Ritz crackers
1 small jar pizza sauce

Mozzarella cheese
Pepperoni (optional)

Spread 4 crackers with pizza sauce. Top with cheese and pepperoni. Place on a paper plate and microwave at 50% for 30-60 seconds or until cheese melts. Rotate after 30 seconds. The more you place in the microwave, the longer it takes to cook. Do not over cook.

Share with Love

Chicken in a Biscuit Crackers

12 cups oyster crackers
2 tablespoons dry chicken
  base

2 tablespoons sour cream and
  onion powder
1 cup Wesson oil

Mix together really well. Bake on cookie sheet for 1/2 hour at 300°. Stir every couple of minutes.

Favorite Recipes from the Heart of Amish Country

Spinach Appetizers

4 eggs, slightly beaten
2 (10-ounce) boxes frozen
  spinach, chopped
1 (16-ounce) box (2 cups)
  Pepperidge Farm Herb
  Stuffing Mix

1 cup grated Cheddar cheese
3/4 cup Parmesan cheese
1/2 teaspoon garlic salt
1/2 teaspoon thyme
1 cup finely chopped onion
3/4 cup oleo, melted

Mix everything together with hands. Let stand for awhile. Roll into balls. Chill for 30 minutes or longer. Bake at 350° for 15-20 minutes. Can be frozen after baked.

Sharing Our Best (Ashland Church of God)

South of the Border Spinach Dip

1 (4-ounce) can chopped
  green chilies, drained
3/4 cup chopped onion
2 tomatoes, chopped
2 teaspoons chopped cilantro
1 (10-ounce) package frozen
  spinach, thawed and squeezed
  dry

1 (8-ounce) package cream
  cheese, softened
2 cups shredded Monterey
  Jack cheese
1/3 cup half-and-half
1-2 dashes Tabasco sauce

Preheat oven to 400°. Butter a 1-quart baking dish. Combine all ingredients. Pour into prepared pan. Bake at 400° for 20-25 minutes. Serve with tortilla chips or toasted pita bread. Makes 8-10 servings.

A Cleveland Collection

Spanakopites
(Greek Spinach Appetizers)

1 pound fresh or frozen filo
pastry leaves
1 (8-ounce) package cream
cheese
1/2 pound feta cheese,
crumbled
1/2 cup Romano cheese,
grated
2 eggs, slightly beaten

2 green onions (some tops),
chopped fine
1 package frozen chopped
spinach, thawed and drained
1/4 teaspoon salt
1/8 teaspoon pepper
1 tablespoon fresh parsley,
minced
1/2 pound butter, melted

Thaw frozen filo dough according to package directions. Cover with Saran wrap and a damp tea towel to prevent drying. Blend cream cheese with feta and Romano cheese; add eggs, onion, spinach, salt and pepper, and parsley, blending well. Refrigerate at least 1 hour. Cut filo in 2 1/2-inch strips. Butter 2 pastry strips; stack together. Put one teaspoon of filling on one end and fold corner over to make a triangle. Continue folding from side to side to end of strip. (Will resemble a folded American flag.) Proceed this way until all filling and filo are used. Put seam-side-down on ungreased cookie sheet, and bake at 350° for 20 minutes. These freeze very well. Do not bake before freezing. Thaw 1/2 hour before baking. Yield: 60.

Angels and Friends Cookbook I

Spinach Pastries

FILLING:

1 (10-ounce) package frozen
 spinach
1/2 cup feta cheese, broken
 up into small pieces
3 tablespoons country Dijon
 mustard

1 small onion, chopped
1/2 cup shredded Mozzarella
 cheese

Thaw spinach in colander. Press spinach well to drain. In a bowl, combine spinach, feta cheese, mustard, and onions. Mix well. Add Mozzarella cheese and mix. Set aside.

PASTRY:

1 (17 1/2-ounce) package
 frozen puff pastry, thawed

Flour for sprinkling
Water for brushing

Unfold pastry sheets. On floured surface, roll out one sheet. Sprinkle pastry sheet with a little flour and roll slightly. Turn sheet over and repeat the process. Cut into 4-inch squares (or any size you prefer). Place a little spinach mixture in middle of square. Brush edges with water. Fold in half and seal with fork. Prick top of pastry with fork to allow steam to escape. Arrange pastries on cookie sheet. Repeat until all pastry sheets are used. Bake in preheated oven at 400° for 20 minutes or until golden brown.

Easy Cooking with Herbs & Spices

Artichoke Cheese Dip

2 cups grated Mozzarella
 cheese
1 cup grated Parmesan
 cheese
1 cup mayonnaise

1 can or little less artichoke
 hearts, chop and discard
 liquid (there are about 6 in a
 can)
1 teaspoon garlic salt

Combine in soufflé dish or 1 1/2-quart casserole. Bake at 375° for 25-30 minutes or until golden brown on top. Serve with onion rounds and enjoy!

Cooking GRACEfully

Black-Eyed Pea and Pepper Salsa

Easy, zesty appetizer with a Southwestern flavor.

2 (15-ounce) cans black-eyed
  peas, rinsed and drained
2 sweet red peppers, diced
1 (11½-ounce) jar hot salsa
3 tablespoons minced onion
4 tablespoons olive oil or
  vegetable oil

4 tablespoons red wine
  vinegar
2 tablespoons snipped fresh
  parsley
1 tablespoon minced jalapeño
  chilies

Combine all ingredients and refrigerate. Allow flavors to blend in refrigerator for 2 hours or overnight. Serve with corn chips or tortillas. Yield: 5 cups.

Five Star Sensations

Pepperoni Pizza Dip

1 (8-ounce) package cream
  cheese, softened
½ cup dairy sour cream
1 teaspoon dried oregano,
  crushed
⅛ teaspoon garlic powder
⅛ teaspoon crushed red
  pepper (optional)
½ cup pizza sauce

½ cup chopped pepperoni
¼ cup sliced green onion
¼ cup chopped green pepper
½ cup shredded Mozzarella
  cheese (2 ounces)
Sweet pepper strips
Broccoli flowerets or
  crackers (optional)

In a small mixer bowl, beat together cream cheese, sour cream, oregano, garlic powder, and red pepper. Spread evenly in a 9- or 10-inch quiche dish or pie plate. Spread pizza sauce over top. Sprinkle with pepperoni, green onion, and green pepper. Bake in a 350° oven for 10 minutes. Top with cheese; bake 5 minutes more, or until cheese is melted and mixture is heated through. Serve with sweet pepper strips, broccoli flowerets or crackers. Makes 1½ cups (12 servings).

Favorite Recipes from Poland Women's Club

Watermelon Fire and Ice Salsa

3 cups watermelon, chopped
and seeded
1/2 cup green pepper,
chopped
2 tablespoons lime juice
1 tablespoon cilantro,
chopped

1 tablespoon green onions,
chopped
1-2 tablespoons jalapeño
pepper, minced
1/2 teaspoon garlic salt
1 cup sour cream
Tortilla chips

Combine first 7 ingredients. Cover and refrigerate one hour. Serve over sour cream with tortilla chips.

Cook, Line & Sinker

Best Vegetable Dip Ever

1/4 cup almonds, toasted
3 cloves garlic, chopped
2 heaping tablespoons
parsley, chopped

4 tablespoons seasoned bread
crumbs
2 cups mayonnaise

Put all ingredients into food processor Blend just until mixed—don't over process. Chill until serving time.

Saturday Night Suppers

Best Vegetable Dip

1 (8-ounce) package cream
cheese, softened
1/2 cup light or dark corn
syrup
1/2 cup sugar
1 cup oil
1/4 cup vinegar

1/4 cup dried minced onion
1 tablespoon lemon juice
1 teaspoon dry mustard
1 teaspoon celery seed
1/2 teaspoon salt
1/4 teaspoon paprika

Combine cream cheese, corn syrup, and sugar in mixer bowl; mix well. Beat in oil. Add remaining ingredients; mix well. Spoon into serving bowl. Chill until serving time. Serve with raw vegetables. Yield: 6 servings.

The Ohio State Grange Cookbook

Corbin's Bean Dip

1 (8-ounce) package cream
  cheese
1 can refried beans

1 (8-ounce) carton sour cream
1 (10-ounce) jar salsa
Shredded Cheddar

Mix first 4 ingredients together; cover with cheese. Bake at 350° until hot and cheese is melted. Serve with corn chips or tortilla chips.

MDA Favorite Recipes

Mean Bean Dip

Bean dips can be pretty bland by themselves. This one is so lively, you'll forget that the chips you're eating with it are low fat.

2 cups fat-free refried beans
1 cup diced onions
1/2 cup salsa
1/4 cup fat-free Ranch
  Dressing

1 package fat-free Cheddar,
  shredded

In the bottom of a 9x9-inch glass cooking dish spread refried beans. Cover with onions and salsa. Microwave on HIGH for 2 minutes. Pour fat-free Ranch Dressing over the pan. Cover with Cheddar. Eat with low-fat tortilla chips.

Serving size: 5 tablespoons. Servings per recipe: 12. Cal 70; Fat 0g; Sat Fat 0g; Chol 2mg; Sod 273mg; Carbo 10g; Fiber 0g; Prot 7g.

The Fat-Free Real Food Cookbook

Mexican Confetti Dip

This is a great source of protein. Great for lunch.

1 (12-ounce) can whole kernel corn, drained

1 (15.5-ounce) can black beans, drained

¹/₃ cup fat-free Italian Salad Dressing

1 (16-ounce) jar of your favorite chunky salsa

Mix all together. Chill. Presto! You're done! Serve with Baked Tostito Chips. Yield: 6 servings (approx. 8 ounces each serving). Per serving: Cal 78; Fat .75g

Variations: 1. Warm a flour tortilla in microwave. Fill center with ¹/₄ cup of dip. Fold up as you would a burrito. 2. Toss ¹/₂ cup with 1¹/₂ cups of your favorite lettuces for a tasty twist to your salad!

Down Home Cookin' Without the Down Home Fat

Artichoke Bread

A hearty appetizer.

1 or 2 loaves frozen bread (1
   if large)
1/2 cup butter
2 tablespoons sesame seeds
2 cloves garlic, crushed
1 1/2 cups sour cream
2 cups cubed Monterey Jack
   cheese

1/2 cup Parmesan cheese
2 tablespoons parsley flakes
1 (14-ounce) can artichoke
   hearts, drained and chopped
1 cup shredded Cheddar
   cheese

Slice through bread horizontally. Scoop center from bread. Sauté bread pieces in butter with sesame seeds and garlic. Remove from stove. Stir in sour cream, Jack cheese, Parmesan cheese, parsley, and artichokes.

Put filling into scooped bread shells. Top with Cheddar cheese. Bake at 350° for 30 minutes, uncovered. Slice bread with bread knife on angle.

Favorite Recipes from Poland Women's Club

Fondue Neuchatel

1 garlic clove, halved
1 1/2 cups white wine
12 ounces shredded
   Emmentaler
12 ounces shredded Gruyère

1 tablespoon cornstarch
3 tablespoons kirsch
Pinch of nutmeg
Pinch of white pepper
Crusty loaf of French bread

Rub garlic on the inside of fondue pot or saucepan. Finely chop garlic and sprinkle in pan. Add wine, heat on medium. When wine is warm, add cheeses, stirring continuously until melted. This is a time-consuming process; be patient and do not let it come to a boil. In a small bowl combine cornstarch and kirsch; stir into cheese mixture. Season with nutmeg and white pepper. Cut bread into 1 1/2-inch cubes to dip into fondue.

Recipes from "The Little Switzerland of Ohio"

Mexican Cheesecake

From the thousands of recipes Betty Rosbottom has demonstrated at LaBelle Pomme Cooking School in Columbus, she circles this south-western appetizer cake as her favorite. The highly seasoned appetizer bakes on a tortilla chip crust in a springform pan. A lesson in how to make yogurt cheese is a bonus.

1 cup finely ground corn
  tortilla chips
2 tablespoons unsalted butter,
  melted
4 tablespoons flour
1 pound light cream cheese
2 cups low-fat yogurt cheese
  (below)
4 large eggs
1 teaspoon dried oregano

1¹/₂ teaspoons cumin powder
¹/₂ teaspoon garlic powder
1 teaspoon chili powder
¹/₂ teaspoon freshly gound
  black pepper
¹/₄ teaspoon ground red
  pepper
¹/₄ teaspoon salt
Salsa, homemade or
  commercial

Spray a 9-inch springform pan with vegetable cooking spray. Combine ground tortilla chips, melted butter, and flour. Mix well and pat onto bottom of pan. Bake in 350° oven about 10 minutes to set; remove, but do not turn oven off.

Beat cream cheese and yogurt cheese with electric mixer until smooth, about 2 minutes. Add eggs, one at a time, and mix to blend. Add seasonings and mix 1 to 2 minutes more.

Pour filling into prepared pan; spread evenly with a spatula. Bake on center rack until firm, 35-40 minutes. Remove from oven and cool completely. Cover and refrigerate.

To serve, remove sides from springform pan and place cheesecake on serving tray. Spread salsa over the top of the cheesecake and place more in serving bowl. Garnish with tortilla chips.

LOW-FAT YOGURT CHEESE:
Make cheese from low-fat yogurt by placing 4 cups of plain yogurt in a fine mesh sieve over a bowl and refrigerating for at least 12 hours. The water, almost half the amount of yogurt, will drain off, leaving a solid mass of yogurt cheese. The cheese can be refrigerated up to 2 days.

Aren't You Going to Taste It, Honey?

Hot Pepper Butter

40 hot peppers*
6 cups sugar
1 quart mustard
1 quart vinegar

1 tablespoon salt
1 1/2 cups flour
1 1/4 cups water

Grind peppers and seeds fine. Add sugar, mustard, vinegar, and salt. Bring to a boil and make thickening (flour and water). Mix (no lumps). Add thickening to pepper mixture. Let boil about 10 minutes. Put in jars and seal. Makes 8-10 pints.

Note: *Peppers will burn hands. Use rubber gloves.

Sharing Our Best (Ashland Church of God)

Green Tomato Pickles

It will take some time but it is worth every minute.

10 pounds green tomatoes
5 pounds white onions
2/3 cup salt
1 quart vinegar (white)
1 1/2 quarts water

1 cup sugar
2 tablespoons celery seed
2 tablespoons white mustard
  seed

Wash tomatoes. Slice. Peel and slice onions. Place tomatoes and onions in large crock in alternate layers. Sprinkle each layer with salt. Cover with a plate that is weighted down. Let stand overnight. Drain. In large kettle place onions and tomatoes. Add 2 cups vinegar and 2 cups water. Heat to boiling. Drain. Add 2 cups vinegar, 4 cups water, sugar, celery seed, and mustard seed. Boil slowly and stir occasionally for 30 minutes. Pack into clean Mason jars. Process in cold packer 20 minutes.

Touches of the Hands & Heart

The Indians called the area around the Mad River *Mac Ack Ocheek*, which means "the smiling valley." After the Civil War, two gentlemen farmers, General Abram Piatt, and his brother, Colonel Donn Piatt built European-like castles there (east of West Liberty): the Castle Piatt Mac-A-Cheek, a 30-room chateau built in 1864; and Castle Mac-O-Chee, built in 1879.

Sliced Zucchini Pickles

They make hamburgers taste better. Also try the dilled version.

1 quart vinegar
2 cups sugar
1/2 cup salt
2 teaspoons ground turmeric
1 teaspoon dry mustard

2 teaspoons celery seeds
4 quarts sliced, unpeeled
  zucchini
1 quart sliced onions

Bring vinegar, sugar, salt, and spices to a boil. Pour over zucchini and onions and let stand one hour. Bring to a boil and cook 3 minutes. Pack in hot jars and adjust lids. Process in boiling water bath (212°) for 5 minutes. Remove jars and complete seals unless closures are self-sealing type. Makes 6-7 pints.

Variation: Dilled Zucchini Pickles: Substitute 2 teaspoons of dill seeds for turmeric.

500 Recipes Using Zucchini

Idiot Pickles

1 (32-ounce) jar Kosher dills
1 3/4 cups sugar

1/4 cup vinegar
1/4 cup water

Drain and rinse pickles. Cut pickles into 3/4-inch pieces and put back in pickle jar. Heat sugar, vinegar, and water together until sugar melts, about 3 1/2 minutes. Pour mixture over pickles and seal. Put in refrigerator. Ready in 3 days.

Cooking with Class

Bread and Breakfast

Lanterman's Mill in Mill Creek Park. Youngstown.

Shaker Daily Loaf

1 envelope or 1 tablespoon
  dry activated yeast
4 tablespoons lukewarm water
1 teaspoon honey
7/8 cup milk
1 tablespoon butter

2 teaspoons sugar
1 teaspoon salt
3-31/2 cups sifted,
  unbleached flour
Melted butter to brush on top

Dissolve yeast in water to which the honey has been added. Scald milk with butter, sugar, and salt and stir until well mixed. Cool until lukewarm, about 90°. Stir in softened yeast mixture, and then enough flour to make a dough that will not stick to your hands. Knead the dough with the palms of your hands about 20 times. Place in a buttered bowl and brush the top with melted butter. Let rise to double its volume. Punch down, to remove excess gas and renew yeast activity. Knead lightly this time and shape into a loaf. Place in a greased and floured loaf pan, 9 inches by 41/2 inches or equivalent, brush again with melted butter and let rise to double its volume.

Bake in a moderate (350°) oven for about 50 minutes. Test loaf by tapping the top; if it sounds hollow, the loaf is done. Remove from pan immediately. Cover lightly with a towel to allow steam to escape. This is an excellent loaf of wholesome, crusty bread.

The Shaker Cookbook

French Bread

2 tablespoons dry yeast
2 tablespoons sugar
2 cups warm water

2 tablespoons vegetable oil
1 tablespoon salt
5 - 51/2 cups flour

Dissolve yeast and sugar in warm water. Add oil, salt, and flour to yeast mixture. Mix well. Knead until smooth. Let rise 10 minutes, then punch down. Repeat 10 minutes rising and punch down 3 more times. Then divide dough into thirds. Roll out dough with a rolling pin. Roll up dough. Place on greased baking sheet. Cut slit in top of bread. Let rise until doubled in size. Bake at 375° for 25 minutes. Brush with melted butter when hot.

175th Anniversary Quilt Cookbook

Italian Style Garlic Butter

Ideal for spaghetti dinner!

1/2 cup butter or margarine	1 teaspoon dried basil,
1/4 cup lite mayonnaise or	crushed
salad dressing	1/2 teaspoon dried oregano,
2 tablespoons grated	crushed
Parmesan cheese	1 clove garlic, minced

Beat together all ingredients with an electric mixer. Store in a covered container in refrigerator up to one month. To serve, spread evenly on slices of French bread or split bagels; place on an ungreased baking sheet. Broil 4 inches from heat 2-3 minutes or until golden. Makes 3/4 cup.

Kinder Kuisine

Bruschetta

This delicious repast is a Roman speciality.

6 slices of large, coarse-	6 tablespoons extra virgin
textured Italian bread, cut	olive oil
about 3/8-inch thick	Freshly ground pepper
3 cloves garlic, cut in half	

METHOD 1:

Toast the bread first, if you have a grill going, toast slices on it. The original way to prepare this dish is to first toast it over a grill. Try to get the bread toasted on outsides while keeping the inside soft. While the bread is still hot, brush with the cut-side of a garlic clove. Dribble with olive oil, grind lots of fresh black pepper over all. Serve immediately.

METHOD 2:

Mince the garlic very fine, add oil. Brush mixture on both sides of untoasted bread. Grind lots of black pepper over bread. Bake at 375° for about 20-25 minutes or until toasted well, turning a few times during process. Serve immediately.

Variation: Cut up small pieces of fresh Roma tomatoes and basil and add them to the above ingredients. Bake as stated above in Method 2, except do not turn during cooking process. It will not take very long before you will become an aficionado of this delicious way of serving bread.

Viva Italia

Poppy Seed Tea Bread

This is our most popular recipe to date. Everyone loves it.

1/3 cup vegetable oil	1 1/2 teaspoons salt
1 (4-ounce) jar strained baby food pears	2 tablespoons poppy seeds
	1 1/2 cups skim milk
2 1/2 cups sugar	1 1/2 teaspoons butter extract
3 eggs	1 1/2 teaspoons almond extract
3 cups flour	
1 1/2 teaspoons baking powder	1 1/2 teaspoons vanilla extract

Preheat oven to 350°. Spray 2 (9x5-inch) bread pans with vegetable oil spray and dust with flour. In large mixing bowl, whisk together vegetable oil, pears and sugar. Add eggs and whisk until well blended. In medium bowl, combine flour, salt, baking powder and poppy seeds; set aside.

Measure milk and add 3 extracts to milk. Add flour mixture to oil mixture alternately with milk, beginning and ending with flour mixture; whisk after each addition. Pour into prepared pans and bake at 350° for 60-70 minutes or until done. Cool for 15 minutes. Leave bread in pans. Prepare glaze.

GLAZE:

1/3 cup orange juice	1/2 teaspoon almond extract
3/4 cup sugar	1/2 teaspoon butter flavor extract
1/2 teaspoon vanilla extract	

Heat orange juice, sugar and extracts in small saucepan, stirring, until sugar melts. Poke holes in bread; pour glaze over. Let stand in pans for 2 hours. Yield: 2 loaves / 14 servings per loaf.

Nutrients per serving: Cal 180; Fat 3.5g (18%); Carbo 35g; Chol 23mg; Sod 157mg; Pro 3g.

Recipe Rehab

Delicious High Fiber Bread

2 teaspoons baking soda
1 cup molasses
3 cups sour milk (or milk with
   3 tablespoons vinegar)

2¹/₂ cups whole wheat flour
2¹/₂ cups bran
1 cup wheat germ
1 cup seedless raisins

Dissolve baking soda in molasses. Add remaining ingredients; mix. Pour into 2 greased loaf pans. Bake at 350° for 45 minutes.

Treasured Recipes from Mason, Ohio

1990s Melt in Your Mouth Dinner Rolls

You had better double this one as they disappear quickly.

1 package dry yeast
¹/₂ cup warm water
1 tablespoon sugar
1 teaspoon baking powder
1 cup milk

¹/₃ cup margarine
¹/₃ cup sugar
Dash of salt
2 eggs, beaten
4¹/₂ - 5¹/₂ cups flour

Add yeast to warm water. Add one tablespoon sugar and baking powder. Let stand for 20 minutes. Meanwhile, scald one cup milk. Add margarine, ¹/₃ cup sugar, and a dash of salt. Cool. Then add eggs and yeast mixture. Add flour and mix. Refrigerate overnight.

   Roll out half the dough as you would for pie and brush with melted margarine. Cut 12 pie-shaped pieces. Roll each from wide end to pointed end. Place on cookie sheet which has been sprayed and let rise. Do the same with remaining dough. Bake at 400° for 10 minutes. Makes 24 rolls.

Touches of the Hands & Heart

Pull-A-Parts

1 (10-count) can biscuits
¹/₄ cup melted butter
2 tablespoons parsley flakes
¹/₂ tablespoon onion flakes

¹/₂ teaspoon celery salt (or
   seed)
Parmesan cheese

Cut biscuits in 4 pieces. Place melted butter, parsley, onion flakes, and celery seed in bottom of pan. Fit in biscuits and sprinkle with Parmesan cheese. Bake at 425° for 20 minutes in 9-inch pie or 8x8-inch square pan.

Oeder Family & Friends Cookbook

Cheese Garlic Biscuits

2 cups Bisquick
2/3 cup milk
1/2 cup shredded Cheddar
  cheese (2 ounces)

1/4 cup (1/2 stick) butter or
  margarine, melted
1/4 teaspoon garlic powder

Preheat oven to 450°. Mix Bisquick, milk and cheese until soft dough forms; beat vigorously for 30 seconds. Drop dough by spoonfuls onto ungreased cookie sheet. Bake 8-10 minutes or until golden brown. Mix margarine and garlic powder; brush over warm biscuits before removing from cookie sheet. Serve warm. Makes about 10-12 biscuits.

Gardener's Delight

Butterscotch Banana Bread

2 cups (4-6) ripe bananas,
  mashed
1 1/2 cups sugar
2 eggs
1/2 cup butter, melted
3 1/2 cups flour
4 teaspoons baking powder
1 teaspoon soda

1 teaspoon cinnamon
1 teaspoon nutmeg
1 teaspoon salt
1/2 cup milk
2 2/3 cups pecans, divided
1 (12-ounce) package
  butterscotch bits

Beat bananas, sugar, eggs and butter until creamy. Add dry ingredients alternately with milk. Mix until well blended. Stir in 2 cups pecans and butterscotch bits. Pour batter into 2 well-greased and floured 9x5x3-inch loaf pans. Sprinkle tops with remaining 2/3 cup nuts. Bake 60 to 70 minutes at 350°. Cool 15 minutes. Remove from pans.

Heavenly Food II

Banana Oatmeal Bread

This is the best banana bread we have ever baked, and goodness knows, in 41 years a lot of over-ripe bananas have been destined for a batch of quick bread. This one is favored because it is made with oatmeal, which keeps it moist. Each time the subject turns to bananas, we recall the day we took six banana baked goods to the ape house at the Toledo Zoo. Along with cookies, bread, cakes, etc., we took a table, lace cloth, and candelabrum to add to the photo setup. When everything was in place, and the monkey stared down at the table in disbelief, the photographer said, "Are you going to get any more crazy ideas?" That was in January. The next summer we took cold soups to be photographed with the polar bears at the zoo. Fortunately, it was a different photographer, which may have saved the food editor's life.

1/2 cup shortening	1/2 teaspoon salt
1 cup sugar	1/2 teaspoon cinnamon
2 eggs	1 1/2 cups mashed bananas,
1/2 teaspoon vanilla	about 3 medium
1 cup flour	1/4 cup milk
1 cup quick oatmeal	1/2 cup chopped raisins
1 teaspoon baking soda	

Cream shortening and sugar. Add eggs and vanilla and beat until fluffy. Combine dry ingredients and add to first mixture alternately with bananas and milk. Mix well and fold in raisins.

Bake in greased 9x5-inch loaf pan 50-60 minutes in 350° oven. Cover for 5 minutes after being removed from oven to keep the moisture in the bread.

Aren't You Going to Taste It, Honey?

Blueberry Pineapple Bread

3 cups flour
2 teaspoons baking powder
1 teaspoon soda
1/2 teaspoon salt
2/3 cup shortening
1 1/3 cups sugar

4 eggs, beaten
1/2 cup milk
1 1/2 teaspoons lemon juice
1 cup crushed pineapple
2 cups blueberries, rinsed and
    drained

Stir flour, baking powder, soda, and salt; set aside. Cream shortening until fluffy, gradually adding sugar. Stir in eggs, milk, lemon juice, and pineapple. Add dry ingredients. Fold in blueberries gently. Pour into 4 small greased loaf pans. Bake 350° for 40-45 minutes. Cool on rack.

Cooking with Class

Coconut Bread

4 eggs
2 cups sugar
1 cup oil
2 teaspoons coconut flavoring
3 cups flour

1/2 teaspoon soda
1/2 teaspoon baking powder
1 cup buttermilk
1 cup coconut
1 cup chopped nuts

In one bowl blend eggs, sugar, oil, and flavoring. In another bowl blend dry ingredients. Alternate flour mixture and buttermilk with egg mixture. Stir in coconut and nuts. Bake in a 325° oven in 2 greased (8 1/2 x 4 1/2-inch) loaf pans or 5 mini-loaves.

GLAZE:

1 1/2 cups sugar
3/4 cup water

3 tablespoons butter
1 teaspoon coconut flavoring

In a saucepan combine sugar, water, and butter. Boil 5 minutes. Add coconut flavoring.

Tumm Yummies

Maple Bread

2 packages yeast
1/4 cup warm water
1 cup rolled oats
3/4 cup boiling water
1 cup hot coffee
1/3 cup butter-flavored Crisco
1/2 cup maple syrup or
  molasses

1/2 cup sugar
2 teaspoons salt
2 beaten eggs
5 cups flour
1/2 cup flour (if needed)

Dissolve yeast in warm water. Mix oats, boiling water, and coffee together; let stand until lukewarm. Mix in Crisco, syrup, sugar, salt, and eggs. Add dissolved yeast. Add flour and knead. Let rise until double in size. Punch down and shape into loaves or rolls. Let rise. Bake at 350° for about 30 minutes.

Our Collection of Heavenly Recipes

Cranberry Pumpkin Bread

2 eggs, slightly beaten
2 cups sugar
1/2 cup oil
1 cup canned pumpkin
2 1/2 cups all-purpose flour
1 tablespoon pumpkin pie
  spice

1 teaspoon baking soda
1/2 teaspoon salt
1 teaspoon cinnamon
1 teaspoon nutmeg
1 cup chopped cranberries

Preheat oven to 350°. Grease 2 (8x4-inch) loaf pans. Combine eggs, sugar, oil, and pumpkin; mix well. In large bowl, combine flour, pumpkin pie spice, soda, salt, cinnamon, and nutmeg. Make well in center. Pour pumpkin mixture into well. Stir until dry ingredients are just moistened. Stir in cranberries. Pour batter into prepared pans. Bake at 350° for one hour or until toothpick inserted in center comes out clean. Yield: 2 loaves.

A Cleveland Collection

Apricot Crescents

4 cups flour
1 pound butter
1 pound cottage cheese (small
  curd)
3 (11-ounce) packages dried
  apricots

1³/₄ cups sugar
3 egg whites
2 pounds ground nuts
2 cups sugar

Mix flour, butter and cottage cheese as for pie dough. Form into about 1-inch balls. Refrigerate overnight. Roll thin; fill and shape into crescents. Cook apricots and put through sieve. Add 1³/₄ cups sugar. With fork, lightly whip egg whites. Brush each horn with egg white and roll or cover with nuts that have been mixed with the 2 cups sugar. Bake in 350° oven for 15 to 20 minutes.

Czech Dancers Polka Club Cook Book

Apple Rolls

Dee-licious warm with milk!

2 cups water
1¹/₂ cups sugar
1 recipe Bisquick shortcake

2 cups pared, sliced or
  chopped apples
1 teaspoon cinnamon

Boil water and sugar 5 minutes. Pour into 9-inch square pan. Prepare shortcake according to recipe on Bisquick box. Roll into ¹/₃-inch thick oblong. Sprinkle with apples and cinnamon. Roll up, cut into 6 slices, and lay cut-side-down in syrup. Bake in 450° oven for 25 minutes.

Treasured Recipes from Mason, Ohio

The Wilds, southwest of Cambridge, is the largest research and conservation center for endangered wildlife in North America. Animals roam freely without cages in an open range habitat incorporating nearly 10,000 acres of grasslands, woodlands, and 150 lakes.

Christmas Morning Rolls

1 bag of 24 frozen dinner rolls
1 (3³/₄-ounce) package
   butterscotch pudding (not
   instant)

¹/₂ cup butter
³/₄ cup brown sugar
¹/₂ cup nuts

Arrange rolls in greased tube pan. Sprinkle dry pudding mix over rolls. Cook butter and remaining ingredients over low heat until sugar is dissolved and mixture is bubbly. Pour over rolls. Cover tightly with foil and let stand on countertop overnight. The next morning, bake at 350° for 30 minutes. Let stand 5 minutes, then invert carefully on serving dish.

Treasured Recipes

Overnight Cinnamon Rolls

1 package yeast
¹/₄ cup warm water
2 eggs, beaten
¹/₃ cup white sugar

¹/₂ teaspoon salt
1 cup milk, scalded
¹/₂ cup oleo
3¹/₂ cups Robin Hood flour

Dissolve yeast in ¹/₄ cup warm water. Add rest of ingredients and refrigerate overnight. Roll out cold dough. Sprinkle with butter, cinnamon and a little brown sugar. Roll up and cut in 1-inch slices. Put pecan topping in bottom of a greased pan, then put rolls on top of that. Let rise 3 hours, then bake at 350° for 15-20 minutes.

PECAN TOPPING FOR ROLLS:

¹/₃ cup butter
¹/₂ cup brown sugar
¹/₂ cup pecan pieces

1 tablespoon corn syrup or
   water

When rolls are done baking flip out on plate.

Favorite Recipes from the Heart of Amish Country

Blueberry Oat Bran Muffins

2¹/₂ cups quick oats, uncooked
¹/₂ cup brown sugar, firmly packed
2 teaspoons baking powder
¹/₂ teaspoon cinnamon

²/₃ cup skim milk (dry powdered)
3 tablespoons canola oil
¹/₂ cup egg beaters, thawed
1 cup fresh or frozen blueberries

Place oatmeal in blender, cover and blend for about one minute. Stir occasionally.

Combine ground oats, brown sugar, baking powder, and cinnamon. Add milk, oil, and egg beaters. Stir until dry ingredients are moistened. Add blueberries. Mix to blend. Fill paper-lined muffin tin. Bake in 400° oven 20-22 minutes or until golden brown. Yield: 1 dozen.

Note: After cool, place muffins in a zip-lock bag and store in freezer. Heat in microwave at HIGH for about one minute before eating.

Heartline Cookbook

Ohio Bran 'n' Raisin Muffins

Best muffins ever.

2 cups bran
1 cup raisins
³/₄ cup milk
²/₃ cup molasses
2 eggs, beaten

¹/₂ cup vegetable oil
1 cup flour
2 teaspoons baking powder
1 teaspoon baking soda
¹/₂ teaspoon salt

Heat oven to 400°. Grease 16 (2 - 2¹/₂-inch) muffin cups. Stir bran, raisins, milk, and molasses in medium-size bowl. Stir well. Allow to stand 15 minutes. Stir in eggs and vegetable oil. Mix flour, baking powder, baking soda, and salt in large bowl. Stir bran mixture into flour mixture until blended. Spoon batter into prepared muffin pan cups. Bake 15-18 minutes until lightly browned and sharp knife inserted in muffins comes out clean. Makes 16 muffins.

Seasoned with Love

Raisin Muffins Superb

2²/3 cups sifted flour
1/3 cup sugar
1 tablespoon + 1 teaspoon
  baking powder
1 teaspoon salt

2 eggs, separated
1 cup milk
1/3 cup margarine, melted
1 cup raisins

In a medium-size bowl, sift dry ingredients together. After separating the eggs, slightly beat egg yolks. In a separate bowl, beat egg whites until stiff. Combine egg yolks, milk, shortening, and raisins. Add all at once to dry ingredients. Mix quickly just enough to moisten all dry ingredients. Fold in beaten egg whites. Line muffin tin with cupcake paper liners. Fill each 3/4 full. Bake at 400° for approximately 20 minutes or until light brown on top. Remove from heat and brush tops with melted margarine. Yield: 1 dozen.

Now That Mom's Not Around

Honey Bran Muffins

Hearty and tasty.

1 quart buttermilk
4 eggs
1 cup salad oil
1 cup honey

5 cups flour
3 cups sugar
5 teaspoons baking soda
1 (15-ounce) box raisin bran

Stir together buttermilk and eggs. Mix in remaining ingredients and stir until just moistened. Let mixture sit for 5 minutes. Spoon into greased muffin tins, filling them 2/3 full. Bake at 350° for 15-20 minutes. Yields 4 dozen muffins.

Chef Charles Tischler, Colonel Crawford Inn.

A Taste of Columbus Vol IV

Thomas Edison, inventor of the light bulb, first saw the light of day in Milan, Ohio, in 1847.

Apple-Pumpkin Streusel Muffins

This is a favorite especially in the fall when the flavors of pumpkin and apples come to mind.

BATTER:

2½ cups flour
2 cups sugar
1 teaspoon ground cinnamon
1 teaspoon baking soda
½ teaspoon ground ginger
½ teaspoon salt
¼ teaspoon ground nutmeg

2 eggs, slightly beaten
1 cup (8 ounces) canned
   pumpkin*
½ cup vegetable oil
2 cups peeled, cored and
   grated all-purpose apples
½ cup finely chopped nuts

TOPPING:

¼ cup sugar
2 tablespoons flour
1 tablespoon butter or
   margarine

½ teaspoon cinnamon

Preheat oven to 375°. In large bowl, combine flour, sugar, cinnamon, baking soda, ginger, salt, and nutmeg. In medium bowl combine eggs, pumpkin, and oil; add to dry ingredients, stir until just moistened. Add apples and nuts. Fill paper-lined or greased muffin cups ¾ full. Combine topping ingredients; sprinkle evenly over muffins. Bake 20-25 minutes or until golden brown. Cool 5 minutes; remove from pans. Makes 18-24 muffins.

Note: *Since pumpkin usually comes packed in 16-ounce cans, use half the can and freeze the remainder for another batch of muffins at a later date. You'll need it, and not much later, either.

Bountiful Ohio

Shenkli
(A Swiss Donut)

³/₄ cup butter
3 cups sugar
8 eggs, beaten
2 lemons, rind only
1 teaspoon lemon flavor

9 - 9¹/₂ cups flour
¹/₂ teaspoon salt
1 teaspoon soda
2 teaspoons cream of tartar

Cream butter and sugar. Add eggs, lemon rind, and flavoring. Mix 4 cups flour, salt, soda, cream of tartar. Sift. Add other flour, 1 cup at a time and mix well. Dough will be very stiff. Roll out by hand in long 1-inch thick rolls. Cut by inch and shape the size of a fat finger. Cool 3-4 hours or overnight in refrigerator. French fry in oil until brown. Drain on paper towels. Can be frozen. Makes 115-125.

Recipes from "The Little Switzerland of Ohio"

Sunshine Coffee Cake

FILLING/TOPPING:

¹/₂ cup brown sugar
2 teaspoons cinnamon
2 tablespoons flour

2 tablespoons melted butter
¹/₂ cup chopped nuts

Blend above ingredients together before mixing coffee cake batter.

BATTER:

1¹/₂ cups flour
3 teaspoons baking powder
¹/₄ teaspoon salt
³/₄ cup sugar

¹/₄ cup shortening
1 egg
¹/₂ cup milk

Preheat oven the 375°. Sift dry ingredients together and cut in shortening. Beat egg well and add milk. Combine liquid with dry ingredients. Spread half the batter in a greased flat pan 8x8- or 6x10-inches. Sprinkle with half of filling. Add the other half of the batter and sprinkle with remaining filling on top. Bake at 375° for 25 minutes. Cut in squares.

The Amish Way Cookbook

Fat-Free Coffee Cake

Coffee Cake is a good guest-for-breakfast or let's fix-something-special-since-Joanie-made-it-to-the-state-sumo-wrestling-championship kind of cake. It's best warm from the oven, but goes with milk as a snack later.

2 egg whites	1/2 teaspoon vanilla
1 cup sugar	1 teaspoon baking soda
1 medium banana	1 tablespoon lemon juice
1 1/2 cups flour	

Preheat oven to 350°. In a large bowl, mix all ingredients, one at a time, stirring well after each addition. Pour batter into a round 9-inch non-stick cake pan that's been lightly coated with cooking spray and dusted with flour.

TOPPING:

1/2 cup brown sugar	2 tablespoons flour
1 tablespoon cinnamon	2 teaspoons egg white

In a small bowl mix all ingredients. Drop the topping in globs over the cake. Bake 30 minutes.

Variation: Want to be really decadent? Ice with 1 1/3 cups powdered sugar, 2 tablespoons boiled skimmed milk, and 2 teaspoons vanilla. Stir until smooth and pour over cake.

Serving size: 1 slice. Servings per recipe: 8. Cal 206; Fat 0g; Sat Fat 0g; Chol 0mg; Sod 247mg; Carb 49g; Fiber 1g; Prot 3g.

The Fat-Free Real Food Cookbook

Coffee Cake

1 box Duncan Hines Yellow Cake Mix (without pudding)	1/2 cup oil
	4 eggs
1 small package French vanilla instant pudding	1/2 cup sugar
	1 cup nuts
1 1/3 cups milk	1 teaspoon cinnamon

Mix cake mix, pudding, milk, oil, and eggs. Set aside. Combine sugar, chopped nuts, and cinnamon. Alternate cake batter with filling mixture in well-greased tube pan. Alternate layers beginning and ending with batter. Bake in 350° oven for 60 minutes.

A Sprinkling of Favorite Recipes

Blueberry Buckle Coffee Cake

4 cups flour
1 1/2 cups sugar
5 teaspoons baking powder
1 1/2 teaspoons salt

1/2 cup shortening
1 1/2 cups milk
2 eggs
4 cups blueberries

TOPPING:
2 cups sugar
2/3 cup flour

1 teaspoon cinnamon
1/2 cup oleo

Blend first 7 ingredients. Beat vigorously 1/2 minute. Carefully stir in blueberries. Spread 1/2 of batter into greased pan. Mix topping ingredients and sprinkle 1/2 of topping over batter. Add remaining batter, then sprinkle rest of topping on top. Bake at 350° 45-50 minutes.

By Our Cookstove

Toad in the Hole

2 slices bacon
1/2 pound pork sausage links,
    cut into 1/2-inch pieces
1 cup all-purpose flour

1 teaspoon baking powder
1 teaspoon salt
3 eggs, beaten
1 1/2 cups milk

Cook bacon till crisp. Drain, reserving 2 tablespoons bacon drippings. Crumble bacon, set aside. In same skillet, brown sausage; drain fat. Stir together flour, baking powder and salt. Add eggs and milk, beat until smooth. Spread reserved bacon drippings in an ovenproof dish. Place sausage pieces in dish; sprinkle with crumbled bacon. Pour batter over all. Bake, uncovered, at 400° till set, 30-35 minutes. Serves 4.

Plain & Fancy Favorites

Ham & Swiss Omelet Squares

Ingredients in () are the quantities to use for 48 portions. Original quantities make 12 portions.

18 large eggs (72)
3/4 cup whole milk (3 cups)
1/2 teaspoon salt (2 teaspoons)
1/4 teaspoon pepper (1 teaspoon)
1 (1-pound, 8-ounce) package hash brown potatoes, thawed (6 pounds)

8 ounces cooked ham (2 pounds)
10 ounces Swiss cheese, shredded (2 pounds, 8 ounces)
3 ounces onion, chopped, or green onion (12 ounces)

Beat together thoroughly eggs, milk, salt and pepper. Combine potatoes, ham, cheese, and onion. Distribute mixture evenly in greased 10x12x2-inch pan for 12 portions, or in 2 (12x20x2-inch) pans for 48 portions. Pour egg mixture evenly over ingredients in pan(s). Bake in preheated 350° oven until golden brown and center is firm: 10x12-inch pan—35-40 minutes; 12x20-inch pan—55-60 minutes; 300° convection oven 10x12-inch pan—25-30 minutes; 12x20-inch pan—40-45 minutes.

St. Gerard's 75th Jubilee Cookbook

Sausage Brunch Casserole

1 package frozen hash brown potatoes, thawed
2 1/2 slices bread, cut in 1/2-inch cubes
1/2 pound bacon, fried or 1 pound sausage, cooked and drained

5 ounces shredded Cheddar cheese
6 eggs
2 cups milk
Salt and pepper
1/2 teaspoon dry mustard

Butter an 8x12-inch dish. Spread hash browns and bread on bottom. Spread meat and cheese over potatoes. Blend eggs, milk, and seasonings and pour over mixture. Bake at 350° for 30-40 minutes. Serves about 12 people.

Treasured Recipes

Cheese Blintz Casserole

This is a wonderful brunch dish, especially for entertaining, as it can be prepared the day before needed.

FILLING:

2 cups small curd cottage cheese

2 egg yolks

1 tablespoon sugar

1 (8-ounce) package cream cheese, softened

BATTER:

1½ cups sour cream

½ cup orange juice

6 eggs

¼ cup butter, softened

1 cup flour

⅓ cup sugar

2 tablespoons baking powder

1 teaspoon cinnamon

Grease a 9x13-inch casserole dish. Beat together all filling ingredients. Set aside.

Combine all batter ingredients in bowl or food processor. Beat or blend until smooth. Pour half of the batter into the casserole dish. Drop filling by teaspoonfuls over batter; spread evenly (the filling will mix slightly with the batter). Pour remaining batter over filling. Cover and refrigerate 2 hours or overnight. Bake, uncovered, at 350° for 50-60 minutes, until light golden brown. Serve with additional sour cream and preserves. Serves 12.

Plain & Fancy Favorites

Stovetop Goetta

Hearty, delicious breakfast food with a couple of eggs, goetta is equally at home at the dinner table. As it fries, it leaves enough residue to make a good gravy.

1 pound ground beef
1 pound ground pork
3 quarts water
2 cups pinhead oatmeal (not
  rolled oats)

1 medium onion, chopped fine
2 teaspoons salt
1/2 teaspoon pepper

Using your heaviest pan, place the ground meat in water, breaking up lumps while bringing the water to a boil. Add the remaining ingredients. Cook for 1 hour. Stir frequently; don't let it stick, the goetta will be very thick when done. (Some people declare the goetta done if a wooden spoon stands upright when stuck in the center of the pot.)

Pour into loaf pans. Refrigerate. The goetta will be firm and can then be sliced and fried to a golden brown. Serve it with applesauce on top or with eggs at breakfast. Yield: approximately 6 pounds.

Cincinnati Recipe Treasury

Shaker Supper Omelet

1/2 cup hot, scalded milk
1/3 cup dry bread or cracker
  crumbs
1 teaspoon salt

1/4 teaspoon pepper
3 eggs, beaten
1 tablespoon butter

Pour hot, scalded milk over crumbs. Let cool. Add salt and pepper and mix in well-beaten eggs. Heat cast-iron skillet over fairly high heat and add butter. Pour in egg mixture and reduce heat to moderate. Fry to a golden brown on the bottom. Be careful not to cook too fast, at too hot a temperature; the egg will toughen and the bottom will burn before the surface is set. When the omelet has set in all but the center, fold in half and slip onto a hot platter. Serve at once. Serves 2.

The Shaker Cookbook

Quickie Stickie Buns

3¹/₄ cups all-purpose flour, divided
2 packages instant blend dry yeast
³/₄ cup milk
¹/₂ cup water
¹/₄ cup butter
¹/₄ cup sugar
1 teaspoon salt
1 egg

In large mixer bowl, measure 1¹/₂ cups flour, add yeast; blend. In medium-size saucepan, measure milk, water, butter, sugar, and salt. Stirring constantly, heat until warm (120-130°); pour into flour-yeast mixture. Add egg. Beat ¹/₂ minute at low speed, scraping bowl. Beat 3 minutes at high speed. By hand, gradually add remaining 1³/₄ cups flour, mixing well. Scrape down batter from sides of bowl. Cover. Let rise in warm place until doubled, about 30 minutes. While dough is rising, prepare topping. Drop topping by tablespoons into well-greased muffin cups, or 10x15-inch jelly roll pan. Stir down batter. Drop by tablespoons into pan. Cover; let rise about 30 minutes. Bake at 375° for 12-15 minutes. Let cool one minute, then invert pan onto pan with waxed paper.

TOPPING:

³/₄ cup butter or margarine
1 cup firmly packed brown sugar
1 tablespoon water
1 teaspoon cinnamon
1 tablespoon light corn syrup
³/₄ cup chopped nuts (optional)

In medium-size saucepan, combine all ingredients. Cook over low heat until butter melts.

Women's Centennial Cookbook

Sticky Bagels

8 ounces fat-free Ultra Promise Margarine
¹/₂ teaspoon vanilla
1 cup brown sugar
2 teaspoons cinnamon
1 dozen bagels cut in half

Beat margarine, vanilla, brown sugar, and cinnamon for one minute on medium speed with blender.

Take bagel and dip top with spread just prepared. If needed, spread with knife. Broil at 450° for 4-5 minutes, until bubbly and brown. Serve warm. Yields 24 servings. Cal 124; Fat .6g.

Down Home Cookin' Without the Down Home Fat

Company French Toast

2 sticks butter, melted
1 cup brown sugar
1 loaf "Texas Toast" bread
Cinnamon

Raisins (optional)
7 eggs
1 teaspoon vanilla
2³/₄ cups milk

Pour melted butter in a 13x9-inch pan and cover with brown sugar. Place a layer of bread (as close as possible) over butter; sprinkle cinnamon and raisins over and cover with another layer of bread. Combine and beat eggs, vanilla, and milk; pour mixture over bread. Cover with plastic wrap and refrigerate overnight. The next morning, bake at 350° for 40 minutes. Let set 5 minutes before slicing. Makes its own syrup.

What's Cooking at Holden School

Peach French Toast

1 cup brown sugar
¹/₂ cup butter or margarine
2 tablespoons water
1 (29-ounce) can sliced
 peaches, drained

12-14 slices French bread
 (1-inch thick)
5 large eggs
1¹/₂ cups milk
3 teaspoons vanilla

Over medium-low heat, stir brown sugar and butter until butter melts. Add water and cook until sauce is thick and foamy. Pour into 13x9x2-inch baking dish. Let cool 10 minutes. Place peaches on top of sauce. Cover with bread, trimming to fit in one layer. Whisk together eggs, milk, and vanilla. Pour over bread. Cover and refrigerate overnight. Bake at 350°, uncovered, 40 minutes or until set and golden. Cover with foil if browning too quickly. Serve with warmed reserved peach syrup, if desired. This is rich and yummy!

The Fifth Generation Cookbook

Clifton Mill, built in 1802, is the largest water-powered grist mill operating in the United States.

Baked Pineapple

Double the recipe—everyone will want seconds!

2 eggs	1¹/₄ cups sugar
1 can crushed pineapple (in	¹/₄ cup water
its own juice)	Butter
2 tablespoons cornstarch	Cinnamon

Slightly beat eggs; add next 4 ingredients. Top with pieces of butter and cinnamon. Egg substitute can be used. Bake at 350° for one hour or until juice is absorbed.

Favorite Recipes from Poland Women's Club

Oven-Fried Apple Rings

8 Winesap apples, peeled and	8 tablespoons brown sugar
cored	2 teaspoons cinnamon
¹/₂ cup butter	1 teaspoon nutmeg
8 tablespoons sugar	

Slice apples into rings. Place half the amount in a 9x13-inch pan. Dot with ¹/₄ cup of the butter. Combine the sugars and spices. Sprinkle half the amount over the apples. Repeat the process for the second layer. Bake at 350° for 55 minutes. Serves 8.

Note: This side dish is great for country ham. Soak ham slices for one hour in cold water; drain well and remove rind from edges. Fry slowly until brown.

Appletizers

Buttermilk Scones

3 cups flour
1/3 cup sugar
2 1/2 teaspoons baking
  powder
1/2 teaspoon baking soda
1/2 teaspoon salt
3/4 cup firm butter

1 teaspoon grated orange peel
1 cup buttermilk
About 1 tablespoon
  half-and-half
1/4 teaspoon cinnamon
2 tablespoons sugar

In large bowl, stir together flour, 1/3 cup sugar, baking powder, soda, and salt until thoroughly blended. Cut butter in until mixture resembles coarse cornmeal. Stir in orange peel. Make a well in center of flour mixture; add buttermilk all at once. Stir mixture with fork until dough cleans side of bowl.

With your hands, gather dough into a ball; turn out onto a floured board. Roll or pat dough into a 1/2-inch circle. Using a 2 1/2-inch circle or heart cookie cutter, cut into individual scones. Place scones 1 1/2 inches apart on lightly greased baking sheets. Brush tops with half-and-half; sprinkle lightly with cinnamon and sugar, mixed. Bake in a 425° oven for 12 minutes or until tops are lightly browned. Makes about 18 scones.

25th Anniversary Cookbook

Sister Lettie's Buttermilk Biscuits

2 cups all-purpose flour
1/2 teaspoon salt
1 tablespoon baking powder
1/2 teaspoon baking soda

3 tablespoons chilled butter
3/4 cup buttermilk, chilled
3 tablespoons melted butter

Sift flour, salt, baking powder, and soda together 3 times. Cut in the butter with a pastry blender or 2 knives, scissors fashion, until mixture resembles coarse meal. Chill the mixture in the refrigerator for about 1 hour or longer.

Add buttermilk and knead lightly, 10-15 times. Roll to 3/4-inch thickness and cut with a 1 1/2-inch round biscuit cutter, and place on lightly greased cookie sheet; or press the dough quickly into a shallow greased and floured pan 9x10x1 1/2-inch and cut the dough into diamond or square-shaped biscuits.

CONTINUED

Brush with melted butter and bake 12 minutes at 450° for round biscuits or at 400° for 18 minutes for pan biscuits. Makes 10 (2-inch) or 15 (1½-inch) round biscuits. The pan biscuits will have tender, soft sides and must be separated. These biscuits are extremely light and delicious. There never seem to be enough!

The Shaker Cookbook

Corn Muffins

Requested in our favorite restaurant dish survey.

¾ cup and 2 tablespoons sugar
1½ teaspoons salt
¾ cup shortening
1½ tablespoons corn syrup
4 eggs
1½ cups milk
2 teaspoons vanilla

3¾ cups and 2 tablespoons cake flour
5¼ teaspoons baking powder
¾ cup and 1 tablespoon yellow corn meal
½ cup water

Cream sugar, salt, shortening, and corn syrup until soft and smooth. Add eggs one at a time, mixing thoroughly after each addition. Gradually stir in milk and vanilla. Set aside. Sift together cake flour and baking powder. Add corn meal. Add the flour-corn meal mixture to first mixture and stir until the flour is absorbed. Add water and mix to a smooth batter (do not overmix or muffins will become tough). Drop batter into well greased muffin tins, filling them about half full. Bake at 400° for 15-20 minutes, or until muffin springs back when center is pressed with a finger. Makes about 36 muffins.

Chef Ed Kromko, French Loaf.

A Taste of Columbus Vol III

Civil War Corn Bread

³/4 cup flour
2 tablespoons sugar
1 teaspoon salt
1 1/2 cups corn meal

2 eggs
1 1/4 cups milk
1/4 cup melted shortening

Sift first 3 ingredients into bowl. Add corn meal, mixing well. Combine eggs and milk in small bowl. Mix. Stir into flour mixture, blending well. Mix in shortening. Spoon into greased and floured 9-inch square pan. Bake at 425° for 30 minutes until golden brown. Yields 6 servings.

Home Cookin' with 4-H

The Best Corn Bread

1 cup sour cream
1 cup cream-style corn
1 cup corn meal
1/2 cup vegetable oil

2 eggs
3 teaspoons baking powder
Pinch of salt

Preheat oven to 350°. In medium bowl combine all ingredients; mix well. Pour into a 9-inch square greased pan or 9-inch cast iron skillet. Bake for 25-30 minutes or until golden brown. Yield: 8 servings.

Cooking on the Wild Side

Baked Crab Sandwich

The bonus is—it's quick to fix.

1¼ pounds King, Lump or
  Snow crabmeat, cut into large
  pieces
1¼ cups mayonnaise
2-3 green onions, chopped
½ head Iceberg lettuce,
  chopped

1 tablespoon salt
½ tablespoon fresh lemon
  juice
12 tomato slices
6 English muffins, split,
  toasted and buttered
12 slices mozzarella cheese

Mix crabmeat, mayonnaise, onions, lettuce, salt and lemon juice together. Place a tomato slice on each muffin; arrange crab salad on top of tomatoes. Top each muffin with a slice of mozzarella. Bake at 350° for 10-15 minutes until cheese is lightly browned. Serve on a plate with fresh fruit garnish.

Angels and Friends Cookbook II

Crab Croissants

½ cup mayonnaise
¼ teaspoon dried dill weed
2 cloves garlic, minced
¼ cup minced fresh parsley
⅛ teaspoon cayenne pepper
⅔ pound crabmeat, flaked
1 cup shredded Monterey
  Jack cheese

1 cup shredded Cheddar
  cheese
1 (2¼-ounce) can sliced ripe
  black olives
1 (10-ounce) package frozen
  artichoke hearts, cooked and
  quartered
4 large croissants

In medium bowl, combine all ingredients. Cover and refrigerate until ready to use. Split croissants horizontally. Spread each croissant half with crab mixture. Place croissants on baking sheet and broil 5 inches from heat for 3-4 minutes or until heated through.

The Kettle Cookbook

Prosciutto-Parmesan Pull-Apart Loaf

3/4 cup (1 1/2 sticks) butter
   or margarine, softened
1/3 cup grated parmesan
   cheese
1/2 cup (2 ounces) coarsely
   chopped prosciutto
1 teaspoon freshly cracked
   pepper

1/4 cup chopped fresh basil or
1/4 cup chopped fresh parsely
   and 1 tablespoon dried basil
1 (1-pound) loaf Italian bread
   or French bread

Combine all ingredients (but bread) in a small bowl. With serrated knife, slice bread diagonally almost all the way through 12 times, at 1 1/2 inch intervals; spread one rounded tablespoonful prosciutto butter between sections, using half of butter mixture. Turn loaf around so that ends are reversed; slice loaf diagonally almost all the way through 12 times, making diamond patterns of 1 1/2 inch sections of bread. Spread with remaining prosciutto butter.

Preheat oven to 450°. Tear off a sheet of heavy-duty aluminum foil 5 inches longer than bread. Center bread on foil. Fold over long sides of foil to come halfway up sides of loaf and fold or crimp short ends of foil to secure. Heat 10 minutes or until crust is crisp and loaf is heated through. Makes 12 servings.

To heat on grill: Bring long sides of foil together over top of bread; fold together one inch of foil. Crease and continue folding foil until it fits loosely over bread. Repeat folding technique at short ends of foil. Place loaf, right-side-up, 5-6 inches from heat. Heat 8 minutes or until loaf is heated through.

Men love this. Although this claims 12 servings, I have gone through almost 2 loaves of this at dinner parties for 8 people.

Cook, Line & Sinker

Granola

6 cups oatmeal
1 cup wheat germ
1 1/2 cups coconut
1 1/2 cups brown sugar

1 1/2 sticks oleo, melted
1/2 cup nuts, chopped
Sunflower seeds (optional)

Mix well then bake in 275° oven. Stir every 20 minutes until browned.

Tasty Recipes

Tuna-Cheese Twist

2 (6¹/2-ounce) cans tuna,
  light chunk, drained
1 (2¹/4-ounce) can ripe
  olives, sliced and drained
¹/2 cup celery, chopped
¹/2 cup green pepper,
  chopped
¹/4 cup onion, chopped
1 can cream of mushroom
  soup

2 cups Bisquick mix
¹/2 cup cold water
1¹/2 cup Cheddar cheese,
  shredded
1 egg
1 tablespoon water
¹/4 cup milk

Mix the first 5 ingredients and ¹/4 cup of the soup. Mix Bisquick and ¹/2 cup cold water until soft dough forms; beat vigorously 20 strokes. Gently smooth dough into ball on floured cloth-covered board. Knead 5 times. Roll dough into 14x11-inch rectangle. Place dough on lightly greased cookie sheet. Spoon tuna mixture lengthwise down center of rectangle; sprinkle with one cup cheese. Make cuts 2¹/2 inches long at 1-inch intervals on 14-inch sides of rectangle. Fold strips over filling. Mix egg and one tablespoon water; brush over dough. Bake at 425° for 15-20 minutes or until light brown. Mix remaining soup and cheese and milk over medium heat, stirring occasionally until hot. Serve over slices of twist. Makes 6 servings.

Note: Chicken can be used instead of tuna.

Mary Yoder's Amish Kitchen Cookbook

Sensational Mandarin Ham Roll-Ups

A garnish of orange slices makes this a pretty springtime dish.

1 (11-ounce) can mandarin
  oranges, drained
1 1/2 cups cooked white rice
1/3 cup mayonnaise
2 tablespoons pecans,
  chopped
2 tablespoons fresh parsley,
  snipped

1 tablespoon green onions,
  sliced
8 large thin slices boiled ham
1/2 cup orange marmalade
1 tablespoon lemon juice
1/4 teaspoon ground ginger

Reserve 8 orange sections. Chop remainder and combine with the cooked rice, mayonnaise, pecans, parsley, and onions. Divide mixture among ham slices. Roll ham around filling and place seam-side-down in 10x6x2-inch baking dish. Combine marmalade, lemon juice, and ginger. Brush on top of rolls. Bake in a preheated 350° oven for 25-30 minutes, brushing occasionally with remaining sauce, and garnish with remaining oranges. Freezes well and may be prepared ahead. Yields: 4 servings.

Simply Sensational

Raspberry Jam

4-5 cups peeled, chopped ripe
  tomatoes
4 cups sugar

1 tablespoon lemon juice
1 (8-ounce) package
  raspberry gelatin

In large kettle, combine tomatoes, sugar, and lemon juice. Stir over high heat until mixture boils. Reduce heat and simmer 15 minutes, uncovered. Remove from heat and stir in gelatin until completely dissolved. Pour into jars or freezer containers. Store in freezer or refrigerator. Makes 8 half-pints.

Cooking with Class

Ham and Spinach Wrap-Ups

A great brunch recipe to celebrate happy memories.

1 can cream of celery soup	2 eggs
1 cup sour cream	1/2 cup onion, chopped
2 tablespoons Dijon mustard	1/4 cup flour
1 cup Minute Rice, uncooked	18 slices boiled ham
1 (10-ounce) package frozen	3/4 cup Pepperidge Farm
spinach, chopped, thawed, and	Stuffing
drained	1/4 cup butter, melted
1 cup small curd cottage	
cheese	

Mix soup, sour cream, and Dijon mustard; reserve half of this mixture for later. Add rice, spinach, cottage cheese, eggs, onion, and flour to half of the soup mixture. Place about 2 tablespoons of mixture on a slice of boiled ham. Roll into log shape and place in baking dish with seam-side-down. Repeat until all 18 slices of ham are used.

Pour remaining half of soup mixture over ham rolls. Combine Pepperidge Farm Stuffing and melted butter and sprinkle over top. Bake in a preheated 350° oven for 45 minutes, covered. Remove lid last 5-10 minutes to toast bread crumbs. Let stand 10-15 minutes before serving. May be prepared ahead and freezes well. Yield: 18 servings.

Simply Sensational

Freezer Strawberry Jam

4 cups crushed strawberries	1 rounded tablespoon Epsom
7 cups sugar	salt

Mix crushed strawberries and sugar well. Boil hard for 5 minutes. Remove from stove and add Epsom salt; stir. Cool in cold water until pieces of berries scatter throughout mixture. Pour in containers. Cool and put in freezer. Delicious!

Our Collection of Heavenly Recipes

Initial Crackers

1/2 cup flour
1/8 teaspoon garlic salt
2 tablespoons sesame seeds

3 tablespoons cold butter
2 tablespoons ice water

Mix flour, garlic salt and sesame seeds. Cut in cold butter until crumbly. Sprinkle on ice water. Mix to form a ball. Roll skinny "snakes." Form your initials. Flatten a bit on ungreased cookie sheet. Bake 15 minutes at 350°. Allow to cool before eating. Serves 6-8.

Cooking with TLC

Soups

The Hower House Museum, a whimsical, well-preserved 28-room mansion built in 1871. Akron.

Bean Soup

Dried beans were used a lot by the Zoar people. This is my recipe and my husband's favorite soup.

1 (2-pound) bag Great
  Northern beans
2 cups diced ham
1 large (46-ounce) can beef
  broth

1 large onion, chopped
2 cups celery, diced
Salt and pepper to taste

Soak beans in water overnight; drain and rinse beans. In large kettle, combine soaked beans, ham, beef broth, onion, celery, and enough water to cover mixture. Salt and pepper to taste. Bring to a boil, then simmer for 3 hours adding a little more water if needed.

Heirloom Recipes and By Gone Days

Cabbage-Bean Soup

1 small onion, chopped (1/4
  cup)
1 large rib celery, sliced thin
  (1/2 cup)
3 medium potatoes peeled
  and diced (2 1/2 cups)
3 tablespoons oil
1 pound cabbage, shredded (6
  cups)

3 cups chicken broth
1 clove garlic, crushed
1 bay leaf
1/2 teaspoon poultry
  seasoning
1/2 teaspoon salt
1/8 teaspoon pepper
1 (16-ounce) can beans with
  tomato sauce

In 3-quart saucepan sauté onion, celery, and potatoes in oil 5 minutes or until onion is tender. Stir in cabbage, broth and seasonings. Cover and cook over moderate heat, stirring occasionally or until potatoes and cabbage are tender. Stir in beans. Cook 10 minutes longer for beans to heat through. Makes 4 generous servings. (I used tomato sauce since beans were in water—took 1 - 1 1/2 hours.) Can be frozen. Also add hamburger to extend.

St. Gerard's 75th Jubilee Cookbook

Savory Winter Vegetable Soup

Tastes even better if prepared ahead 3-4 days.

8 tablespoons butter, divided	1/2 teaspoon basil
2 cups onion, chopped	1/2 teaspoon white pepper
6 tablespoons flour	3-4 carrots, julienned
6 cups rich chicken broth	6 large mushrooms, sliced
2 cups potatoes, diced	2 large leeks, julienned
1 bay leaf	1 cup celery, diced
1 1/2 teaspoons salt	1/2 - 3/4 cup whipping cream

Sauté onion in 4 tablespoons butter until soft but not brown. Add flour and stir over moderate heat for about 2 minutes. Gradually add chicken broth, whisking until smooth. Add potatoes and seasonings; simmer, uncovered, until potatoes are almost tender. Sauté strips of carrots, mushrooms, and leeks in 4 tablespoons of butter until just softened, but not brown. When potatoes in the soup are just barely cooked, add the chopped celery, which should remain crisp. Add the whipping cream, stir until smooth. Taste for seasonings, adding salt and pepper, if needed. Serve very hot, garnished with strips of leeks, carrots, and mushrooms. Yields: 6 servings.

Variation: Add 2 cups cooked, cubed chicken.

Simply Sensational

Chili Soup

1 pound hamburger	1 can kidney beans
1 onion, chopped	1 can tomato juice
2 tablespoons flour	Chili powder
1/4 cup brown sugar	

Brown hamburger and onion. Drain grease. Add 2 tablespoons flour and brown sugar, stir. Add kidney beans and tomato juice. Add chili powder to taste. Simmer for 15 minutes.

Salem Mennonite Cookbook

Beside The Point's Split Pea Soup

Akron's fabulous West Point Market, under the direction of proprietor Russ Vernon, has become known as one of the most elegant and innovative food and wine stores between New York and California.

Carol Moore is director of "A Moveable Feast," catering division. This is Carol's choice of a "typically Ohio" recipe. Strictly Midwestern in origin, split pea soup is enhanced by West Point's special touches.

8 cups water
1 (1-pound) bag split peas,
  rinsed and drained
1 ham bone with meat or 1
  large ham hock
2 large onions, chopped
2-4 leeks, white part only,
  chopped
2 ribs celery, chopped
  (include some leaves)

1 large carrot, peeled and
  chopped
1 cup dry white wine
1 clove garlic, finely chopped
$1/2$ teaspoon marjoram leaves
$1/4$ teaspoon thyme leaves
Salt
Pepper

In large kettle, combine all ingredients except salt and pepper; bring to a boil. Reduce heat, cover and simmer 2 - $2^{1}/2$ hours or until peas are soft. Remove ham bone; cool slightly. Remove meat from bone; return to kettle. Add salt and pepper to taste. Makes about 2 quarts.

Bountiful Ohio

Hodge Podge Soup

$1^{1}/2$ pounds hamburger
$3/4$ cup chopped onion
1 clove garlic (or garlic
  powder)
3 cans minestrone soup
1 (31-ounce) can pork and
  beans

3 cups water
$1^{1}/2$ cups chopped celery
1 tablespoon Worcestershire
  sauce
$1/2$ teaspoon oregano

In a large saucepan cook hamburger, onion, and garlic until brown and tender. Stir in minestrone soup, pork and beans, 3 cups water, celery, Worcestershire sauce, and oregano. Simmer on low, covered, for 30 minutes.

Recipes & Remembrances

Spinach and Meatball Soup

1 pound ground beef
1 cup Italian-style bread
 crumbs
3/4 cup grated Parmesan
 cheese
2 eggs, lightly beaten
1/2 cup water
7 cups chicken broth

1 cup finely chopped onion
1 cup finely chopped carrots
1 (10-ounce) package frozen
 chopped spinach, thawed and
 drained
1 tablespoon oregano leaves,
 crushed

In a bowl, combine beef, bread crumbs, Parmesan cheese, eggs, and water. Shape into 3/4-inch balls; set aside. In a large saucepot, combine chicken broth, onion, and carrots. Bring to a boil. Reduce heat and simmer, covered, for 10 minutes. Stir in spinach and oregano. Return to a boil. Add meatballs. Reduce heat and simmer, covered, until meatballs are cooked, about 10 minutes. Serve with additonal Parmesan cheese if desired. Makes 6-8 servings.

Cook, Line & Sinker

Hearty Italian Soup

1 pound mild sausage
1 pound hot sausage
4 carrots, peeled
1 1/2 pounds zucchini
2 green peppers
1 cup onions, finely chopped
2 cloves garlic, minced
1 cup white cooking wine

10 cups chicken broth
2 large cans peeled, whole
 tomatoes
2 teaspoons dried basil
1 teaspoon dried oregano
Black pepper to taste
1 cup uncooked orzo
1 1/4 cups Parmesan cheese

Remove casings from sausage. Brown in soup pot and drain fat. Dice vegetables. Add onions and garlic to pot, stirring until soft. Add all remaining ingredients except orzo and cheese and bring to boil.

When boiling, add orzo and cook for 20 minutes. Serve and sprinkle with Parmesan cheese. Serves 12.

The Kettle Cookbook

Greek Lemon Soup

4 quarts chicken stock	1/3 - 1/2 cup lemon juice
4 eggs, well beaten	(adjust to taste)
1/2 cup vermicelli noodles	1/2 teaspoon salt
(nested type, crushed)	1/4 teaspoon pepper

Bring chicken stock to a boil. Add noodles and cook until done, about 5 minutes. In a separate bowl, beat the eggs with the lemon juice. When noodles are cooked, remove from heat and SLOWLY add the hot soup to the egg mixture until about 1/2 of the soup is combined. Reverse procedure and then SLOWLY add egg mixture back to rest of the soup in the pot. Salt and pepper to taste. Serve immediately and serve hot.

Now That Mom's Not Around

Carrot Vichyssoise

Should be made ahead and chilled.

1 medium onion, chopped fine	2 ounces margarine
1 large leek, sliced	1 teaspoon salt
3 large potatoes, sliced	Dash of pepper
4 carrots, sliced	1/2 teaspoon sugar
Ham, cubed and cooked	2 1/2 cups homogenized milk
2 1/2 cups chicken bouillon	Julienne carrots

Sauté onion and leek until yellow. Add potatoes, carrots, ham, bouillon, and butter. Bring to quick boil. Reduce heat. Simmer until potatoes and carrots are tender, about 20 minutes. Remove from heat. Add seasoning to taste. Put into blender for 2 minutes. Return to pot. Add milk. Heat. (Do not boil.) Chill. Serve with julienne carrots (raw).

The Kettle Cookbook

Noodle Soup

The Zoarites ate a lot of soup. With more than one family living in each house, soup was a good way to stretch a meal.

2 cups diced celery
1 tablespoon minced onion
1/4 cup grated carrots
2 large (46-ounce) cans
    chicken broth

1 (8-ounce) bag Inn Made
    "fine" noodles

Cook the celery, onion and carrots in a little water for 1/2 hour. Add the chicken broth and bring to a boil, then add noodles. Boil gently for 20 minutes.

Heirloom Recipes and By Gone Days

Broccoli Cheese Noodle Soup

8 ounces butter
1 cup flour
1 quart chicken broth
1 pound broccoli, frozen or
    fresh (can precook to speed
    cooking process)

1 quart milk
8 ounces Velveeta cheese
Salt and pepper to taste
Kluski-style noodles or fine
    egg noodles (precook)

Melt butter in pan on stove at low-medium heat. Add flour and stir until well coated. Add chicken broth and stir until thickened by bringing to a boil. Reduce heat; add remaining ingredients except noodles and simmer until broccoli is done. Add precooked noodles. Serve in bread bowls or jumbo soup bowls.

Note: Mushrooms may also be added.

Cooking with TLC

German Cabbage Soup

2 (10½-ounce) cans
  condensed beef broth
2½ cups water
1 (8-ounce) can tomato sauce
2 teaspoons lemon juice
3 cups shredded cabbage
2 cups diced apples

⅓ cup sliced onions
1 tablespoon caraway seed
¼ teaspoon garlic powder or
  1 fresh clove crushed garlic
1 teaspoon sugar
⅛ teaspoon black pepper

In large saucepan combine broth, water, tomato sauce and lemon juice. Bring to a boil. Add remaining ingredients. Cover and simmer 20 minutes or until cabbage is tender. Serves 6-8.

The Amish Way Cookbook

Potato Cheese Soup

6-8 potatoes, peeled and
  diced
2-3 carrots, sliced
1-2 celery stalks, sliced
1 onion, chopped
1 (8-ounce) package cream
  cheese

¼ cup butter or margarine
1 (10¾-ounce) can cream of
  chicken soup, undiluted
2 cups milk
Salt and pepper to taste
4 bacon strips, fried and
  crumbled

Place potatoes, carrots, celery and onion in a large kettle; cover with water. Cook until tender. Meanwhile, in a mixing bowl, combine cream cheese, butter and soup; stir well. Add milk, seasoning and bacon; add to vegetables and heat through. Yield: 10-12 servings.

175th Anniversary Quilt Cookbook

Swiss Potato Soup

12 slices bacon, coarsely
  chopped
1 onion, coarsely chopped
2 leeks (or 4 scallions)
  coarsely chopped
1 pound cabbage, coarsely
  chopped

4 potatoes, peeled and diced
6 cups chicken stock
2 cups Gruyère cheese,
  grated
1 cup light cream
1 tablespoon dill weed
Salt and pepper

Sauté bacon in a large kettle for 3 minutes. Add onions, leeks, and cabbage and continue to cook for 5 minutes. Add potatoes and chicken stock; bring to a boil, lower heat and simmer uncovered for 40 minutes.

Pour into blender, a little at a time, and spin until smooth. Pour back into kettle. Add cheese gradually and stir over medium heat until melted. Do not boil.

Just before serving, add cream, dill weed and season to taste. Serve with buttered croutons. This is a very hearty soup. Can be made ahead, but should not be frozen. Serves 10-12.

The Kettle Cookbook

Potato Soup

3 tablespoons butter
5 medium potatoes, peeled
  and cut in cubes
1 medium onion, diced
2 cups water

1 teaspoon salt
Pepper to taste
1/8 - 1/4 teaspoon dill
1 chicken bouillon cube
2 cups milk

Cook potatoes and onion in hot butter until golden, about 10 minutes. Add water, salt, pepper, dill, and bouillon cube; heat over high heat till boiling. Reduce heat and simmer 15 minutes or until potatoes are tender. Remove from heat. Mash potatoes with potato masher. Add milk; heat through.

The PTA Pantry

Baked Potato Soup

4 large baking potatoes
2/3 cup butter or margarine
2/3 cup all-purpose flour
6 cups milk (2%)
3/4 teaspoon salt
3/4 teaspoon pepper

4-8 green onions, divided
16 slices bacon, cooked and
   crumbled, divided
1 1/2 cups shredded Cheddar
   cheese, divided
1 1/2 cups sour cream

Wash potatoes and prick several times with fork. Bake at 400° for one hour or until done. Let cool. Peel and partially mash, leaving chunks. Melt butter in saucepan over low heat. Add all-purpose flour, stirring until smooth. Cook one minute, stirring constantly.

Gradually add 6 cups milk. Cook over medium heat, stirring constantly until mixture thickens and bubbles. Add potatoes, salt, pepper, 4 tablespoons green onions, 1/2 cup bacon, and one cup cheese. Cook until thoroughly heated; stir in sour cream. Add extra milk, if needed, for desired thickness. Serve with remaining onions, bacon, and cheese or you can put all in soup at one time. After adding sour cream, do not boil. Makes 20 servings.

Per serving: Cal 348; Prot 12g; Fat 19g; Chol 34g.

Wadsworth-Rittman Hospital Cookbook

French Onion Soup

1 pound sliced onions
1/2 stick butter
Salt and pepper
1 bay leaf
1 ounce dry sherry wine
1 can beef consommé

2 cans College Inn Broth
6 large croutons
6 teaspoons grated Parmesan
   cheese
6 slices Provolone cheese

Sauté onions in butter until light brown. Add salt, pepper, and bay leaf. Add the sherry wine and simmer for a few minutes. Add beef consommé and chicken broth. Cook for approximately 20 minutes. Let boil for 10 minutes. Ladle into 6 French onion soup bowls. To each bowl, add one crouton and 1/2 teaspoon Parmesan cheese. Lay one slice of Provolone cheese over each bowl and cover with another 1/2 teaspoon of Parmesan cheese. Bake in broiler (or oven) until cheese is bubbly and brown.

Cooking GRACEfully

Tomato Bisque

In earlier days, it was common practice to home can tomatoes, not only by themselves, but also in the form of concentrated soup base. To make tomato soup, all you had to do was heat the soup base in one pan and an equal amount of milk in another, then combine them. Most older community cookbooks in Ohio contain at least one recipe for cream of tomato soup, sometimes called tomato bisque.

2 cups chicken broth or stock
1 (14¹/₂-ounce) can whole
    tomatoes, undrained and
    broken up
¹/₂ cup chopped celery
¹/₂ cup chopped onion
3 medium tomatoes, peeled,
    seeded and chopped

3 tablespoons butter or
    margarine
3 tablespoons flour
2 cups half-and-half or light
    coffee cream
1 tablespoon sugar

In large saucepan, combine broth, canned tomatoes, celery, and onion; bring to a boil. Reduce heat; cover and simmer 20 minutes. In blender or food processer, purée mixture in small batches until all mixture is puréed. In same pan, cook fresh tomatoes in butter about 5 minutes; stir in flour. Add half-and-half; over low heat, cook and stir until thickened. Stir in broth mixture and sugar; heat through (do not boil). Makes about 1¹/₂ quarts.

Bountiful Ohio

Cheesy Chicken Chowder

1 quart chicken broth
1 quart milk
4 tablespoons butter
³/₄ cup flour
1 tablespoon chicken base
1 teaspoon salt

¹/₄ teaspoon pepper
2 cups Velveeta cheese
2 cups peas, carrots, and
    potatoes, cooked
3-4 cups chicken, cooked and
    cut up

Cook together broth, milk, butter, flour, chicken base, salt, and pepper. Add cheese to melt. Last add cut-up vegetables and chicken.

Favorite Recipes from the Heart of Amish Country

Salmon Chowder

Keep an open mind when you see all of the canned products in this recipe. It's a winner. Trust the food editor who made it for a friend recovering from surgery. She was almost like new the next day.

1 (15-ounce) can salmon, preferably red	2 soup cans milk
2 tablespoons butter	1 (12-ounce) can cream-style corn
1 small onion, chopped	1 (12-ounce) can whole kernel corn
2 celery ribs, diced	
2 (10½-ounce) cans cream of celery soup	1 tablespoon dill weed

Remove skin and center bone from salmon. Sauté onion and celery in butter until soft. Add remaining ingredients and heat soup. Do not boil.

Aren't You Going to Taste It, Honey?

Turkey Soup

2-3 chicken bouillon cubes	3 large carrots, thinly sliced
2½ cups water	1 (9-ounce) package frozen lima beans
Leftover turkey (approximately 2 cups)	⅛ teaspoon thyme leaves
⅛ teaspoon pepper	1 small bay leaf
1 teaspoon salt	1 (16-ounce) can tomatoes, undrained and cut up
1 cup converted rice	

Add chicken bouillon cubes to water and boil until dissolved. Simmer broth while adding rest of ingredients. Cook 30 minutes on low until rice and vegetables are done. Remove bay leaf. Makes 12 (1⅓-cup) servings.

Per serving: Cal 150; Prot 13g; Carbo 21g; Fat 2g; Chol 25mg; Sod 670mg; Pot 380mg.

Oeder Family & Friends Cookbook

Home-Made Chicken Soup

1 (6-pound) chicken-pullet, cut in pieces	1 medium parsnip, peeled (optional)
Chicken giblets	3 stalks celery, including leaves
1 1/2 teaspoons salt	
Water, to cover	1/2 bunch parsley, tied with white thread
1 large onion	
2 large carrots, peeled	2 stems of fresh dill (optional)

Place chicken pieces in large soup pot. Add water to cover chicken, but no more; add salt. Bring to a boil; skim off top. Add onion, carrots, parsnip, celery, and fresh dill. Cover. Cook until chicken is tender, adding parsley 15 minutes before soup is done. Taste and add salt if needed. Remove chicken and serve separately. You can add noodles, rice or matzo balls to soup before serving.

Generation to Generation

Wedding Soup

MEATBALLS:

1 pound ground beef	1/2 teaspoon oregano
1/2 pound ground pork	Parsley
1 egg	Parmesan cheese
Pepper	1/4 cup Italian bread crumbs

Combine all ingredients. Shape into tiny balls. Boil meatballs a few at a time. Meatballs are done when they rise to the top of boiling water.

20 cups water (5 quarts)	Acini de pepe (1/2 - 3/4 box)
20 chicken bouillon cubes	2 eggs, beaten with Parmesan cheese
3 packages chopped spinach	

Bring water to boil. Add bouillon and stir. Add spinach and boil until spinach is thawed. Add meatballs and bring back to boil. Add acini de pepe and cook until tender. Remove from heat. Slowly add egg/cheese mixture, stirring constantly. Freezes well.

Cooking GRACEfully

White Chili

Chili-heads, those guys who live for a bowl of red, keep their recipes a secret and wear outlandish clothes when they enter chili contests, probably don't have much to do with even the name White Chili, let alone the taste of it. But for the rest of the world, it has been a real "Wow!" since it arrived on the chili scene five years ago. White beans, chicken breasts, and broth keep the name honest.

1 pound great northern beans
2 pounds boneless chicken
  breasts
1 tablespoon olive oil
2 medium onions, chopped
4 garlic cloves, minced
2 (4-ounce) cans chopped
  mild green chilies

2 teaspoons ground cumin
1 1/2 teaspoons dried
  oregano, crumbled
1/4 teaspoon ground cloves
1/4 teaspoon ground red
  pepper
5 cups canned chicken broth
1 (7-ounce) bottle beer

OPTIONAL:
1/2 teaspoon each: white,
  lemon and black pepper
3 cups grated Monterey Jack
  cheese

Sour cream and salsa

Cover beans with water and soak overnight. Drain. Place chicken in large saucepan. Add cold water to cover and bring to a simmer. Cook until just tender, about 15 minutes. Drain and cool. Remove skin; cut into small pieces.

Drain beans. In same pot, sauté onion in oil until translucent; stir in garlic, chilies, cumin, oregano, cloves, and ground red pepper; sauté 2 minutes. Add beans, broth, and beer. If desired, stir in optional peppers. Bring to a boil; reduce heat and simmer until beans are very tender, about 2 hours. Stir occasionally.

Add chicken and one cup cheese; stir until cheese melts. Season with salt to taste. Serve with remaining cheese, sour cream, and salsa for guests to spoon onto chili if they wish.

Aren't You Going to Taste It, Honey?

French Market Soup

1 bag 15 varieties dry bean
  mixture
3 quarts water
1 tablespoon salt
1-2 ham hocks or 1 ham bone
  with some meat remaining
1 bouquet garni bag
1 large can diced tomatoes

2 cups chopped onion
2 cups chopped celery
2 cloves garlic, minced
1 pound skinless smoked
  sausage, sliced and browned
  slightly
2 raw boneless chicken
  breasts, chopped

Wash and drain beans. Add to water, salt, ham, and garni bag in a large pot. Simmer, covered, 2½ - 3 hours. Add tomatoes, onion, celery, and garlic. Simmer, uncovered, 1½ hours, until creamy. Add sausage and chicken. Simmer 40 minutes. Serve with scoop of cooked rice and chopped parsley. Serves 10-12.

Note: Flavor improves with age and is best made the day before.

Cook, Line & Sinker

Wedding Soup
(Italian)

1 stewing chicken	2 cups diced celery
1 tablespoon salt	1 whole onion
3 sprigs parsley	6 quarts water

Cook chicken with salt, parsley, celery, and onion in about 6 quarts of water, 3 hours, or until chicken is tender. Remove onion. Strain. Debone chicken and return to soup.

MEATBALLS:

1 pound lean ground beef, or veal	1 tablespoon parsley, chopped
2 eggs	2-3 tablespoons grated Romano cheese
3/4 cup seasoned bread crumbs	Salt and pepper to taste

Mix beef or veal, eggs, bread crumbs, parsley, cheese, salt, and pepper together. Make tiny meatballs and fry until brown, or brown in oven. Drain on paper towels.

CROUTONS:

1 cup bread crumbs	12 eggs, well beaten
1 cup grated Romano cheese	1 teaspoon chopped parsley
1 tablespoon baking powder	

Mix bread crumbs, Romano cheese, baking powder, eggs, and parsley together and pour on a cookie sheet that has been lined with brown paper and buttered. Bake at 350° until brown, about 20 minutes. While still hot, cut into cubes.

1 (10-ounce) package frozen chopped spinach, cooked and drained, or	1 pound fresh escarole or endive, cooked and chopped

Add spinach or escarole and meatballs to soup; mix well and heat. Serve piping hot with croutons over top of each serving. Pass grated Romano cheese. Serves 8-10.

Angels and Friends Cookbook I

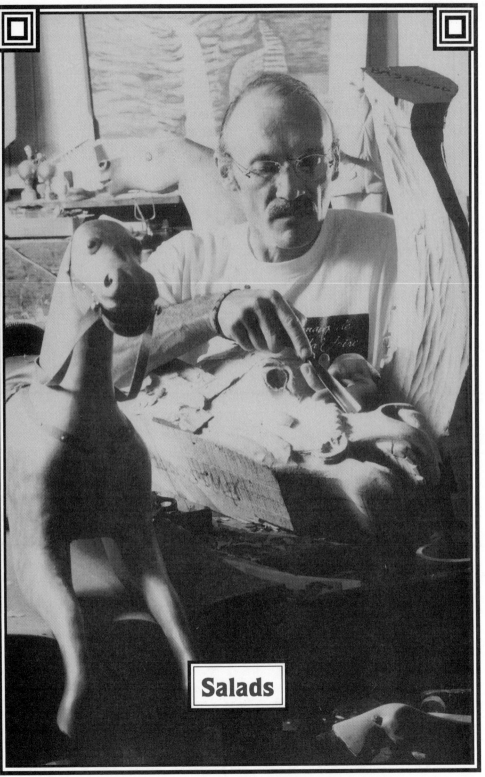

Salads

Woodcarving at the Merry-Go-Round Museum. Sandusky.

Dilled Broccoli Salad

4 cups broccoli flowerettes
  (about 2 bunches)
2 cups diced celery
1 large red onion, diced
1/2 cup diced roasted red
  pepper

3/4 cup sour cream
3/4 cup mayonnaise
1/4 cup minced fresh dill (do
  not use dried)

Boil broccoli briefly until crisp tender, 2-3 minutes. Drain, refresh under cold water and drain again. Place in bowl with other vegetables. Mix sour cream and mayonnaise with dill. Toss with broccoli mixture. Serves 8.

Saturday Night Suppers

Blueberry Salad

1 (6-ounce) package
  raspberry Jello
1 cup boiling water

1 (21-ounce) can blueberry
  pie filling
1 medium can crushed pineapple

TOPPING:

1 cup sour cream
1 (8-ounce) package cream
  cheese, softened

1/2 cup sugar
1 cup chopped nuts (optional)

Mix Jello, water, pie filling, and pineapple. Pour into 9x13-inch dish and refrigerate until firm. Combine sour cream, cream cheese, sugar and nuts, and spread over gelatin mixture. Chill before serving. Serves 16.

Treasured Recipes

7-Up Salad

2 boxes lemon gelatin
2 cups boiling water
1 (20-ounce) can crushed
   pineapple, drained (reserve
   juice)
2 cups 7-Up
2 cups small marshmallows

4 large bananas, diced
2 tablespoons flour
1/2 cup sugar
1 egg, beaten
1 cup pineapple juice
2 tablespoons butter
1 cup heavy cream, whipped

Dissolve gelatin in water; cool. Add pineapple, 7-Up, marshmallows, and bananas. Chill until firm. Mix flour and sugar; add egg, then pineapple juice. Cook, stirring constantly. Take from heat and add butter. When cool, add cream, whipped. (Dream Whip may be used.) Spread on gelatin layer.

Women's Centennial Cookbook

Lemon Jello Salad

1 (3-ounce) box lemon gelatin
1 (3-ounce) package cream
   cheese
1 small can crushed
   pineapple, drained

2 cups frozen whipped topping
1/2 cup nuts, chopped

Dissolve gelatin in hot water according to package directions. Melt cream cheese in hot gelatin. Set in refrigerator until it begins to thicken. Add pineapple and return to refrigerator. When gelatin mixture is almost set, fold in whipped topping. Add nuts. Put in mold or bowl and return to refrigerator until completely set.

It is sometimes easier to soften the cream cheese in the microwave and fold it into the Jello using an electric mixer. It gives the salad a smoother texture and sets faster.

25th Anniversary Cookbook

Red Raspberry-Rhubarb Salad

1 (10-ounce) container frozen
  red raspberries
1 (16-ounce) box frozen
  rhubarb, cooked as directed
1 family-size box red
  raspberry Jello

1³/₄ cups boiling water
1 (8-ounce) can crushed
  pineapple, drained
²/₃ cup chopped celery
2 cups chopped nuts

Put raspberries in cooked rhubarb while the rhubarb is still hot. Combine Jello and boiling water. To Jello add rhubarb mixture, drained pineapple, chopped celery and chopped nuts.

Recipes from "The Little Switzerland of Ohio"

Hidden Pear Salad

1 (16-ounce) can pears, liquid
  drained and reserved
1 (3-ounce) package lime
  Jello
1 (3-ounce) package cream
  cheese, softened

¹/₄ teaspoon lemon juice
1 envelope whipped topping
  mix
Lettuce leaves

In a saucepan, bring pear liquid to a boil. Stir in Jello until dissolved. Remove from heat and cool at room temperature until syrupy. Meanwhile, purée pears in a blender. In a mixing bowl, beat cream cheese and lemon juice until fluffy and smooth. Add puréed pears; mix well. Prepare whipped topping according to package directions; fold into pear mixture. Fold in cooled gelatin. Pour into a oiled 4¹/₂-cup mold. Chill overnight. Just before serving, unmold salad onto a lettuce-lined platter. Yield: 6-8 servings.

Tasty Recipes

Ice Cream Salad

50 butter crackers, crushed
1/2 cup melted butter
2 (3-ounce) packages banana
    instant pudding mix
1 1/2 cups milk

1 1/2 quarts vanilla ice cream,
    softened
2 envelopes whipped topping
    mix

Combine cracker crumbs (reserve 1/2 cup) and melted butter in bowl; mix well and press remaining crumbs into 9x13-inch glass dish. Combine pudding mix and milk in mixer bowl; beat until well mixed. Add ice cream; mix well. Pour over crumb crust. Prepare whipped topping mix using package directions. Spread over ice cream layer; sprinkle with reserved 1/2 cup crumbs. Chill in refrigerator until set. Yield: 12 servings.

The Ohio State Grange Cookbook

Strawberry Pretzel Salad

2 cups coarsely crushed
    pretzels
3/4 cup margarine, melted
1 cup plus 3 tablespoons
    sugar, divided
1 (8-ounce) package cream
    cheese, softened
1 (8-ounce) carton frozen
    non-dairy whipped topping,
    thawed

1 (6-ounce) package
    strawberry-flavored gelatin
1 cup boiling water
1/2 cup mini-marshmallows
2 (10-ounce) packages frozen
    strawberries, thawed

Combine pretzels, margarine, and 3 tablespoons sugar; mix. Press into 13x9x2-inch dish. Bake at 400° for 8 minutes. Remove from oven; cool.

In large bowl with electric mixer, beat cream cheese and remaining one cup sugar until well blended. Fold in whipped cream and spread over pretzels. Chill.

In mixing bowl, dissolve gelatin in boiling water. Add marshmallows; stir till melted. Add strawberries. Let stand 10 minutes. Pour on cream cheese. Keep refrigerated.

Cooking with Hope Ridge Families

Deviled Potato Salad

8 hard-boiled eggs
3 tablespoons vinegar
3 tablespoons prepared
  mustard
1 cup mayonnaise
1/2 cup sour cream

1/2 teaspoon celery salt
1 teaspoon salt
2 teaspoons chopped onion
6 medium potatoes, cooked
  and cubed

Cut eggs in half; remove yolks and mash. Blend yolks, vinegar, mustard, mayonnaise, sour cream, celery salt, and salt. Mix well. Chop egg whites and onions. Combine with mixture and add to potatoes. Chill and garnish with tomato wedges, cucumber slices, and/or hard boiled egg slices. Yield: 6-8 servings.

Sharing Our Best (Elizabeth House)

Tropical Pork Tenderloin Salad

2 pork tenderloins, 1 1/2 - 2
  pounds total
1 recipe Ginger-Lime
  Marinade
1 medium-size fresh pineapple
2 cups red seedless grapes
2 ripe avocados
Crisp lettuce leaves

1 recipe Ginger-Lime
  Dressing
1/2 cup toasted pine nuts
1/2 cup toasted shredded
  coconut
Lime slices and mint leaves,
  for garnish

Trim the tenderloins of all fat and silver skin. Place in a gallon-size, heavy-duty, zip-top plastic bag and add the marinade; seal tightly. Place in the refrigerator for several hours or overnight.

Remove the tenderloins from the marinade and place on a hot grill, or roast, in a shallow pan on a rack, in a pre-heated 425° oven for 20-25 minutes or until pork reaches 155-160° internal temperature.

Remove and cool. Wrap and chill until ready to use. Peel the pineapple and cut into bite-sized chunks. Cut grapes in half. Peel and slice the avocados.

Line a large platter or large shallow bowl with the lettuce leaves. Slice the tenderloin into 1/4-inch slices and toss in half of the dressing. Place in the center of the lettuce. Arrange the fruit in an attrac-

CONTINUED

tive fashion around the pork. Drizzle with the remaining dressing. Sprinkle the pine nuts and coconut over the top and garnish with lime slices and mint leaves. Serve immediately. Serves 8-10.

GINGER-LIME MARINADE:

1/4 cup peanut, or vegetable
oil
Juice and grated rind of 2
medium to large limes
1 large clove garlic, minced
1 tablespoon minced ginger
root

2 tablespoons chopped fresh
cilantro leaves
1 teaspoon salt
1/2 teaspoon Tabasco sauce
1 teaspoon sugar

Whisk together until well blended.

GINGER-LIME DRESSING:

3/4 cup peanut oil
1/4 cup fresh lime juice
1 tablespoon "hot and sweet"
mustard

1/2 teaspoon salt
1 tablespoon honey
1 teaspoon grated ginger root

Whisk together until well blended. (Or mix in blender or food processor.) Makes about one cup.

More Cooking with Marilyn Harris

Japanese Salad

3 or 4 chicken breasts,
cooked and slivered
1 1/2 heads lettuce, torn
4 green onions and tops,
thinly sliced

1 small can Chinese noodles
1 package slivered almonds
1/4 cup poppy seeds

Combine salad ingredients and stir.

DRESSING:

4 tablespoons sugar
2 teaspoons salt
1/2 teaspoon pepper

4 tablespoons vinegar
1/2 cup salad oil

Combine sugar, salt, pepper, vinegar, and salad oil and shake well. Pour over salad and toss. Serves 8.

Angels and Friends Cookbook I

Hot Baked Turkey Salad

SALAD:

3 cups cubed chicken or
turkey
1 cup diced celery
1 (8-ounce) can water
chestnuts
1 (2-ounce) jar chopped
pimento
1/2 cup toasted croutons

1/2 teaspoon salt
1/2 cup toasted sliced
almonds
3/4 cup mayonnaise
3/4 cup sour cream
2 tablespoons lemon juice
2 teaspoons grated onion

TOPPING:

1/2 cup buttered crumbs

1/4 cup grated Parmesan cheese

Combine salad ingredients. Spoon into a greased 2-quart casserole. Combine topping mixture and sprinkle over top. Bake, uncovered, at 350° for 25-30 minutes until heated through.

Heavenly Dishes

Chicken Salad in Melon Rings

This dish can be prepared up to 4 hours before serving. In fact, the flavors improve. Keep everything chilled and assemble just before serving.

2 cups cooked chicken
breast, cut into bite-size
pieces
1 1/2 cups seedless green
grapes, halved
1/2 cup celery
1/2 cup toasted slivered
almonds
2/3 cup mayonnaise
1 teaspoon soy sauce
1/2 teaspoon curry powder,
optional

Salt and freshly ground black
pepper to taste
Chilled lettuce leaves
2 medium cantaloupes
Toasted slivered almonds for
garnish
Green and red grapes and/or
strawberries for additional
garnish, if desired

In a large bowl, combine chicken, grapes, celery, and 1/2 cup almonds. In a small bowl, combine mayonnaise, soy sauce, curry powder, salt and pepper; mix thoroughly. Toss with the chicken mixture and chill.

CONTINUED

Just before serving, place lettuce leaves on individual plates. Cut the cantaloupe into 1 - 1^{1}/$_{2}$-inch thick circular slices. Remove rind, seeds, and stringy pulp. Place on top of lettuce leaves. Fill each with chicken salad. Garnish with toasted almonds on top of salad and red and green grapes and/or whole strawberries on side of plate. Serves 6.

Variation: Honeydew melon or peach slices can be substituted for the cantaloupe. Red leaf lettuce adds a nice color to the plate.

Plain & Fancy Favorites

Cobb Salad
with Buttermilk Herb Dressing

Light, pretty salad with an excellent dressing.

1/2 head iceberg lettuce	4 scallions, chopped
1/2 head red leaf lettuce	2 hard-cooked eggs, chopped
1/2 bunch watercress,	2 whole chicken breasts,
chopped	cooked and cubed
2 medium tomatoes, diced	1 large avocado, diced
1/2 cup crumbled bleu cheese	Chopped parsley for garnish
6 slices bacon, cooked and	
crumbled	

Cut lettuce into small pieces. Toss lightly in a bowl with watercress and arrange on a serving platter. Arrange tomatoes, bleu cheese, bacon, scallions, eggs, chicken, and avocado in rows across lettuce. Garnish with parsley and chill.

BUTTERMILK HERB DRESSING:

1/2 cup buttermilk	1/2 teaspoon freshly ground
1/2 cup mayonnaise	pepper
1 large shallot, minced	1 tablespoon minced chives
1 large clove garlic, minced	1/2 teaspoon ground thyme
1/2 teaspoon coarse salt	1 teaspoon minced parsley

Whisk buttermilk, mayonnaise, shallot, and garlic in a medium bowl. Add the salt, pepper, chives, thyme, and parsley, blending well. To serve, pass the salad with dressing on the side. Yield: 6 servings.

Note: Dressing best made at least 24 hours before serving.

Five Star Sensations

Cashew Chicken Salad

A wonderful luncheon idea.

¹/₂ cup Thousand Island
dressing
3 cups cooked, cubed chicken
breast
1¹/₄ cups chopped celery

2 tablespoons pickle relish
¹/₂ cup chopped red onion
¹/₂ cup salted cashews
1 (11-ounce) can Mandarin
oranges, drained

In a large bowl, combine all ingredients except oranges. When mixed, gently fold in oranges. To serve, line serving plates with lettuce and spoon on mixture. Serves 6.
Chef Judith Parsons, Red Door Tavern.

A Taste of Columbus Vol IV

Corn and Pasta Salad

Cleveland is a city of great ethnic diversity. Most Italian immigrants arrived in the early 1900s. Those who came from Sicily, a fruit-growing region, helped make the neighborhood called Big Italy the center of the city's fruit industry. In turn, Italian merchants like Frank Catalano built Cleveland into the state's center of the produce industry. They gave us our taste for oranges, bananas, garlic, olive oil and other delicacies.

Like other Americans, many Italians married members of other ethnic groups. This recipe is a marriage, too: it shows what can happen when Italian pasta meets Midwestern produce.

2 cups rotini pasta, cooked
and drained
1 (17-ounce) can whole kernel
corn, drained
¹/₂ cup each: chopped green
pepper, red onion, and sliced
radishes

¹/₂ cup bottled Italian salad
dressing
¹/₂ cup salsa or picante sauce
¹/₄ teaspoon salt
¹/₈ teaspoon pepper

In large bowl, combine pasta, corn, green pepper, onion, and radishes. In small bowl, combine dressing, salsa, salt and pepper. Pour over pasta mixture; toss lightly. Refrigerate at least 2 hours to blend flavors. Makes 6-8.

Bountiful Ohio

Salmon Caesar Salad

12 ounces salmon	1 head romaine lettuce,
1/2 cup water	washed and cut into bite-size
1/2 cup Chablis	pieces
Salt to taste	1 cup Caesar salad dressing
3 tablespoons lemon juice	4 tablespoons freshly grated
Freshly ground black pepper	Parmesan cheese
1 cup seasoned croutons	

Poach the salmon in the water, wine, lemon juice, salt and pepper for 10-12 minutes, just until cooked. Remove from liquid and cool. Reserved liquid may be frozen for later use. When salmon is cooked, flake.

Toss romaine, croutons, salmon, and Parmesan cheese with the Caesar dressing.

The Watermark Restaurant, Cleveland.

Best Recipes of Ohio Inns and Restaurants

Rotini Salad

8 ounces rotini	3 tomatoes
1 1/2 green (bell) peppers,	3/4 cup onion
diced	

Cook rotini in water. Do not overcook; drain, rinse, and chill. Dice peppers, tomatoes, and onion.

DRESSING:

1/2 teaspoon Italian seasoning	1/8 teaspoon pepper
mix	1 1/3 cups vinegar
1 teaspoon paprika	1 1/3 cups sugar
2 teaspoons sesame seeds	1/3 cup oil
1 teaspoon salt	

Combine all ingredients except oil. Stir to blend. Add oil. Add diced vegetables to chilled rotini. Add dressing and toss. Chill overnight.

Ottoville Sesquicentennial Cookbook

Hot German Potato Salad

1 tablespoon + 1 teaspoon
  margarine
3/4 cup finely chopped onion
2 tablespoons flour
1/3 cup sugar
1 teaspoon salt
Pepper to taste
1/2 teaspoon celery seed

2/3 cup water
5 tablespoons vinegar
2 drops liquid smoke
4 medium boiling potatoes,
  cooked, peeled, sliced
1 tablespoon imitation bacon
  bits

Put margarine in a 1 1/2-quart casserole dish and microwave on HIGH for 30 seconds or until melted. Add onion and microwave on HIGH for 2-3 minutes or until onion is transparent. Stir in flour, sugar, salt, pepper to taste and celery seed. Microwave on HIGH for one minute. Stir in water, vinegar and liquid smoke. Microwave on HIGH 3-4 minutes or until mixture boils. Add potatoes and imitation bacon bits, stirring gently to coat. Yield: 4 servings.

Lifetime Warranty

Spinach-Pasta Salad

A new look for an old standard.

1 (7-ounce) package of frozen
  or 1 cup dried tortellini
  (cheese filled) or 1 cup veggie
  pasta corkscrews
6 cups torn, fresh spinach
1 1/2 cups bibb lettuce or
  endive

4 slices bacon, cooked and
  crumbled or 2 tablespoons
  crumbled bacon bits
4 green onions, thinly sliced
1/2 cup red wine and vinegar
  bottled salad dressing

Cook pasta according to directions. Drain. In large bowl combine pasta, spinach, lettuce, bacon and onion. Cover and chill. Just before serving, toss mixture with dressing. Makes 8-10 servings.

Kinder Kuisine

Spaghetti Salad

1 pound thin spaghetti	1 (2.75-ounce) jar Salad
1 green pepper	Supreme
1 medium tomato	1 (8-ounce) bottle Italian
1 red or white onion	dressing
1 cucumber	

Cook spaghetti following directions on package. Dice all the vegetables and toss with spaghetti. Add 3/4 - 1 jar of Salad Supreme; toss. Add Italian dressing; toss. Refrigerate at least 4 hours.

Cooking with Class

Marinated Zucchini and Mozzarella Cheese Salad

12 ounces mozzarella cheese	1 clove garlic, chopped
1 large tomato	1 tablespoon fresh basil or 1/2
1 medium zucchini	teaspoon dried
1/4 cup oil	1/4 teaspoon salt
1/4 cup white vinegar	1/2 teaspoon sugar

Cut cheese into 6 slices. Place in 8-inch square dish. Cut tomato into 6 slices. Place tomato slices on top of cheese. Slice zucchini into 1/4-inch slices. Arrange slices in dish. Combine remaining ingredients and shake. Pour over zucchini. Cover dish and refrigerate.

Treasured Recipes from Mason, Ohio

Parsley Salad

1 bunch parsley	Lime juice
1 medium red onion, chopped	Salt to taste

Discard any discolored or spoiled parsley leaves. Wash well and drain water. Pat dry with paper towels. Finely chop parsley and add onion. Add lime juice and salt to taste. Mix well with hand. Use a little extra lime juice for better taste. Serve with rice and curry.

Easy Cooking with Herbs & Spices

Artichoke Heart Salad

2 jars marinated artichoke
  hearts, drained
2/3 cup Hellman's mayonnaise
3/4 teaspoon curry powder
1 (4³/4-ounce) package
  chicken-flavored rice mix
  (cook ahead and cool)

6 green onions, chopped
1/2 green pepper, chopped
12 stuffed green olives
1 cup chopped mild green
  chiles (optional)

Drain juices from artichoke hearts and combine with mayonnaise and curry powder. In a large bowl, gently toss cooked, cooled rice with remaining ingredients. Pour dressing over all, toss well. Serves 12.

Note: This recipe should be made ahead, but should not be frozen.

The Kettle Cookbook

Calico Salad

1/2 cup packed brown sugar
1/3 cup cider vinegar
2 teaspoons celery seed
1/4 teaspoon ground turmeric
Salt and pepper to taste
2 tablespoons chopped onion

1 (16-ounce) can cut green
  beans, drained
1 (16-ounce) can sliced
  carrots, drained
1 (16-ounce) can whole kernel
  corn, drained

Combine brown sugar, vinegar, celery seed, turmeric, salt and pepper in bowl; mix well. Add onion, well-drained green beans, carrots, and corn; stir gently to coat. Chill, covered, overnight. Yield: 6 servings.

The Ohio State Grange Cookbook

Broccoli Salad

DRESSING:

1 cup Hellmann's mayonnaise
1/2 cup sugar
2 tablespoons vinegar

1 teaspoon prepared mustard
1 teaspoon paprika

SALAD:

2 bunches broccoli florets
1 cup chopped purple onion
1 cup raisins
1 cup sliced fresh mushrooms

1 small can drained mandarin
  orange
1/2 cup cashew pieces
8 slices fried bacon, crumbled

Mix dressing ingredients until smooth. Cover and refrigerate overnight. Just before serving, pour over remaining ingredients. Serves 8-12.

Heavenly Food II

Broccoli Salad

1 bunch broccoli (flowerettes
  only)
Chopped red onion (to your
  taste)
Golden raisins (1/4 cup or
  more if you like)

3 - 4 strips bacon, cooked
  crispy
4 ounces shredded Cheddar
  cheese

SAUCE:

3/4 cup mayonnaise
2 teaspoons white vinegar

1/2 cup sugar

A day ahead of serving, cut broccoli flowerettes very small (no stems) and place in mixing bowl. Chop red onion for color and to your taste and add to bowl of broccoli. Sprinkle golden raisins over mixture. Crumble bacon up into small bits and add, then sprinkle Cheddar cheese over all.

Mix sauce ingredients thoroughly and toss salad mixture with it. Let it set in the refrigerator overnight. When ready to serve, toss again to make sure all the vegetables are coated in the sauce. Very refreshing.

The PTA Pantry

Luncheon Strawberry Spinach Salad

1 pound asparagus spears
1/2 cup bottled poppy seed
 dressing
1 teaspoon grated orange peel
1 tablespoon orange juice
8 cups torn fresh spinach or
 assorted greens

2 cups sliced fresh
 strawberries and/or whole
 blueberries
3/4 - 1 pound cooked turkey,
 cut into 1/2-inch cubes
1/4 cup pecan halves

Snap off and discard woody bases from asparagus. Cut into 1-inch pieces. Place asparagus in a 1-quart microwave-safe baking dish with 2 tablespoons water. Microcook, covered, on 100% power for 5-7 minutes, until crisp tender, stirring once. Drain asparagus. Rinse with cold water. Let stand in cold water till cool; drain.

Meanwhile, for dressing, in a medium mixing bowl, stir together poppy seed dressing, orange peel, and orange juice; set aside. In salad bowl, combine asparagus, greens, berries, and turkey. Add dressing mixture and toss. Top with pecans. Makes 4 main-dish servings. Serve with bran muffins.

Per serving: Cal 390; Fat 26g; Chol 59g; Prot 33g; Carbo 18g; Dietary fiber 8g; Sod 376mg.

Hint: This would taste great with strips of grilled chicken or with smoked turkey.

Cook, Line & Sinker

Spinach Salad

6-8 strips of crisp bacon,
 crumbled
2 hard-boiled eggs, chopped
1/2 cup sliced mushrooms

Fresh spinach and leaf
 lettuce, torn into bite-size
 pieces
Small purple onion, sliced

DRESSING:

1 cup oil
3/4 cup sugar
1/3 cup ketchup

1/4 cup vinegar
1 teaspoon Worcestershire
 sauce

Mix dressing ingredients and heat to dissolve sugar. This dressing may be warm or at room temperature, but should be poured over the salad ingredients immediately before serving.

Favorite Recipes

Spinach-Apple-Cheese Salad

2 hard-cooked eggs, diced
1 large apple, diced
1 small onion, diced
1/4 pound bleu cheese,
   crumbled

1/2 cup mayonnaise
1/2 cup sour cream
Salt and pepper to taste
1 pound spinach, washed

Combine all ingredients except the spinach. Break the spinach into bite-size pieces. Add the salad mixture to the spinach just before serving. Serves 4-6.

Appletizers

Fresh Corn Salad

This is unusual, delicious, and makes a great dish for a cookout.

3 cups cooked, drained corn
   (about 6 ears fresh, or can use
   frozen or canned)
1 large onion, diced
2 medium zucchini, unpared,
   cubed
1 bunch green onions, sliced
1 sweet red pepper, chopped
1 green pepper, chopped
1/4 cup minced fresh parsley

1 clove garlic, minced
1/4 teaspoon salt
1/8 teaspoon black pepper
2 teaspoons sugar
1 teaspoon cumin
2 teaspoons Dijon mustard
1/2 teaspoon hot sauce
3 tablespoons vegetable oil
1/4 cup water
1/2 cup white wine vinegar

In large bowl, combine corn, onion, zucchini, green onion, and red and green peppers. In small bowl, combine remaining ingredients and whisk together. Pour dressing over vegetable mixture and toss lightly until well mixed. Refrigerate until serving time. Yield: 12 servings.

Nutrients per serving: Cal 90; Fat 4g (35%); Carbo 14g; Chol 0mg; Sod 70mg; Pro 2g.

Recipe Rehab

Everyone's heard of The McGuffey Reader... Professor William Holmes McGuffey, known as the "Schoolmaster of the Nation," wrote the first of the classic textbooks in Oxford during the 1830s.

Sauerkraut Salad

1 large can sauerkraut	1 cup carrots
1 cup mango	1 cup sugar
1 cup celery	1/2 cup white vinegar
1 cup onion	1/4 cup salad oil

Wash and drain sauerkraut. Chop first 4 ingredients. Whip sugar, vinegar, and salad oil until white. Mix with sauerkraut. Refrigerate 2 hours.

Treasures and Pleasures

Jane's Orange Salad

Great any time of year. A nice presentation for company.

SALAD:

1 head lettuce	Chopped red onion to taste
1 cup grape halves	1/2 cup toasted almonds
1 can cold mandarin oranges, drained	1 avocado, diced

DRESSING:

2/3 cup salad oil	Dash dry mustard
1/3 cup orange juice	1 teaspoon celery seed
1/4 cup sugar	2 tablespoons chopped
3 tablespoons vinegar	parsley

Tear lettuce into bite-size pieces. Toss with remaining ingredients. Combine all dressing ingredients; mix well. Chill. Shake well before pouring over salad. Mix salad and dressing just prior to serving.

MDA Favorite Recipes

Pea Salad

1 (2-pound) bag frozen peas	1/3 cup cashew halves
3/4 cup red onion, chopped	2 1/2 teaspoons curry powder
1 cup Monterey Jack cheese, cubed	1/2 cup mayonnaise
1 cup medium Cheddar cheese, cubed	Cashews (for garnish)

Cook peas according to directions on bag. Rinse under cold water; drain. Add remainder of ingredients. Chill until cool.

Ottoville Sesquicentennial Cookbook

Marilyn's Thanksgiving Salad

This crunchy, colorful salad is so named because for years I have made a version of it to serve with that annual feast.

2 large heads Belgian endive
3 large Red Delicious apples,
  cored and halved
2 tablespoons fresh lemon
  juice
4 large ribs celery, strings
  removed
1 cup walnut halves

1/2 cup white raisins
1 recipe Lemon-Walnut
  Dressing
1 medium head romaine,
  washed, dried, and chilled
4 ounces fresh goat cheese
Watercress sprigs

Wash the endive, separate it into individual leaves, wrap in paper towels, place in a plastic bag, and chill for at least one hour. Slice the apple halves into thin slices. Toss gently in the lemon juice. Slice the celery into thin slices. Toss together the apples, celery, walnuts and raisins with the dressing. Shred the romaine. Arrange 3 or 4 endive leaves on an individual salad plate. Make a bed of shredded romaine in the center of the leaves. Top with a large spoonful of the apple mixture. Crumble the goat cheese and sprinkle some on the top of each salad. Garnish with a watercress sprig. Serve immediately. Serves 8.

LEMON-WALNUT DRESSING:

1/2 cup walnut oil
2 tablespoons fresh lemon
  juice
1 teaspoon finely chopped
  lemon zest

2 teaspoons honey
Pinch salt

Blend together until well mixed. Makes about 3/4 cup.

Cooking with Marilyn

Orange-Almond Salad

DRESSING:

$1/2$ teaspoon salt
Dash of pepper
2 tablespoons sugar
2 tablespoons red wine
 vinegar

$1/4$ cup oil
1 tablespoon parsley, chopped

Combine all ingredients in blender and then refrigerate. Shake well before using.

SALAD:

$1/4$ cup sliced almonds
4 teaspoons sugar
$1/4$ head iceberg lettuce
$1/4$ head romaine
1 cup celery, chopped
2 green onions, thinly sliced
$1/2$ cup green olives

1 cup artichoke hearts
$1/2$ cup fresh mushrooms,
 sliced
1 can cocktail baby corn
1 (8-ounce) can mandarin
 oranges, drained

In small saucepan, cook almonds and sugar over low heat. Stir constantly until sugar is melted and almonds are coated, about 3 minutes. When sugar is liquid, pour onto waxed paper. Cool and break apart, as for brittle. This can be done one day ahead. Store at room temperature.

Tear lettuce and romaine into bite-size pieces. Place greens, celery, onions, green olives, artichoke hearts, mushrooms, and baby corn in large bowl. Pour dressing on about 5-10 minutes before serving. Arrange in serving bowl or individual salad dishes. Garnish with mardarin oranges and almonds.

Generation to Generation

Candle Salad

1 slice pineapple
$1/2$ banana
~~2 tablespoons mayonnaise~~

1 tablespoon peanut butter *with*
1 maraschino cherry
Try Heavy Sweet Cream
= or cream
Cheese
+ Ranch
Sugar

Place pineapple slice on a leaf of lettuce. Put banana (candle) into hole of pineapple with pointed end up. Mix mayonnaise and peanut butter (candle wax) and pour over banana. Put maraschino cherry (flame) on top. Serves one.

Share with Love

Pineapple & Mango Salad

1 medium half-ripe fresh
  pineapple
2 half-ripe mangoes
3 tablespoons red wine
  vinegar

1 tablespoon Dijon rough
  mustard
1 tablespoon paprika
1 teaspoon sugar

Discard crown of pineapple. Cut off skin. With point of knife, re-move eyes and discard. Cut pineapple in half and into quarters. Discard hard core. Cut pineapple into bite-size pieces. Transfer to glass salad bowl. Peel mangoes. Slice and cut into bite-size pieces. Transfer to salad bowl. Discard seeds or if preferred add to bowl. Add vinegar, mustard, paprika, and sugar. With wooden spoon, toss and mix well. Chill and serve.

Easy Cooking with Herbs & Spices

Cranberry Salad

1 pound cranberries
1 cup sugar
1 cup dark grapes
1 cup nuts (walnuts or pecans)

18 large marshmallows, cut up
  (or 8 small for 1 large)
1 pint whipping cream

Grind cranberries and add one cup of sugar. Mix and refrigerate overnight. Next day, add grapes, nuts, and marshmallows. Whip whipping cream and add to other ingredients. Put in oblong dish. Makes 15 servings.

Per serving: Cal 244; Prot 3g; Fat 16g; Chol 25g.

Wadsworth-Rittman Hospital Cookbook

The Richland Carousel in Mansfield opened in 1992. Comprised of 52 animals and two chariots, it is the first all-wood, hand-carved carousel built in this country in nearly sixty years. The open year-round pavilion is heated in winter.

Golden Raisin Coleslaw

VINAIGRETTE:

4 tablespoons golden raisins
3 tablespoons red wine
   vinegar
2 tablespoons olive oil
1/2 cup water

2 tablespoons onion, finely
   chopped
1 teaspoon Dijon mustard
Salt and pepper to taste

In a small saucepan, combine the above ingredients and boil the mixture, stirring, for 30 seconds. In a blender purée the vinaigrette until it is smooth.

COLESLAW:

2 cups cabbage, grated
1 carrot, coarsely grated

1/2 cup golden raisins

Combine the cabbage, carrot, and raisins. Pour vinaigrette over coleslaw and toss. Serves 6.

Light Kitchen Choreography

Different Slaw

This great blend of flavors makes this recipe one of the most re-quested at Cincinnati Zoo potlucks.

1 package Ramen Noodles,
   uncooked
1 cup sunflower seeds
1 cup sliced almonds
6-8 green onions with tops,
   chopped

1 (16-ounce) package
   prepared slaw cabbage or 1
   medium head of cabbage,
   shredded

DRESSING:

3/4 cup oil
1/2 cup sugar
1/3 cup white vinegar

Flavoring package from
   Ramen Noodles

Mix together noodles, seeds, almonds, onions, and cabbage. Just before serving, combine dressing ingredients; mix well. Pour over slaw mixture; toss to coat. Serve immediately to prevent sogginess. Yield: 10-12 servings.

Note: This works well using half water/half oil and a sugar substitute to cut calories and fat intake.

Cooking on the Wild Side

Pickled Beets and Eggs

This one gets the vote for Cincinnati's most widely-known unusual recipe. After the mixture sits overnight, the eggs are bright purple. Sliced in a salad or used as deviled eggs, they are lovely. Some eat the eggs with a drop or two of Worcestershire sauce on the yolk. This offers a wise solution after Easter when there are multitudes of hard-cooked eggs sitting around waiting for a recipe.

6-8 hard-cooked eggs	2 cinnamon sticks
2 (16-ounce) cans small whole beets, slices or wedges	2 whole cloves
	2 black peppercorns
1 cup cider vinegar	1/4 teaspoon salt
1-1 1/2 cups sugar	1 large onion, sliced thickly

Carefully crackle the shells for peeling, without gouging the eggs. Peel beneath cool running water to help ease off the shells. Drain the juice from the beets into a measuring cup and add enough water to equal 2 cups of liquid. Pour the liquid into a saucepan and add the vinegar, sugar, cinnamon, cloves, peppercorns, and salt. Bring to a boil, and then set aside. Place the beets, eggs, and onion slices into a large-mouth jar or a non-metallic bowl, alternating ingredients. Pour the liquid over, cover, and refrigerate overnight. To serve as a relish or salad, drain off the pickling liquid or remove as many eggs and vegetables from the jar or bowl as needed. Slice the eggs in half and surround with the tangy, chilled beets and onion rings. Yield: 8-10 servings.

Note: To use fresh beets (about 1 1/2 pounds) reserve 2 cups of the cooking liquid and add no water. Although the mixture will keep for several weeks, the eggs and onions tend to get rubbery after a few days.

Cincinnati Recipe Treasury

Pickled Kraut

1 (29-ounce or 32-ounce) package sauerkraut	1 cup sugar
	Onion, chopped
1/2 cup oil	Green pepper, chopped
1/2 cup water	Celery, chopped

Drain sauerkraut. Do not squeeze! Add onion, green pepper, and celery to taste. Mix well. Allow to stand before serving. Refrigerate. This is great with a sandwich.

A Sprinkling of Favorite Recipes

Celery Seed Dressing

An old standby recipe. Try it on avocado, cottage cheese, fruit or green salad.

1 cup vegetable oil	9 tablespoons sugar
1 medium onion, quartered	1/2 cup cider vinegar
1 teaspoon salt	1 tablespoon celery seed
1 teaspoon dry mustard	

In the food processor, combine oil, onion, salt, mustard, and sugar. Process until well blended. With the processor running, slowly add the vinegar and celery seed. Refrigerate. Remove from refrigerator 30 minutes before serving. Yield: about 2 cups.

The Heritage Tradition

Seafood, Pasta, Rice, Etc.

Cincinnati, on the beautiful Ohio River.

Baked Fish of Sole

1 small onion, chopped
1/4 teaspoon minced garlic
1 teaspoon olive oil or canola
  oil
7 ounces fillet of sole
Lemon juice
1/4 teaspoon parsley flakes

1/4 teaspoon dried chives
1/8 teaspoon black pepper
1/4 teaspoon Salt Sense, if
  diet permits
1/8 teaspoon paprika
Homemade Soy Sauce

Sauté onion and garlic in olive oil. Set aside. Spray small baking dish with nonstick cooking spray. Brush fish with lemon juice. Place in prepared dish. Sprinkle fillet with parsley, chives, pepper, paprika, and salt. Add soy sauce last—use it liberally because it tends to evaporate quickly. Bake at 375° about 25 minutes or until fish flakes easily. Serves one.

HOMEMADE SOY SAUCE:

3/4 cup water
2 tablespoons instant chicken
  bouillon granules
2 teaspoons wine vinegar

1 tablespoon molasses
1/8 teaspoon ground ginger
1/8 teaspoon black pepper
1/4 teaspoon minced garlic

In a small saucepan combine water, bouillon, wine vinegar, molasses, ginger, pepper, and garlic. Boil gently, uncovered, for 5 minutes or until mixture is reduced to 1/2 cup. Store in refrigerator. Stir or shake before using. Yield: 1/2 cup.

Heartline Cookbook

Sweet 'n' Sour Baked Fish

1 onion, chopped
1 green pepper, cut into strips
1 tablespoon olive oil or
   canola oil
1 teaspoon ginger
1 tablespoon brown sugar
1 tablespoon cornstarch

1 tablespoon Homemade Soy
   Sauce
1/4 cup tarragon vinegar
1 (24-ounce) can crushed
   pineapple with juice
1 - 1 1/2 pounds fish fillets

Sauté onion and pepper in oil until tender. Add the next 6 ingredients. Cook, stirring until blended and thickened.

Spray a baking dish with a nonstick cooking spray. Arrange fillets in it. Season with black pepper and Salt Sense, if diet permits. Cover with soy sauce. Bake at 350° for 30 minutes.

Heartline Cookbook

Pufferbelly Sole Crown Florentine

3 (7-8-ounce) filets of sole
Salt
1 cup Florentine Stuffing

1/3 cup dry white wine
1/4 teaspoon paprika
1/8 teaspoon pepper

Wash fish and pat dry, place skin-side-up and salt lightly. Place 1/3 cup stuffing in center of each filet. Roll up, securing with toothpick. Stand on end, "crown fashion," in greased baking pan. Pour wine over crowns, season, and bake at 325° for 25-35 minutes or until flaky. Do not overbake. Makes 1 serving.

FLORENTINE STUFFING:

1 1/2 cups spinach, washed,
   drained, and chopped or 3/4
   cup frozen spinach, thawed
   and drained
1/2 cup sour cream
1/2 cup cracker crumbs

2 ounces margarine
1/2 cup minced onions
4 ounces sliced mushrooms
1 ounce slivered almonds
Salt and pepper

Blend spinach with sour cream and crumbs. In skillet, melt margarine, add onions, mushrooms, and almonds, and stir until slightly cooked. Season, blend with spinach mixture, and chill. Yields 4 servings.

The Pufferbelly Restaurant, Berea Ohio.

Dining in Historic Ohio

Red Snapper
with Sesame Ginger Marinade

A delicate hint of ginger is a perfect flavor companion to snapper.

1 tablespoon sesame seeds
$^1/_2$ teaspoon sesame oil
2 tablespoons soy sauce
1 tablespoon white wine
  vinegar
2 tablespoons fresh minced
  ginger

1 teaspoon minced garlic
$^1/_4$ teaspoon cayenne pepper
1 pound fresh snapper fillets
Parsley
Orange slices

Spread sesame seeds in a microwave-safe dish and microwave on HIGH, uncovered, for one minute. Set aside. Mix the sesame oil, soy sauce, vinegar, ginger, garlic, and cayenne pepper in a cup. Arrange the fish on a microwave-safe plate, skin-side-down with the thickest parts to the outside of the plate.

Pour the marinade over the fish and let stand for 15 minutes. Cover the fish with plastic wrap, vent in 2 places and microwave on HIGH 4-5 minutes or until the thickest portion just turns opaque. Let stand 5 more minutes to finish cooking. Unwrap, spoon some juice over fillets and sprinkle with toasted sesame seeds. Garnish with parsley and orange slices. Yield: 4 servings.

Cooking on the Wild Side

Orange Roughy with Puff Topping

Almost no work is involved in this dish. The raspberry mustard gives the puffy mustard-mayonnaise topping a lovely flavor. If you prefer, substitute any white-fleshed fish such as sole or flounder for the Orange Roughy.

$^1/_3$ cup mayonnaise
$^1/_3$ cup Robert Rothschild
  Red Raspberry Mustard

$1^1/_2$ pounds orange roughy
  fillets

Preheat oven to 350°. In a small bowl, mix mayonnaise and mustard. Place fish in a shallow ovenproof pan. Spread mayonnaise mixture over the fish, covering completely. Bake at 350° for 10-15 minutes, just until fish is done. If top is not lightly browned, place fish under the broiler for a minute or so. Yield: 4 servings.

Robert Rothschild Recipes

Fried Fish Batter

Is there any question about the consistency of a batter made with yeast and beer? It is guaranteed to be light and crispy. Just remember to have the fish dry so the batter will adhere and be sure the oil is hot enough to brown the batter. How hot? Really hot. If you can find a thermometer, do what it says for fried fish.

2 cups flour	1 package dry yeast,
2 eggs, beaten	dissolved in 1/4 cup warm
1 can beer	water

Mix all ingredients and let stand at room temperature for 2 hours before using. Leftover batter can be covered and kept refrigerated for about 3 weeks.

Aren't You Going to Taste It, Honey?

Baked Seafood Cakettes

These Seafood Cakettes are an economical and delicious way to introduce seafood into your party lineup. They can be assembled the night before or at least several hours before, chilled on a lightly greased baking sheet, and popped into a hot oven before the guests arrive. Make a lot—they always go quickly and, with the help of the food processor, they are easy to prepare.

2 tablespoons olive oil	1 tablespoon fresh lime juice
1/2 cup chopped onion	1/4 teaspoon hot pepper
2 cloves garlic, minced	sauce
3/4 pound raw shrimp, peeled	1/2 teaspoon salt, or to taste
and deveined	2 tablespoons chopped fresh
1/2 pound raw scallops	cilantro
1/4 cup mayonnaise	2 cups fresh bread crumbs
1 egg, lightly beaten	

Heat oil in a skillet. Sauté onion and garlic for 2-3 minutes. Remove and cool. Finely chop the shrimp and scallops in a food processor; mix with the onion and garlic. Add mayonnaise, egg, lime juice, hot pepper sauce, salt, and cilantro. Stir in 1/2 cup of the bread crumbs. (Use slightly stale white or whole-wheat bread. Break it into large pieces, including crusts, and place in a food processor with steel blade. Process until fine crumbs are formed.) Form into small oval cakes, roll in remaining crumbs to coat, and place on a well-greased baking sheet. Cover and chill until serving time.

When ready to serve, place in a preheated 400° oven for 15 minutes or until golden brown. Serve warm with Zesty Tartar Sauce for dipping. Makes about 24 small cakes.

ZESTY TARTAR SAUCE:

1 cup mayonnaise	2 tablespoons chopped
1 tablespoon fresh lime juice	cilantro
1 tablespoon Dijon mustard	2 tablespoons chopped
1/2 teaspoon hot pepper	scallions
sauce	2 tablespoons capers

Stir together the mayonnaise, lime juice, mustard, and pepper sauce until smooth. Fold in remaining ingredients. Cover and chill until ready to serve. Makes about 1 1/4 cups.

Cooking with Marilyn

Baked Imperial Crab

1 tablespoon chopped
  pimiento
1 tablespoon chopped green
  pepper
2 tablespoons mayonnaise
1 tablespoon prepared
  mustard

¹/₂ teaspoon Worcestershire
  sauce
6 saltines, slightly crushed
Pinch of salt
1 egg
1 pound back fin crab

Mix first 8 ingredients. Add one pound back fin crabmeat. Mix very lightly. Put crab imperial in clam shell dishes or any small heat resistant dish. Cook until heated through in moderate oven. Do not overcook.

Tumm Yummies

Shrimp Veracruzana

A super dinner-party recipe, easily made ahead and reheated. Add a tossed green salad with some avocado slices and some warm, buttered flour tortillas to round out the meal.

1 clove fresh garlic, minced
1 large onion, sliced
3 tablespoons extra-virgin
  olive oil
1 large red sweet pepper, cut
  into strips
1 large green pepper, cut into
  strips
2 large ripe tomatoes, peeled,
  seeded, and chopped
1 cup canned tomato purée
1 teaspoon sugar
2 jalapeño peppers, chopped
2 tablespoons red wine
  vinegar

2 tablespoons dry sherry
¹/₂ teaspoon dried leaf
  oregano
¹/₄ teaspoon ground
  cinnamon
¹/₄ teaspoon cloves
¹/₄ cup chopped fresh cilantro
Salt to taste
1 tablespoon capers
1¹/₂ pounds medium-sized
  raw shrimp, peeled and
  deveined
10 each black and green
  pitted olives

Sauté fresh garlic and onion in oil; add pepper strips and sauté for 3 minutes, stirring. Set aside. Simmer remaining ingredients, except shrimp and olives, for 20 minutes. Stir in shrimp and olives and cook 3-4 minutes longer. Add the onion mixture and cook 2 minutes more. Top with parsley and more olives, if desired. Serve over rice. Serves 6.

Cooking with Marilyn

Shrimp Quesadillas

Use your imagination when serving this dish. The combinations of sauces and fillings are endless. Our favorite filling is shrimp but leftover chicken, pork, cooked and seasoned beef and mushrooms, or just cheese and green chiles are equally good.

18 medium shrimp, cooked	1-2 tablespoons vegetable oil
6 medium flour tortillas	
6 slices Monterey Jack cheese	

Lay a flour tortilla flat on the table. Place 1/2-slice of cheese on half of the tortilla. Place 3 shrimp on top of the cheese. Lay second half-slice of cheese on top of shrimp. Fold top half of tortilla over top of cheese and shrimp, forming 1/2 circle. Proceed with remaining tortillas.

Heat one tablespoon of oil in a skillet over medium-high heat. Fry each quesadilla one minute on each side, until nicely browned. Remove to paper towels to drain. Repeat with remaining quesadillas. You may need to add more oil to your skillet as you fry the quesadillas.

To serve, cut into thirds. Place on a bed of your favorite sauce: Pico de Gallo, Yellow Pepper Sauce, Salsa, Guacamole, or a combination of 2. Yield: 6 servings.

YELLOW PEPPER SAUCE:

4 tablespoons chicken stock or white wine	1 small onion, chopped
2 large yellow bell peppers, chopped	1 garlic clove, finely chopped
	1 pinch salt
	2 tablespoons butter

In a saucepan, simmer chicken stock or wine, peppers, onions, garlic, and salt for 25 minutes. Remove from heat. Purée in food processor or blender. Strain. Return to another saucepan. Over medium heat, whisk in 2 tablespoons of butter until pepper sauce is heated and the butter absorbed. Yield: about one cup.

The Heritage Tradition

Pasta Scampi

4 tablespoons olive oil
4 cloves garlic, minced
2 pounds shrimp, peeled and
deveined
1 each medium red and green
bell peppers, cut into strips
1 cup dry white wine
4 tablespoons lemon juice
1 teaspoon dried basil or
oregano

4 tablespoons fresh parsley,
chopped
6 ounces spaghetti
6 quarts boiling water
1/4 cup water
1 tablespoon cornstarch
Grated Parmesan cheese

Heat oil in a nonstick frying pan. Add garlic, shrimp, and pepper strips, sauté, stirring frequently, until shrimp are pink. Add liquids and spices and cook for several minutes longer. Meanwhile, prepare spaghetti in boiling water and drain when tender. Mix cornstarch with 1/4 cup water and add to the shrimp mixture stirring until mixture thickens. Serve spaghetti topped with shrimp mixture. Sprinkle with grated Parmesan cheese.

Note: Scallops may be used in place of shrimp if preferred.

Tried and True by Mothers of 2's

Italian Shrimp and Pasta Toss

1 cup sliced fresh mushrooms
1/2 cup chopped onion
2 cloves garlic, minced
1 teaspoon basil leaves
2 tablespoons olive oil
1/2 cup water
2 tablespoons lemon juice
2 teaspoons chicken bouillon
1 pound medium raw shrimp,
peeled and deveined

1 cup chopped green pepper
1 large tomato, seeded and
chopped
8 ounces angel hair pasta,
cooked
2 tablespoons grated
Parmesan cheese

In large skillet, cook mushrooms, onion, garlic, and basil in oil until tender. Add water, lemon, and bouillon; bring to a boil. Reduce heat; add shrimp and pepper. Simmer, uncovered, 5-8 minutes or until shrimp are pink. Stir in tomato. In large bowl, toss shrimp mixture with hot noodles and cheese. Serve with additional cheese if desired.

Cook, Line & Sinker

Rookwood Pottery Pasta Alla Roma

4 ounces spinach noodles,
cooked
1 1/2 ounces mushrooms,
diced
2 ounces diced tomatoes
2 ounces cauliflower florets
2 ounces broccoli florets

3 ounces ham, diced
3/4 teaspoon minced garlic
Butter for sautéeing
4 ounces tomato sauce
1 ounce heavy cream
Parmesan cheese for topping

In large skillet, sauté noodles, mushrooms, tomatoes, cauliflower, broccoli, ham, and garlic. Blend in tomato sauce and cream. Place on ovenproof serving dish, top with Parmesan cheese, and run under broiler to brown. Makes one serving.
Rookwood Pottery, Cincinnati, Ohio.

Dining in Historic Ohio

Mom's Homemade Noodles

2 cups flour
3 tablespoons water

2/3 cup egg yolks
2 tablespoons vinegar

Measure flour into a medium mixing bowl. Make a well in the flour with a fork. Add remaining ingredients. Mix well scraping sides often. On floured surface roll dough to desired thickness. Allow to dry slightly. Cut dough to favorite widths. Spread noodles in single layer on floured surface. Dry fully. Store in airtight container.

A Matter of Taste

Spaghetti Pie

6 ounces spaghetti
2 tablespoons butter or
  margarine
2 eggs, well beaten
1/3 cup Parmesan cheese
1 cup creamed cottage cheese

1 pound ground beef or 1/2
  pound beef and 1/2 pound
  sausage
12-ounce jar Prego
1/2 cup provolone or
  Mozzarella cheese

Cook spaghetti; drain. Add butter, eggs and Parmesan cheese. Press in 10-inch pie or quiche dish (greased). Spread cottage cheese on top of spaghetti. Brown ground meat and mix with spaghetti sauce. Heat; spread on top of pie. Bake, uncovered, at 350° for 25 minutes. Remove and top with shredded provolone or Mozzarella cheese. Return to oven 5 minutes until cheese is melted.

Heavenly Food II

George's Spaghetti Pie

6 ounces spaghetti
2 tablespoons butter or
  margarine
1/2 cup grated Parmesan
  cheese
2 well-beaten eggs
1 cup (8 ounces) cottage
  cheese
1 pound ground beef
1/2 cup chopped onion
1/4 cup chopped green
  peppers

1 small package fresh
  mushrooms
1 (8-ounce) can tomatoes, cut
  up
1 (6-ounce) can tomato paste
1 teaspoon sugar
1 teaspoon dried oregano
1/2 teaspoon garlic salt
1 cup Mozzarella cheese,
  shredded

Cook spaghetti. Drain. Stir butter or margarine into hot spaghetti. Stir in Parmesan cheese and eggs. Form spaghetti mixture into a crust in a buttered 10-inch pie pan. Spread cottage cheese over bottom of spaghetti crust.

In skillet, cook ground beef, onion, peppers, and mushrooms until tender. Drain. Stir in undrained tomatoes (chopped), paste, sugar, oregano, and garlic salt. Heat through. Pour into spaghetti crust. Bake uncovered at 350° for 20 minutes. Sprinkle Mozzarella cheese on top; bake 5 minutes longer.

25th Anniversary Cookbook

Stuffed Manicotti

1 pound mild bulk pork
  sausage
1 (6-ounce) can tomato paste
2 (15-ounce) cans Italian
  tomato sauce
1/4 cup water
1/2 - 3/4 tablespoon light
  brown sugar
1 (15-ounce) carton ricotta
  cheese

3 cups shredded Mozzarella,
  divided
1 egg
1 teaspoon parsley flakes
8 manicotti noodles (cooked,
  rinsed and drained)
Grated Parmesan cheese
  (optional)

In large saucepan, brown sausage and drain. Remove half and set aside. Stir tomato paste, sauce, water, and brown sugar into sausage; simmer 15 minutes. Meanwhile, in medium bowl, combine remaining sausage, ricotta, 2 cups Mozzarella cheese, egg, and parsley. In 13x9x2-inch pan, pour 1/3 of sauce mixture. Stuff noodles with cheese and sausage mixture and place on top of sauce. Pour rest of sauce over noodles. Sprinkle remaining cup of Mozzarella cheese and Parmesan on top. Bake uncovered in a 350° oven for 20 minutes.

Oeder Family & Friends Cookbook

Unbelievable Lasagna

1 pound hamburger
4-5 cups spaghetti sauce
8 ounces lasagna noodles
1 pound cottage cheese

1/2 pound Mozzarella cheese
1 cup grated Parmesan
  cheese

Brown and drain hamburger and add to spaghetti sauce. In 13x9x2-inch baking dish, spread one cup sauce. Arrange a layer of uncooked lasagna noodles. Top with one cup sauce, 1/2 cottage cheese, 1/2 Mozzarella cheese, 1/2 Parmesan cheese and one cup sauce. Repeat, gently pressing lasagna noodles into cheese mixture. End with final layer of sauce. Make sure all lasagna pieces are covered with sauce. (Lasagna will expand to ends of pan.) Bake at 350° for 55 minutes. Allow to stand 15 minutes after heat is turned off. Cut into squares and serve.

By Our Cookstove

White Lasagna

A tasty variation of a family favorite.

8 ounces lasagna noodles
1 pound ground beef
1 cup celery, finely chopped
3/4 cup onion, chopped
1 clove garlic, minced
2 teaspoons basil
1 teaspoon oregano
3/4 teaspoon salt
1/2 teaspoon pepper
1/2 teaspoon Italian seasoning
1 cup light cream

1 (3-ounce) package cream cheese, cubed
1/2 cup dry white wine
2 cups Cheddar cheese, shredded
1 1/2 cups Gouda cheese, shredded
1 egg, beaten
12 ounces cottage cheese
12 ounces Mozzarella cheese, sliced

Cook noodles to al dente. Brown meat and drain grease. Add celery, onion, and garlic. Cook until done. Add herbs, cream, and cream cheese. Cook over low heat to melt cream cheese. Add wine and gradually add Cheddar and Gouda cheeses, stirring until nearly melted. Remove from heat. Stir egg and cottage cheese together. In greased 9x13-inch pan, layer one-half of each: noodles, meat, cottage cheese, and Mozzarella. Repeat layers. Bake, uncovered, in a preheated 375° oven for 30-35 minutes. Let stand 10 minutes before cutting. May be prepared ahead. Freezes well. Yield: 6-8 servings.

Simply Sensational

Vegetarian Lasagna

Lasagna noodles
1 pound fresh spinach
2 cups fresh mushrooms, sliced
1 cup grated carrots
1/2 cup chopped onion
1 tablespoon cooking oil
1 (15-ounce) can tomato sauce
1 (6-ounce) can tomato paste
1/2 cup chopped ripe olives
1 1/2 teaspoons oregano
2 cups (16 ounces) cream-style cottage cheese
16 ounces Monterey Jack cheese, sliced
Grated Parmesan

Cook lasagna noodles in boiling unsalted water for 8-10 minutes, or until tender; drain. Rinse spinach, cook covered (no extra water), for 5 minutes, turning.

In saucepan cook sliced mushrooms, carrots, and onions in hot oil till tender, but not brown. Stir in tomato sauce, tomato paste, olives, and oregano. In greased 9x13x2-inch baking dish, layer half each of the noodles, cottage cheese, spinach, Jack cheese, and sauce mixture; repeat layers, reserving several cheese slices for top. Bake at 375° for 30 minutes. Let stand 10 minutes before serving. Pass the Parmesan.

A Taste of Toronto—Ohio, that is

Black Beans and Pasta
(Lowfat)

1 teaspoon olive oil
1 small green pepper,
    chopped
1 small onion, chopped
1/2 teaspoon dried oregano
1 clove garlic, minced
1/2 teaspoon cumin
2 (8-ounce) cans low-sodium
    tomato sauce

1 (15-ounce) can black beans,
    rinsed and drained
Hot pepper sauce to taste
8 ounces macaroni, cooked
1/2 cup shredded nonfat
    Cheddar cheese

Over medium heat, warm oil; sauté pepper, onion, oregano, garlic, and cumin till vegetables are tender.

Add tomato sauce, beans, and hot pepper sauce; bring to boil. Reduce heat to low. Cook about 10 minutes. Toss with hot macaroni. Top with Cheddar cheese.

Down Home Cooking from Hocking County

Roasted Red Pepper Sauce with Pine Nuts

8 large sweet red peppers
1/2 cup olive oil
4 cloves garlic, sliced thin
3/4 pound thin spaghetti
1 1/2 tablespoons coarse salt
    for pasta water
1/2 cup fresh basil, or 2
    teaspoons dried

3 tablespoons pine nuts,
    roasted for 10 minutes at 350°
Freshly ground black pepper
Freshly grated Parmigiano-
    Reggiano cheese

Roast the peppers for about one hour at 400°. Turn a few times. When the skins are blistered and blackened, remove from oven and place in a paper bag for 20 minutes. Take out, peel, core and discard seeds. Cut into strips, saving juices that run off.

Put the oil and garlic in a large fry pan. Sauté garlic until just before golden. In a separate pot, heat 5 quarts of water for pasta. Add the pepper pieces to the fry pan and cook for an additional few minutes. Cook pasta until al dente, and toss with the sauce in the fry pan. Add the basil, pine nuts and grind some black pepper over all. Serve with the grated cheese. Serves 4-6.

Viva Italia

Freezer Tomato Sauce

Delicious on spaghetti!

20 large tomatoes	4 tablespoons sugar
4 large onions	2 tablespoons salt
4 large carrots	3/4 teaspoon pepper
1 mango	4 tablespoons oregano

Peel and cut up tomatoes. Peel and cut up onions. Wash and cut up carrots. Chop mango. Put in large kettle. Add sugar, salt, pepper, and oregano. Cook until vegetables are tender and thick (about one hour). Stir often. Blend slightly in blender. Blending too long will cause air bubbles. Put into containers and freeze.

Note: Can add one can tomato paste.

Recipes & Remembrances

Baked Herb Rice with Pecans

1 cup sliced fresh mushrooms	1 tablespoon Worcestershire
1/2 cup chopped shallots	sauce
1/4 cup plus 2 tablespoons	1 teaspoon dried whole thyme
butter, melted	1 teaspoon dried whole
1 cup long-grain rice	rosemary
1/2 cup chopped pecans,	2 bay leaves
toasted	Hot sauce to taste
1 1/4 cups canned undiluted	Salt and freshly ground
chicken broth	pepper to taste
1 1/4 cups water	Additional chopped toasted
1 (2-ounce) jar diced	pecans
pimiento, drained	
2 tablespoons chopped fresh	
parsley	

Sauté mushrooms and shallots in butter in a large Dutch oven until tender. Add rice and 1/2 cup pecans; stir well. Add chicken broth and remaining ingredients except additional pecans. Bring to a boil. Remove from heat; cover and bake at 350° for 45 minutes to one hour or until rice is tender and liquid is absorbed. Remove and discard bay leaves. Serve, garnished with additional pecans.

Plain & Fancy Favorites

Majic Jambalaya

2 medium carrots, sliced thin
1 medium zucchini
1 teaspoon margarine
1 (8-ounce) can stewed
  tomatoes, undrained
2¹/₂ ounces sliced
  mushrooms

1 cup water
¹/₄ teaspoon each basil and
  thyme
16 ounces Slovenian kielbasa
  cut into pieces
1¹/₂ cups uncooked instant
  rice

Sauté carrots and zucchini in margarine in 10-inch skillet over medium heat for 3 minutes. Add tomatoes and juice, mushrooms, water, basil, thyme, and kielbasa. Bring to boil. Reduce heat to low, cover and simmer 5 minutes. Stir in rice. Cover, remove from heat and let stand 8 minutes, stirring after 4 minutes. Season with hot sauce to taste. Mmmmmmmmm good! Serves 5.

Hats Off to "Real Men Cook" Cookbook

Rice Zucchini Bake

1 pound ground beef
1 large onion, chopped
¹/₂ cup uncooked rice
¹/₂ cup parsley, chopped
¹/₂ teaspoon dried savory
1¹/₂ cups water

Salt and pepper to taste
1 zucchini (large), about 3
  pounds
³/₄ cup grated Cheddar
  cheese

In a large skillet, brown ground meat. Add onion, rice, parsley, savory and water. Cover and cook until rice is tender, about 20 minutes. Add salt and pepper to taste. Stir occasionally.

Cut zucchini in half. Scoop out seeds and sprinkle with a little salt. Stuff with the rice and meat filling. Sprinkle with grated cheese. Cover with foil and place in a flat baking dish. Bake at 350° for 30-35 minutes or until squash is tender.

500 Recipes Using Zucchini

Granville is one of Ohio's prettiest villages. Originally settled by transplanted New Englanders, the landmark inns, museums, restaurants, shops, homes, churches, and a hilltop campus (Dennison University) make for fine small-town strolling. Half of the village is on the National Register of Historic Places.

Pizza Rice Casserole

3/4 pound ground beef
1 onion, chopped
2 cups tomato sauce
1/4 teaspoon garlic salt
1/4 teaspoon oregano
1 teaspoon parsley flakes

1 teaspoon sugar
1 teaspoon salt
Dash pepper
2 cups cooked rice
1 1/2 cups cottage cheese
1/2 cup shredded cheese

Brown ground beef and onion in a large skillet. Add tomato sauce and spices. Cover and simmer 15 minutes. In another container, combine cooked rice and cottage cheese. Put 1/3 of rice mixture in a buttered 2-quart casserole. Top with 1/2 of meat and tomato sauce. Continue to alternate layers, ending with sauce. Sprinkle with cheese. Bake at 325° for 30 minutes or until hot and bubbly.

175th Anniversary Quilt Cookbook

Shrimp-Rice-Broccoli Casserole

1 teaspoon minced garlic
1 stalk celery, chopped
1 small onion, chopped
1 green pepper, chopped
1 bay leaf, crumbled
2 tablespoons olive oil or
   canola oil
2 pounds medium shrimp,
   cleaned and cooked

1 cup brown rice, cooked
1 cup steamed broccoli
2 cups chicken stock (or
   canned broth)
2 tablespoons cornstarch
1/8 teaspoon pepper, black or
   white
1 (4-ounce) can sliced
   mushrooms, drained

Sauté garlic, celery, onion, green pepper, and bay leaf in oil. Pre-cook shrimp and rice; drain both and set each aside. Steam broccoli. Thicken chicken stock with the cornstarch. Combine all ingredients in a casserole dish that has been sprayed with a nonstick cooking spray. Heat in the oven or in the microwave before serving. Serves 4.

Heartline Cookbook

Polish Reuben Casserole

2 cans mushroom soup
1 1/3 cups milk
1/2 cup chopped onion
1 tablespoon prepared
  mustard
2 (16-ounce) cans sauerkraut,
  rinsed and drained
1 (8-ounce) package
  uncooked medium-wide
  noodles

1 1/2 pounds Polish sausage,
  cut in 1/2-inch pieces
2 cups (8 ounces) shredded
  Swiss cheese
3/4 cup whole-wheat bread
  crumbs
2 tablespoons butter, melted

Combine soup, milk, onion, and mustard. Blend well. Spread sauerkraut in greased 9x13-inch pan. Top with uncooked noodles. Spoon soup mixture evenly over top. Top with sausage; then cheese. Combine crumbs and butter in bowl. Sprinkle over top. Cover pan tightly with foil. Bake at 350° for one hour or until noodles are tender.

Favorite Recipes

Tomato-Salami Quiche

1 (10-inch) prepared pastry shell, unbaked

1 cup (4 ounces) shredded Cheddar cheese

4 eggs

2 cups diced tomatoes, seeded and well drained (about 3 medium tomatoes)

1/4 pound thinly sliced hard salami, cut into small pieces

1 cup milk (or half-and-half, if preferred)

1 tablespoon instant minced onion

2 tablespoons freshly minced parsley

1 teaspoon dried oregano, crushed

1/2 teaspoon garlic salt

Freshly ground black pepper

Line a 10-inch pie plate or quiche pan with highstanding rim with pastry and have oven preheating to 450°. Prick bottom of pie shell with fork. Bake for 8 minutes. Remove from oven. Do not reduce oven temperature.

While pie shell is baking, prepare shredded cheese, tomatoes, and salami. Be sure tomatoes are well drained. In prebaked pie shell, sprinkle half the cheese, salami, and tomatoes. Repeat layers. In medium mixing bowl, beat the eggs to blend. Add milk, minced onion, parsley, oregano, garlic salt, and pepper. Beat well and pour evenly over quiche ingredients. Spread parsley with tines of fork, if it tends to clump. Bake quiche at 450° for 10 minutes; reduce temperature to 325°; bake 30-35 minutes more. Let stand 5 minutes before cutting. Serves 8.

Herbs: From Cultivation to Cooking

Ski Cheese Pie

PHYLLO CRUST:

1 package of phyllo	1 tablespoon olive oil
1 egg white	Olive oil spray

Thaw phyllo according to package directions. Mix egg white with olive oil. Spray pie plate with olive oil spray. Working quickly with phyllo, place one sheet of phyllo over pie plate allowing sheet to drape over the sides. With hands, press sheet to fit well of pie plate while outer edges drape over sides. Quickly brush some egg mixture over phyllo only on the inside of the pie plate.

Place another sheet of phyllo over first at right angles to the first sheet and again using a pastry brush, spread with egg mixture. Repeat until there are 4 layers of phyllo dough. Take the overlapping edges of phyllo and "scrunching them up," form a pie rim. Dab pie rim or edge with egg mixture. Fill and bake.

PIE:

2 cups reduced-fat sharp Cheddar cheese, shredded	8 slices turkey bacon, diced
2 tablespoons flour	1/4 cup skim milk
1/2 teaspoon salt	2 eggs and 2 egg whites beaten together
1/4 teaspoon dry mustard	1 (8-ounce) can tomato sauce
1/4 cup onion, chopped	

Preheat oven to 350°. Toss cheese with flour and seasonings. Set aside. Cook onion and bacon in skillet for 10 minutes, adding cold water in 1/4-cup increments as necessary to prevent burning.

Combine bacon, onions, skim milk, beaten eggs, tomato sauce and mix well. Add cheese mixture; be sure to combine well. Pour into Phyllo Crust. Bake at 350° for 40-45 minutes. Serves 8.

Note: It may be necessary to cover edges of Phyllo Crust with foil halfway through baking to prevent burning.

Light Kitchen Choreography

The former home and farm of sausage-maker Bob Evans is a major attraction. Wagon tours take visitors around the nineteenth-century homestead and village in Rio Grande.

Cheese Pita

1 box filo leaves
1 (24-ounce) small curd
    cottage cheese
1 (8-ounce) cream cheese,
    softened
3/4 cup Parmesan cheese

2 eggs
2 tablespoons parsley
1/2 teaspoon salt
Melted butter for brushing on
    filo
2 cans spinach, drained

In advance, thaw filo leaves according to package directions. Mix all ingredients, except filo, spinach and butter, in large bowl. Spread out 3-4 sheets of filo on towel. Brush with melted butter. Spread several large spoonfuls of filling across one short end of filo rectangles, about 2 inches from the top and one inch from each side. Sprinkle layer of drained spinach on top of cheese mixture. Roll up, starting at the end with cheese (jelly-roll fashion) and put lengthwise into 9x13-inch pan, brushed with melted butter. Bake at 350° until browned. Cool slightly before cutting.

Note: Filo sheets can be cut into strips and folded flag-style. They make great appetizers.

25th Anniversary Cookbook

Cheesy Green Onion Quiche

Pastry for bottom of quiche
    dish
8 slices bacon, cooked and
    crumbled
3/4 cup (3 ounces) shredded
    Swiss cheese
4 eggs, beaten
1 (8-ounce) carton
    commercial sour cream

1/2 cup half-and-half
1/4 cup sliced green onion
1 tablespoon all-purpose flour
3/4 teaspoon salt
1/8 teaspoon pepper
Dash dried crushed red
    pepper

Line a 9-inch quiche dish or pie plate with pastry. Trim excess pastry around edges. Prick bottom and sides of pastry with a fork. Bake at 400° for 3 minutes. Remove from oven and gently prick with fork. Bake 5 minutes longer.

Sprinkle bacon and cheese into pastry shell. Combine remaining ingredients and mix well. Pour into pastry shell and bake at 375° for 40-45 minutes until set.

Treasured Recipes

Vegetables

Skiing at Mad River Mountain. Near Bellefontaine.

Sauerkraut

Wash, quarter, core and shred cabbage. Weigh. Thoroughly mix 1/2 cup salt to 10 pounds shredded cabbage. Firmly pack into stone jar. Cover with a white cloth and inner plate or glass pie plate. Remove scum when it forms. Be sure it's covered with liquid at all times. Sauerkraut is cured and ready to can in 10 days or 2 weeks. Pack sauerkraut into pint or quart jars, leaving 1/2-inch head space. Tighten lid and store in a cool place.

One Nation Under Sauerkraut

Summer Squash & Onion Sauté with Sour Cream & Fennel

As soon as yellow squash appear at a nearby farm, we make this dish and serve it as long as the squash are available. It's a good accompaniment to grilled fish or chicken.

2 tablespoons vegetable oil
3 small yellow squash,
trimmed and cut into 1/4-inch
slices
1 small onion, sliced
2 tablespoons minced fennel
fronds

1/4 cup low-fat sour cream
Kosher salt and freshly
ground black pepper
1 tablespoon minced fresh
chives

Heat oil in a nonstick skillet over medium heat. Add squash and onions and toss until vegetables are coated with oil. Reduce heat to low, cover and cook, stirring from time to time, until vegetables are just tender, about 6 minutes.

Stir in fennel and sour cream; season with salt and pepper to taste. Cook, uncovered, just until heated through, 1-2 minutes. Sprinkle with chives and serve. Serves 4.

Onions, Onions, Onions

 Findlay Market has an incredible array of fresh fruits, vegetables, meats, and flowers. The open-air market has been a tradition in Cincinnati for over 140 years.

Glass Jar Sauerkraut

5 pounds shredded cabbage
  including cores

3¹/₂ tablespoons coarse
  uniodized salt

Weigh the shredded cabbage accurately. Sprinkle with the salt which should be "a little more than level but not heaping" tablespoons. Mix well by hand so that the salt draws the water out of the cabbage. Pack "very, very tightly" into quart glass jars.

Make sure plenty of juice is created. Do not fill jars any higher than the shoulder. Seal with 2-piece lids and set in a dark place and cover with newspaper. Do not move for six weeks as the kraut "works" (ferments). Juice will run over the top of jars. At the end of 6 weeks, turn jars upside down to check for leakage. Should a jar leak replace the lid with a new one. Tighten lids and store.

Note: For an interesting flavor contrast, use half cabbage and half shredded turnips, relatives of the cabbage. For a delicious cold relish make turnip kraut using the same amount of turnips and coarse salt.

One Nation Under Sauerkraut

Mrs. Yutzey's Sauerkraut

2 tablespoons butter (no
  margarine)
¹/₂ cup chopped onions
1 quart sauerkraut

1 grated potato (³/₄ cup)
1 teaspoon caraway seed
2 cups boiling water

Melt butter in kettle and cook until golden. Stir in sauerkraut and cook 8 minutes. Mix in onion, potato, and caraway seed. Pour in boiling water. Cook uncovered over low heat for 30 minutes. Cover and cook another 30 minutes. Serves 6-8.

Note: You can add a little brown sugar or chopped apple for a different taste.

One Nation Under Sauerkraut

Baked Sweet Sauerkraut
with Tomatoes and Bacon

The Ohio Sauerkraut Festival is held in Waynesville, population 2,000 the second week of October and attracts thousands of people. Remember, this state was settled by Germans; they flock to sample the food and buy crafts at the festival's five hundred booths. It is sort of like a krauty Mardi Gras.

This old, old recipe is a real treasure. The few ingredients—all listed in the title—would have been in any Ohio kitchen at the turn of the century. The dish is baked quite a long time, until the top caramelizes, the liquid cooks away, and the kraut is nearly transparent.

1 (14-ounce) can tomatoes, coarsely chopped, undrained
1 (16-ounce) can sauerkraut, undrained
1 cup sugar
6 slices raw bacon, cut in ¹/₂-inch pieces
¹/₂ teaspoon freshly ground pepper

Preheat the oven to 325°. Grease a flat (see Note) 2-quart glass baking dish. Place all the ingredients in the dish and combine thoroughly. (You may have to use your hands to distribute the bacon evenly.) Bake, uncovered, for 2 hours and 15 minutes, or until the top begins to brown deeply and most of the liquid has cooked away.

Note: It is important to use a flat dish so the liquid evaporates as it cooks.

Heartland

Sauerkraut and Sausage

1 (27-ounce) can sauerkraut, rinsed
1 medium apple, peeled and chopped
1 small onion, chopped or use minced onion
1 tablespoon caraway seed
2 tablespoons brown sugar or more according to taste
Several shakes coarsely ground pepper
¹/₂ package smoked sausage cut in small chunks

Cook over low to medium heat on top of stove or bake at 350° for an hour.

Recipes from "The Little Switzerland of Ohio"

Reuben Casserole

1 cup sour cream
1 small onion
10 slices rye bread
1/2 cup Thousand Island
 dressing
1 small can sauerkraut

1/2 pound corned beef
12 ounces Mozzarella cheese,
 shredded
8 ounces Swiss, shredded
1 1/4 cups melted butter

Combine sour cream and onion. Layer 5 slices of bread on bottom of a large casserole dish, then sour cream/onion mixture, then Thousand Island dressing, sauerkraut, corned beef, and cheese. Put 5 slices of rye bread on top, broken into pieces. Drizzle butter over top. Bake uncovered for 30 minutes at 350°. Makes enough for 18-24 servings.

What's Cooking at Holden School

German Sauerkraut Pita

1 1/2 pounds bulk pork
 sausage
1 medium onion, chopped
1 clove garlic, minced
1 teaspoon caraway seeds

1 pound sauerkraut, drained
1/2 cup sherry
Pepper to taste
Pita bread

Brown sausage with onion, garlic and caraway seeds, then drain. Add sauerkraut, sherry, and pepper, and simmer 20-30 minutes. Serve in pita bread.

One Nation Under Sauerkraut

Short Cut Cabbage Rolls

4 cups shredded cabbage
1 1/2 pounds hamburger
  (cooked and drained)
3 tablespoons minced onion
1 1/2 teaspoons salt
1/4 teaspoon pepper

1/2 teaspoon paprika
1/8 teaspoon garlic
1 (8-ounce) jar sauerkraut
  drained
1 (8-ounce) can tomato sauce

Spread a layer of shredded cabbage and then hamburger in bottom of casserole dish. Put onion, salt, pepper, paprika, and garlic on the top of hamburger. Then add sauerkraut and spread tomato sauce over the top of it. Bake at 300° for 1 1/2 hours. Then spread one cup sour cream on top; return to 400° oven for 8-10 minutes.

One Nation Under Sauerkraut

Haluski

1/4 cup chopped onion
1/4 cup chopped green pepper
2 sticks margarine, divided
1 head cabbage, chopped

1 (16-ounce) package kluski
  noodles
Salt and pepper to taste

Sauté the onions and green peppers in one stick of margarine. Add the chopped cabbage, and sauté till tender. In the meantime, prepare the noodles as directed. Add the drained noodles to the onion, pepper, cabbage mixture.

Add remaining stick of margarine and salt and pepper to taste. This will fill a crock pot—great to take to a covered dish dinner.

A Taste of Toronto—Ohio, that is

Cabbage and Onion Casserole

8 cups chopped cabbage
3 cups chopped onion
4 tablespoons butter
4 tablespoons flour
1/4 teaspoon pepper

1 1/2 cups milk
1 pound Velveeta cheese
2 cups croutons
1 pound sausage, browned
  and drained

Parboil cabbage and onion on stove for 7 minutes; drain. Melt butter; add flour and pepper; add milk and cubed cheese. Cook until melted. Layer 1/2 cabbage and onion mixture, 1/2 croutons, 1/2 sausage, 1/2 cheese. Layer again in same order. Let stand 5 minutes. Bake in 3-quart dish at 350° for 1/2 hour.

Treasures and Pleasures

Cabbage and Noodles

Chop one head of sweet cabbage and one large onion. Cook in salted water. Drain and squeeze out excess water. Fry cabbage and onion in butter. Then add hot fried cabbage to cooked noodles. Mix well. Serve hot.

Favorite Recipes

Sloppy Beans and Cornbread

SLOPPY BEANS:

1 pound dry lima beans
1/2 pound pork, ham, or sausage
Cayenne pepper pod

1 large onion, chopped
1 potato, chopped (optional)
Salt and pepper to taste

Soak the beans overnight in cold water. Put them on to cook the next day, adding the meat and pepper pod. Simmer, covered, 2-3 hours. When the beans are getting soft, add the onion, potatoes, salt, and pepper. The vegetables should only cook the last half an hour or so. At the time you add the vegetables, make the cornbread.

CORNBREAD:

2 strips bacon
1 cup cornmeal
1 cup white or whole wheat
   flour
1 cup sour milk or buttermilk
1 tablespoon sugar

2 teaspoons baking powder
1/2 teaspoon baking powder
1/2 teaspoon salt
3 tablespoons fat, oil, or
   melted butter
1 egg, beaten

Fry the bacon in a 10-inch iron skillet. Preheat the oven to 400°. Remove the bacon and crumble. Pour off all but about 2 table-spoons of the bacon grease, using in the cornbread for fat if de-sired. Keep the skillet hot. In a small bowl mix together the re-maining cornbread ingredients. Stir in the bacon bits. Pour the batter into the hot skillet and place it in the oven for about 20 minutes. It is done when set, and there will probably be a crack down the center. Serve the Sloppy Beans in a bowl, with the Cornbread and plenty of butter on the side.

Cincinnati Recipe Treasury

Killer Baked Beans

2 large bell peppers, chopped
2 large onions, chopped
2 pounds ground sirloin
4 (20-ounce) cans
  pork-n-beans
3 (16-ounce) cans kidney
  beans

3 cans green lima beans
1 tablespoon nutmeg
1 tablespoon cinnamon
1 pound sugar
2 sticks butter

Mix all ingredients and cook (at least 3 hours) at 325° until thick, stirring occasionally.

Hats Off to "Real Men Cook" Cookbook

Calico Beans

1 pound hamburger, browned
1/2 pound bacon, cooked,
  drained
1 can pork and beans
1 can kidney beans

1 can lima beans, drained
3/4 cup brown sugar
1/2 cup catsup
2 tablespoons vinegar
1/2 cup onion

Mix all ingredients together. Put in crock pot until all heated through, or put in oven for approximately 30-45 minutes at 350°.

Ottoville Sesquicentennial Cookbook

Swiss Vegetable Medley

1 (16-ounce) package
  California Blend vegetables,
  thawed and drained
1 can cream of mushroom
  soup
1 cup shredded Swiss cheese,
  divided

1/3 cup sour cream
Pepper to taste
1 (4-ounce) jar chopped
  drained pimentos (optional)
1 (2.8-ounce) can French-fried
  onions, divided

Combine vegetables, soup, 1/2 cup cheese, sour cream, pepper, pimentos, and 1/2 can French-fried onions. Pour into greased 1-quart casserole. Bake, covered, for 30 minutes at 350°. Top with remaining cheese and onions. Bake, uncovered, 5 minutes longer.

Our Collection of Heavenly Recipes

Beata's Six Bean Casserole

This is a favorite at family get-togethers!

1 pound sausage, browned
2 medium onions, diced
1 cup celery, diced
1 can chili-flavored beans
1 can pork and beans
1 can lima beans (green)
1 can yellow wax beans

1 can kidney beans
1 can green beans (cut)
2 tablespoons mustard
1 cup brown sugar
1 cup tomato soup
1 (6-ounce) can tomato paste
2 slices bacon

Sauté sausage, onions and celery. Add chili-flavored beans and pork and beans. Drain and add all other beans. Add mustard, brown sugar and tomato soup. Place in large baking dish. Spread tomato paste on top. Criss-cross 2 strips of bacon on top. Bake uncovered in preheated 350° oven for one hour.

Cooking with TLC

Cindy's Green Beans

Serve hot or cold.

2 pounds green beans, cooked*
1 bunch green onions, chopped

1/2 pound bacon, fried and crumbled
1/4 pound bleu cheese, crumbled

Cook green beans in boiling water until just cooked; drain. Add green onions to beans in serving bowl. Toss beans with Dill Dressing. Top with crumbled bacon and bleu cheese. Can be served hot or cold.

DILL DRESSING:

1 cup vegetable oil
1/4 cup balsamic vinegar
3 tablespoons lemon juice
1/2 teaspoon black pepper

1/4 teaspoon paprika
1/2 teaspoon dry mustard
1-2 cloves minced garlic
Fresh dill

Combine all ingredients.

Note: *Fresh green beans are best in summer, but frozen work well.

Favorite Recipes from Poland Women's Club

Broccoli Casserole

Easy and delicious.

1 (20-ounce) package broccoli, cut	1 (8-ounce) package Velveeta cheese
1 stick butter, divided	20 Ritz crackers

Cook broccoli; drain very well. Melt 1/2 stick of butter with Velveeta cheese. Crumble crackers and other half of butter (melted). Mix broccoli with melted butter and cheese. Spread crackers on top and bake at 350° for 15-20 minutes.

Incredible Edibles

Baked Sweet Potatoes and Apricots

Anyone with a "sweet tooth" will love this dish!

6 fresh medium sweet potatoes or 2 large cans of sweet potatoes, drained	1 tablespoon cornstarch
	1/4 teaspoon salt
	1/2 teaspoon cinnamon
1 (17-ounce) can apricot halves in light syrup, cut into thirds	1/3 cup golden raisins
	1/4 cup dry sherry
	1 teaspoon grated orange peel
1 1/2 tablespoons brown sugar	

Cook fresh sweet potatoes in boiling water until tender, 30-35 minutes. Peel and halve potatoes lengthwise. Place in 9x13x2-inch baking dish.

Drain apricots, reserving syrup; add water to syrup, if necessary, to equal 1 cup of liquid and set aside. Arrange apricots over potatoes.

In saucepan, combine brown sugar, cornstarch, salt, and cinnamon. Stir in apricot syrup and raisins. Cook and stir over high heat until mixture comes to a boil. Stir in sherry and orange peel. Pour mixture over potatoes and fruit.

Bake, uncovered, in a 350° oven, basting occasionally for 20 minutes or until well glazed. Serves 6.

Light Kitchen Choreography

Spiced Apple and Sweet Potato Casserole

1 (18-ounce) can sweet
potatoes, sliced
1 (20-ounce) can sliced apples
³/₄ teaspoon cinnamon

¹/₂ teaspoon nutmeg
¹/₃ cup pineapple juice
¹/₄ cup butter
Parsley flakes

Arrange sweet potato slices and apples in alternating layers in an 8-inch square baking dish. Sprinkle each layer with cinnamon and nutmeg. Add pineapple juice. Dot with butter. Cover and bake at 375° for 15 minutes. Uncover and continue baking 20 minutes. Garnish with parsley flakes. Makes 6 servings.

Incredible Edibles

Sweet Potato Casserole

3 cups mashed sweet potatoes
¹/₂ cup brown sugar
2 eggs, beaten
¹/₂ teaspoon salt
¹/₂ stick oleo, melted
¹/₂ cup milk

1¹/₂ teaspoons vanilla
¹/₃ cup flour
¹/₂ cup brown sugar
1 cup chopped nuts
¹/₂ stick oleo

Mix potatoes, ¹/₂ cup brown sugar, eggs, salt, ¹/₂ stick oleo, milk, and vanilla. Pour into 1¹/₂-quart baking dish. Mix flour, brown sugar, nuts, and ¹/₂ stick oleo together. Spread over sweet potatoes. Bake at 350° for 35 minutes.

Cooking GRACEfully

Mashed Sweet Potato Bake

6 small sweet potatoes
1/2 teaspoon grated orange
   peel
2 tablespoons orange juice
2 tablespoons brown Sugar
   Twin

1 tablespoon margarine
1/2 teaspoon salt (optional)
1/4 teaspoon ground
   cinnamon
1 egg
1/2 cup skim milk

Prepare and cook sweet potatoes. Drain and mash with a potato masher or on low speed of electric mixer. Add orange peel, juice, brown sugar substitute, butter, salt, and cinnamon. Add egg and skim milk, that have been beaten together. Beat sweet potato mixture until fluffy. Add additional skim milk if needed. Turn into a 1-quart baking dish that has been sprayed with vegetable spray. Cover and bake in a 350° oven for 45-50 minutes. Yields 6 servings. Exchange: 1 serving=1 bread, 1/2 fat. Cal 105.

Tried and True Volume II: Diabetic Cookbook

Make-Ahead Mashed Potatoes

5 pounds potatoes, peeled
   and cooked
1/2 cup butter or oleo
1/2 cup sour cream
1 (8-ounce) package cream
   cheese

1/2 - 1 cup milk
2 eggs, beaten
1 package Good Seasons
   Italian Dressing*

Mash potatoes; add rest of ingredients. Whip together; put in a buttered casserole dish. Set in refrigerator overnight (a couple of days doesn't matter). Bake at 350° for 45 minutes to one hour, uncovered.

Note: *The Good Seasons Dressing mix is optional but it sure is good. Maybe you'll just want salt and pepper.

Heavenly Dishes

 Annie Oakley made her mark traveling with Buffalo Bill Cody's Wild West Show, but she learned to shoot in the woods of Darke County, Ohio, and was born near Greenville.

Crunch-Top Potatoes

¹/₃ cup oleo
3 or 4 large baking potatoes,
  peeled and sliced
³/₄ cup crushed cornflakes

1¹/₂ cups shredded sharp
  cheese
1¹/₂ teaspoons paprika
Salt, if desired

Melt oleo in 8x8-inch pan at 375°. Add single layer of potatoes; turn in the oleo. Mix remaining ingredients; sprinkle over. Bake ¹/₂ hour until done.

Tumm Yummies

Garlic Roasted Potatoes

4 large baking potatoes,
  peeled
4 cloves garlic
6 tablespoons butter

³/₄ cup Parmesan cheese
Salt to taste
Pepper to taste

Cut potatoes in half lengthwise; slice ¹/₄-inch thick. Rinse in cold water; drain thoroughly on paper towels. Mince garlic or put through press. Melt butter in small saucepan; add garlic and cook on medium heat for one minute. Place potatoes in large bowl; add butter/garlic, half the cheese and seasonings. Stir until potatoes are well coated; pour into shallow pan. Top with remaining cheese; bake at 400° uncovered until golden brown, about 30 minutes. Do not stir or turn during baking. Yield: 8 servings.

175th Anniversary Quilt Cookbook

Garlic Potato Straw Surprise

2 pounds baking potatoes,
  peeled and coarsely
  shredded, divided
1 tablespoon vegetable oil
10 garlic cloves, peeled

1 tablespoon fresh parsley,
  chopped
1/2 teaspoon salt
1 tablespoon butter

Preheat oven to 400°. Squeeze any excess liquid from shredded potatoes. Heat oil in a large cast iron skillet on medium-high heat. Add half of the potatoes, tossing to coat. Push the garlic cloves into the potato and sprinkle with parsley and salt.

In a separate skillet, heat butter on medium heat and toss remaining potatoes in the melted butter. Immediately layer potatoes on top of the potato/garlic mixture, spreading evenly over the first layer. Bake in 400° oven for 45 minutes or until potatoes are golden brown and crisp. Serves 4.

Light Kitchen Choreography

Garlic Mashed Potatoes

1 pound (about 4 medium)
  potatoes, peeled and halved
1 small head garlic, peeled
4 cups chicken stock

1/2 cup butter
Salt and pepper, to taste
1/2 cup light cream

Place potatoes in saucepan with garlic and chicken stock. Bring to a boil. Reduce heat. Simmer until potatoes are soft; drain. Gently mash potatoes and garlic with butter, salt, pepper, and cream. Serves 4.

A Cleveland Collection

Potato Puffs

We serve this recipe at our banquets. They hold well, are different and good.

4 pounds potatoes, boiled	1 cup grated Cheddar cheese
3/4 - 1 1/4 cups milk	2 egg yolks
1/4 cup butter	1 cup crushed cornflakes
1 1/2 teaspoons salt	3 tablespoons toasted sesame
2 teaspoons sugar	seeds

Peel potatoes. Boil until soft; drain and mash. Heat milk, butter, salt, and sugar together. Gradually whip in until potatoes are smooth and fluffy. Add cheese and egg yolks and chill. Form into balls. Roll in mixture of cornflakes and sesame seeds. Can serve, or freeze and package.

To serve: Place frozen puffs on baking sheet. Brush lightly with melted butter. Bake in hot oven at 400° for 20 minutes for small puffs, 30 minutes for medium puffs. Makes 48 small.

The Fifth Generation Cookbook

Cheesy Scalloped Potatoes

They'll think you've been cooking all day.

2 tablespoons regular mayonnaise	1 cup shredded lowfat (4-5 grams per ounce) Cheddar cheese
6 tablespoons low fat (1 gram per tablespoon) mayonnaise	4 cups thinly sliced, peeled raw potatoes
2 tablespoons flour	2 tablespoons grated fat-free Parmesan cheese
1/8 teaspoon black pepper	
1 cup skim milk	

Spray 10x6-inch baking dish with vegetable oil spray. Preheat oven to 350°. In medium saucepan, combine regular mayonnaise, low fat mayonnaise, flour and pepper. Over medium heat, gradually add milk, stirring until thickened. Add Cheddar cheese; stir until melted. Place potatoes in prepared baking dish; pour sauce over potatoes. Sprinkle with Parmesan cheese and spray with vegetable oil spray. Bake at 350° for 55-60 minutes or until potatoes are tender. Yield: 6 servings.

Nutrients per serving: Cal 295; Fat 8g (24%); Carbo 47g; Chol 14mg; Sod 428mg; Pro 11g.

Recipe Rehab

Potato and Mozzarella Cheese Puff

3 beaten egg yolks or egg
  substitute
1/4 cup skim milk
6 ounces shredded
  Mozzarella cheese (light)
3 cups mashed potatoes

2 tablespoons chopped
  parsley
1 tablespoon finely chopped
  onion
3 egg whites, beaten

Spray a 2-quart baking dish. Combine egg yolks and milk. Add remaining ingredients, except egg whites; beat well. Fold beaten egg whites into mixture. Put in baking dish. Bake at 375° for 40-45 minutes or until knife inserted in middle comes out clean and top is browned. Serve immediately. Yields 6 servings. Exchange: 1 bread, 1 1/2 meats, Cal 185.

Tried and True Volume II: Diabetic Cookbook

Surprise Scalloped Potatoes
(Lowfat)

1 (2-pound) package frozen
  hash browns (partly thawed)
1 (16-ounce) carton sour
  cream (fat free)
2 cups shredded Colby or
  sharp (use low or no fat
  cheese)
1 cup shredded Monterey
  Jack

1/2 cup onion
1/2 cup chopped bell pepper
1 (2-ounce) jar pimento,
  drained
1 tablespoon chicken bouillon
1/8 cup margarine

Combine all ingredients, except 1/2 cup Colby; mix. Turn into buttered baking dish. Bake at 350° for 55-60 minutes. Top with remaining cheese. Bake 5 minutes. Let stand another 5 minutes.

Down Home Cooking from Hocking County

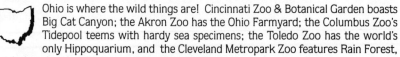

Ohio is where the wild things are! Cincinnati Zoo & Botanical Garden boasts Big Cat Canyon; the Akron Zoo has the Ohio Farmyard; the Columbus Zoo's Tidepool teems with hardy sea specimens; the Toledo Zoo has the world's only Hippoquarium, and the Cleveland Metropark Zoo features Rain Forest, an indoor jungle with its own thunderstorms.

Skillet Potato Cake
with Shallots & Chives

We bake this cake of grated potatoes and shallots in a hot cast-iron skillet in the oven and frequently serve it with chicken dishes.

8 large russet potatoes
1/2 cup minced shallots
3 tablespoons minced fresh
  chives
1 tablespoon chopped fresh
  rosemary leaves or 1 1/2
  teaspoons dried
1 tablespoon minced fresh
  parsley

2 teaspoons kosher salt
1 tablespoon freshly ground
  black pepper
1/2 cup (1 stick) unsalted
  butter
Chopped chives and chive
  blossoms, for garnish
  (optional)

Early in the day, bake potatoes until just tender but still a bit firm. Cool thoroughly. Preheat oven to 450°. Peel potatoes and coarsely grate into a large mixing bowl. Add shallots, chives, rosemary, parsley, salt and pepper and mix well.

Melt butter in a 9-inch cast-iron skillet. Pour 3/4 of it (6 tablespoons) into potato mixture. Thoroughly coat the skillet with remaining 2 tablespoons butter. Place the skillet in the oven and preheat until hot, about 5 minutes.

When the skillet is hot, carefully remove from the oven, fill with potato mixture, and press firmly to make a compact cake. Bake until the edges are browned, about 45 minutes.

Remove the skillet from the oven and let stand for a few minutes. Invert over a platter and cut potato cake into wedges. Sprinkle with more chives and chive blossoms and serve. Serves 8-10.

Onions, Onions, Onions

Beer-Battered Sweet Onion Rings

This batter gets shiny and crisp in frying. If it is a tad too thin, it may slip off here and there—but that's nothing serious. After you've made these once, you'll get the hang of it.

1 cup plus 2 tablespoons unbleached flour	**¹/8 teaspoon cayenne**
1 teaspoon kosher salt	**1 cup beer**
¹/2 teaspoon freshly ground black peper	**1 large (at least 1-pound) Vidalia, Walla Walla, Maui or other sweet onion**
¹/2 teaspoon freshly ground white pepper	**4-8 cups vegetable oil for deep-frying**

Combine flour, salt, black and white peppers, and cayenne in a large mixing bowl. Add beer, all at once, and whisk until smooth. Set aside for 30 minutes. Cut onion into slices at least ¹/2-inch thick. Separate into rings.

Pour oil into a deep-fat fryer or wok to a depth of 2-3 inches and heat to 375°. Preheat the oven to warm (250°).

Stir batter. It should be somewhat thicker than pancake batter, so that onions will get a nice coating. It if is too thick, thin by gradually adding a bit more beer. Working in batches of 3 or 4, dip onion rings into batter.

Add battered onion rings, 3-4 at a time, to oil. Fry, without crowding, until golden brown, about 3 minutes, turning if necessary. Drain well on paper towels and keep warm in the oven. Repeat until all onion rings are fried. Sprinkle with salt and serve.

Onions, Onions, Onions

Onion Patties

Tastes just like onion rings!

3/4 cup flour
1 tablespoon sugar
1 tablespoon cornmeal
2 teaspoons baking powder

2 teaspoon ssalt
3/4 cup milk
2 1/2 cups onion, finely
   chopped

Mix dry ingredients together; then add milk. Batter should be fairly thick. Add onions and mix thoroughly. Drop by tablespoonfuls into 1/2 inch of oil in skillet. Flatten slightly when you turn them. Brown on both sides until crisp.

The Amish Way Cookbook

Vidalia Onion Casserole

6-7 large Vidalia onions,
   sliced
1 stick oleo

1 sleeve Ritz crackers,
   crushed
Parmesan cheese

Sauté onions in oleo until soft. Layer 1/2 onions in casserole dish. Place 1/2 of crackers on top. Sprinkle with cheese; repeat layers. Bake 350° for 35-40 minutes until brown on top.

Cooking with Class

Onion Casserole

2 or 3 large onions, peeled
3 tablespoons margarine
1 (10-ounce) can cream of
   chicken soup
1 cup milk

8 ounces Swiss or sharp
   Cheddar cheese, shredded
1 teaspoon soy sauce
Bread crumbs

Cut onions into slices; separate slices into single rings. Sauté onions in margarine in skillet until clear. Remove to greased 6 1/2x9-inch casserole. Add chicken soup and milk to pan drippings; mix well. Cook until heated through, stirring until smooth. Add cheese; stir until melted. Stir in soy sauce. Pour over onions; sprinkle with bread crumbs. Bake at 350° for 30 minutes or until hot and bubbly. Yield: 10 servings.

The Ohio State Grange Cookbook

Swiss Cheese Onion Dish

Good and different.

2 tablespoons butter
3 large sweet onions, sliced
2 cups shredded Swiss cheese
Pepper to taste
1 can cream of chicken soup
(undiluted) or 2 packages dry
soup with proper amount of
water added

²/₃ cup milk
2 teaspoons soy sauce
8 slices French bread,
buttered on both sides

In skillet, melt butter. Sauté onions until slightly browned. Layer onions, two-thirds cheese, and pepper in 2-quart casserole dish. In saucepan, heat soup, milk, and soy sauce; stir to blend. Pour soup mixture into casserole and stir gently. Top with bread slices. Bake at 350° for 15 minutes. Push bread slices down under sauce; sprinkle with remaining cheese. Bake 15 minutes more. Yield: 8-10 servings.

The Fifth Generation Cookbook

Broccoli-Corn Casserole

1 package broccoli, thawed
1 can cream-style corn
¹/₄ cup cracker crumbs
1 egg, beaten
2 tablespoons melted butter

1 onion or 1 tablespoon
instant
¹/₂ teaspoon salt
2 tablespoons melted butter
¹/₄ cup cracker crumbs

Mix all but last 2 ingredients together and put in 1¹/₂-quart greased casserole. On top, put 2 tablespoons melted butter mixed with cracker crumbs. Bake at 350° for 45 minutes.

Heavenly Dishes

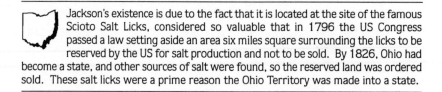

Jackson's existence is due to the fact that it is located at the site of the famous Scioto Salt Licks, considered so valuable that in 1796 the US Congress passed a law setting aside an area six miles square surrounding the licks to be reserved by the US for salt production and not to be sold. By 1826, Ohio had become a state, and other sources of salt were found, so the reserved land was ordered sold. These salt licks were a prime reason the Ohio Territory was made into a state.

Skillet Scalloped Corn

1/4 cup chopped green onions	1/4 teaspoon paprika
2 tablespoons margarine	Pepper to taste
2 tablespoons flour	3/4 cup milk
1/4 teaspoon salt	1 egg, beaten
1/4 teaspoon dry mustard	1 (12-ounce) can corn, drained

Sauté green onions in margarine in skillet until tender. Stir in flour, salt, mustard, paprika, and pepper. Cook until bubbly, stirring constantly. Add mixture of milk and egg gradually, stirring constantly. Cook until thickened, stirring constantly. Stir in corn. Heat to serving temperature.

The Ohio State Grange Cookbook

Corn Soufflé

1 stick margarine, melted	1 (8-ounce) can whole corn
2 eggs, beaten	1 (8-ounce) can creamed corn
8 ounces sour cream	1 box Jiffy cornbread mix

Add margarine to beaten eggs. Add sour cream. Mix in corn and Jiffy mix. Pour into greased 8x8-inch pan. Bake at 350° 45 minutes to an hour or until done. Should be like very moist cornbread, not soupy. Serves 6.

Heavenly Food II

Best Roasted Corn-on-the-Cob

Fresh corn-on-the-cob, unshucked	Butter, salt, and pepper to taste

Plunge the corn into a bucket of cold water and let it sit at least 2 hours. While the coals are heating, shuck the corn almost to the bottom of the cob and remove as much of the silk as possible. Rub with butter and sprinkle with salt and pepper. Pull the shucks back up and tie at the top with a piece of shuck or string. Place the corn on an outdoor grill and cover them with a wet, wrung-out gunny sack to keep in the steam. Roast 15-20 minutes, turning frequently, or until the corn is cooked through and smells irresistible.

Cincinnati Recipe Treasury

Spaghetti Squash with Garlic and Parmesan

Molly and Ted Bartlett own Silver Creek Farm in Hiram, an organic farm raising fresh produce certified by the Ohio Ecological Food and Farm Association. Molly gets many requests for recipes using what they grow. Customers are always looking for new ways to prepare the many varieties of squash. This is one of her favorites. Micro-wave cooking makes spaghetti squash quick and easy to prepare.

1 (2 to 3-pound) spaghetti squash	2-3 cloves garlic, finely chopped
1/4 cup grated Parmesan cheese	Salt
2 tablespoons butter or margarine	Pepper
	Chopped fresh parsley

Pierce squash in several places with large fork or knife. Place on paper towel in microwave oven. Cook on 100% power for 10 minutes or until squash yields to pressure and feels soft. Cool slightly; halve crosswise. Scoop out seeds and fibers; twist out long strands of pulp with fork, place in 2-quart microproof baking dish. Add remaining ingredients, except parsley; mix well. Cover; cook at 100% power (HIGH) for 4-6 minutes or until heated through. Top with parsley. Makes 6-8 servings.

Bountiful Ohio

Zucchini with Tomatoes

3 pounds zucchini, cut into 1/4-inch slices	2 teaspoons salt
3 medium onions, sliced	1/8 teaspoon pepper
1 clove garlic, sliced	2 teaspoons oregano
1/3 cup salad oil	1 teaspoon wine vinegar
1 (1-pound, 12-ounce) can tomatoes (about 3 1/3 cups)	3 tablespoons grated Parmesan cheese

Arrange zucchini slices in a greased 3-quart baking dish. Sauté onions and garlic in oil until lightly browned and tender. Add tomatoes, seasonings and vinegar. Heat to boiling and simmer for 1 minute. Pour tomato/onion mixture over zucchini slices in baking dish. Top with cheese. Bake at 400° about one hour, or until zucchini slices are tender. Serves 8-10 people.

Treasured Recipes from Mason, Ohio

Zucchini Undercover
(Cheese and Vegetables, Burrito-Style)

1/2 cup finely chopped onion
1 clove garlic, minced
3 medium zucchini, chopped
1 (4-ounce) can chopped
  green chilies
1 teaspoon dried basil leaves,
  crushed
1/2 teaspoon dried oregano,
  crushed
1/4 teaspoon ground cumin

1/4 teaspoon salt
Small amount of cooking oil
1 cup grated Monterey Jack
  cheese
3/4 cup toasted wheat germ
6-8 flour tortillas (large,
  refrigerated type)
Dairy sour cream
Fresh minced parsley

In large skillet or griddle, sauté onion, garlic, zucchini, chilies, basil, oregano, cumin, and salt in a tablespoon of oil over medium heat 5 minutes. Stir in cheese and wheat germ, stirring until cheese melts and is blended with vegetables.

Have tortillas at room temperature and spoon vegetable mixture onto center of each, dividing evenly. Roll as for crêpes, long and cigar-shaped. Fry bundles in small amount of oil until golden, turning once. Watch carefully. Over moderate heat, flour tortillas brown quickly and will burn. Top with sour cream and minced parsley. May be prepared ahead, browned, then chilled. Reheat in oven at 350° or microwave according to instructions. Serves 4.

Herbs: From Cultivation to Cooking

Zucchini Ripieni Con Tonna

8 medium zucchini
2 tablespoons olive oil
1 (6½ - 7-ounce) can tuna
fish, drained and flaked
2 tablespoons grated Parmesan
or Romano cheese
⅓ cup chopped sweet fresh
cucumber pickles

1 teaspoon salt
⅛ teaspoon pepper
½ cup Italian-style bread
crumbs
1 cup creamed cottage cheese
1 egg, slightly beaten

Wash zucchini and pat dry. Use sharp paring knife to cut slice from one [long] side of each squash. Scoop out centers, reserving ¼-inch thick shells. Chop pulp. Sauté in 2 tablespoons of oil until tender and lightly browned. Cool. Combine with tuna, Parmesan cheese, pickles, salt, pepper, and bread crumbs. Sprinkle shells with additional salt, if desired. Stuff with tuna mixture. Combine cottage cheese and egg in electric blender or electric mixer. Spread over tuna filling. Brush zucchini with oil. Place in lightly oiled 13x9x2-inch baking pan. Bake in a 375° oven for 35-40 minutes or until tender. Makes 4 servings.

500 Recipes Using Zucchini

Cheese Stuffed Zucchini

2 (5-ounce) zucchini
2 teaspoons olive oil
1 cup sliced mushrooms
1 teaspoon fresh minced
garlic
4 ounces Mozzarella cheese,
diced
1 tablespoon chopped fresh
basil or 1 teaspoon dried

1 tablespoon chopped fresh
parsley
Dash each of salt, pepper and
ground nutmeg
2 teaspoons grated Parmesan
cheese

Trim ends of both zucchini. Slice each in half lengthwise and scoop out pulp, reserving shells. Heat oil in small saucepan. Add pulp, mushrooms, and garlic. Sauté until all is soft. Place in a bowl. Cool slightly. Add Mozzarella cheese, basil, parsley, and seasonings. Stuff zucchini shells. Sprinkle one teaspoon of Parmesan cheese on each shell. Cover and bake at 350° for 30 minutes. Remove cover and bake for 15 minutes more. Serves 4.

500 Recipes Using Zucchini

Baked Zucchini and Rice

1 tablespoon olive oil
1 medium onion, chopped
2 pounds small zucchini,
  sliced into 1/4-inch rounds
2 cloves garlic, minced
Freshly ground black pepper
1 (28-ounce) can crushed
  Italian plum tomatoes

1 cup uncooked long grain
  rice
2 tablespoons parsley,
  chopped
1/4 cup Parmesan cheese,
  grated, divided
1/4 cup bread crumbs

Heat oven to 425°. Heat oil in large skillet; add onion and cook until lightly browned. Add zucchini and garlic; stir-fry for about 3 minutes until zucchini is partially cooked. Season to taste with black pepper.

Add tomatoes and simmer gently, uncovered, about 4 minutes. Stir in rice, parsley, and 1/8 cup Parmesan cheese. Spoon into buttered baking dish and sprinkle top with crumbs and remaining cheese. Bake [covered] at 425° for 30-35 minutes, or until top is golden. Serves 6.

Light Kitchen Choreography

Steamed Cauliflower

1 head cauliflower

1 jar Cheez Whiz, melted

Weigh head of cauliflower. After removing leaves, rinse cauliflower, giving 1-2 shakes to remove excess water. Place on plate, cover with plastic wrap, leaving a 1-inch vent opening. For each pound the head weighs, microwave on HIGH for 7 minutes. When done, carefully remove plastic wrap and pour melted Cheez Whiz over top. Garnish as desired.

Gardener's Delight

Carrot Casserole

We often double the recipe. You can use canned or frozen carrots, but fresh is better.

4 cups carrots sliced diagonally, ¹/₂-inch thick	¹/₂ cup water
	Salt

Cook until soft; drain.

SAUCE:

2 tablespoons butter or margarine	1 cup grated Velveeta cheese
1¹/₂ tablespoons flour	1 (13¹/₂-ounce) can French fried onion rings
1 cup milk	

Combine first 4 ingredients over low heat on stove, stirring frequently, till thickened. Spray casserole dish with vegetable spray. Add a layer of carrots, a layer of onions, and repeat, ending with carrots. Add sauce and bake for 15 minutes at 350°. Sprinkle top with remaining onions. Bake 5 minutes more.

Treasures and Pleasures

Cinnamon Baked Carrots

Our family holiday dinners are not complete without Cinnamon Baked Carrots. Even when the children were young, they loved carrots. These carrots can be made ahead and frozen for future use.

2 pounds carrots	1 teaspoon salt
1 cup butter	2 teaspoons cinnamon
1 cup sugar	1 cup water

Wash and peel carrots. Cut into 4-inch sticks. Place carrots in a deep baking dish. Melt butter and sugar together. Add salt and cinnamon. Stir. Add water. Heat mixture until it starts to bubble. Pour over carrots. Bake 1½ hours uncovered at 350°. You may serve with a slotted spoon, but some will want the baking juices with their carrots. Yields 8-10 servings.

The Heritage Tradition

Tally Ho Tomato Pudding

Toledo claims this sweet pudding to be its very own and traces it to the Tally Ho Restaurant. It is customary for Toledo hosts to prepare it for out-of-town dinner guests, and the tradition continues at the Columbian House, an 1827 stage coach inn, in Waterville, Ohio. The buttered bread cubes bake through the pudding and turn a golden brown when it is completed. Then it must be served quickly before it falls.

1 cup brown sugar	2 cups dry bread cubes,
1 cup tomato purée	crusts removed
¹/₄ cup water	¹/₂ cup melted butter

Combine brown sugar, tomato purée, and water. Cook 5 minutes. While tomato mixture is cooking, put bread cubes in casserole and pour melted butter over. Pour on hot tomato mixture. Do not stir. Bake 50 minutes in a 325° oven. The drier the bread cubes, the more crusty the pudding will be.

Aren't You Going to Taste It, Honey?

Baked Cheese-Stuffed Tomatoes

6-8 medium-size tomatoes	¹/₂ teaspoon marjoram
1¹/₂ cups Swiss cheese,	1 teaspoon prepared mustard
grated	2 tablespoons butter, melted
1 egg, beaten	¹/₃ cup herb stuffing mix
5 tablespoons onion, chopped	

Cut off top of tomato. Gently scoop out and coarsely chop pulp. Combine ³/₄ of tomato pulp with remaining ingredients. Spoon mixture into tomato shells and sprinkle with a few stuffing crumbs. Place in a 9x13-inch casserole and bake at 350° for 25 minutes or until tender.

The PTA Pantry

Stan Hywet Hall in Akron is often described as Ohio's most beautiful home, as well as its largest (65 rooms). Built from 1911 to 1915 by rubber baron Frank Seiberling, it is the best place to see how tycoons lived in the days before there was a national income tax.

Sister Luella's Tomato Fritters

2 cups heavy tomato purée
1½ cups fine cracker
  crumbs
2 tablespoons minced onion
1½ teaspoons sugar

1 tablespoon flour
½ teaspoon salt
⅛ teaspoon pepper
3 eggs, beaten
3 tablespoons butter

Mix all ingredients together except butter. Heat butter in a skillet over moderate heat and drop in mixture by spoonfuls. Fry to a delicate brown. Serves 4-6.

The Shaker Cookbook

Corn Fritters

2 eggs, separated
2 tablespoons flour
1 tablespoon sugar (optional)
1 teaspoon salt

Pepper to taste
2 cups corn or 1 can creamed
  corn

Beat egg yolks; add flour, sugar, salt, and a little pepper. Add corn and fold in stiffly beaten egg whites. Drop by spoonful on greased griddle or frying pan. Do not cook too fast.

Sharing Our Best (Elizabeth House)

Herbed Spinach Phyllo Roll

Phyllo pastry is easily available in the frozen food section of most supermarkets. There were times in the past when phyllo was hard to find. The spinach filling is a somewhat traditional filling for phyllo triangle hors d'oeuvres. Making a single long spinach roll instead enables you to use this recipe as a vegetable with your meal. If cut into large slices, it could be a tasty luncheon dish when served with a salad.

1 tablespoon butter
1/2 cup chopped onion
8 green onions, chopped
1 cup chopped mushrooms
  (about 1/4 pound)
3 cups fresh spinach, finely
  chopped (about 1 1/2 pounds)
1/4 cup parsley, finely
  chopped
1 tablespoon fresh tarragon,
  chopped (or 1/2 teaspoon
  dried)

1/2 teaspoon salt
1/4 teaspoon pepper
3 eggs, beaten
1/4 pound Feta cheese,
  crumbled
1/3 cup Parmesan or Romano
  cheese
5 phyllo leaves at room
  temperature
3 tablespoons butter, melted

Sauté onion and green onions in one tablespoon butter in a large skillet over low heat for 5 minutes, until soft. Add mushrooms. Cook until almost all the liquid evaporates. Remove onions and mushrooms from skillet. Reserve.

Add spinach to skillet. Cook over medium heat until limp, about 2 minutes. Remove from heat. Press out excess moisture.

In a bowl, combine onion and mushrooms, spinach, herbs, salt, pepper, eggs, and cheeses. Stir until well blended. Reserve. Cool. Preheat oven to 375°. Unfold phyllo leaves. Keep covered with a barely damp towel while working. Place one phyllo leaf on clean dry surface. Brush leaf with melted butter. Place another leaf on top of first, brush with butter. Repeat with the 3 remaining leaves.

Spoon spinach mixture along long edge of phyllo leaf to within one inch of short edges. Fold short edges over one inch. Roll up phyllo leaves, beginning at the long edge.

Place the roll seam-side-down on a buttered or oiled baking sheet. Bake 40-45 minutes until crisp and lightly browned. Cool slightly. Slice. May be served with Hollandaise sauce, if desired. Yield: 6-10 servings.

The Heritage Tradition

Sautéed Chick Peas

1 tablespoon vegetable oil
1 medium red onion, halved
and finely sliced
2 small green chili peppers,
seeded and finely sliced

Dash of mustard seed
2 cups canned chick peas,
drained and rinsed
1 teaspoon paprika

Heat nonstick skillet until warm, add oil. On medium heat, sauté onions and chili peppers until soft. Add mustard seed and sauté slightly. Add chick peas and paprika. Sauté 2-3 minutes. Remove from heat and serve hot or cold.

Easy Cooking with Herbs & Spices

Exotic Eggplant

1 medium eggplant, peeled
and cut into small pieces
3/4 teaspoon oregano
2 tablespoons Robert
Rothschild Extra Virgin Olive
Oil
1 1/2 teaspoons brown sugar

3 tablespoons Robert
Rothschild Italian Garden
Vinegar
Salt and pepper to taste
1 (4-ounce) jar whole
pimentos, drained and cut into
half-inch squares

Cook eggplant for 15 minutes in boiling water. Drain and set aside. Preheat oven to 375°. Simmer oregano in olive oil for 5 minutes, add eggplant. Sprinkle with brown sugar and cook for 10 minutes, turning. Sprinkle with vinegar and salt and pepper to taste, and mix gently. Lightly oil a 1-quart casserole. Layer in the eggplant and pimento. Bake for 30 minutes.

Robert Rothschild Recipes

Grilled Caponata

2 small to medium eggplants,
  about 1 pound each
1 large red bell pepper
1 large yellow bell pepper
1 large red Spanish onion (or
  other sweet onion)
6 fresh Roma tomatoes
Extra-virgin olive oil
1/2 cup golden raisins
1 tablespoon light brown
  sugar
1/4 cup red wine vinegar
4 cloves roasted garlic
3 tablespoons capers
3 tablespoons chopped fresh
  parsley
1 tablespoon chopped fresh
  basil
Salt to taste
1/2 teaspoon Tabasco sauce
  (or to taste)

Wash and trim stem from eggplants. Cut in half lengthwise. Score the surface, cutting about 1/4-inch into the eggplant. Brush the surface with olive oil, using just enough oil to coat. Place the eggplant, cut-side-down, on a medium-hot grill. Cover and cook 20-30 minutes or until tender when pierced with the top of a sharp knife. Remove and cool.

After the eggplant is on the grill, add the peppers, which have been halved and lightly brushed on both sides with the olive oil, and the onion, which is also halved and lightly brushed with oil. Grill both until crisp-tender, 10-15 minutes. Remove and cool.

Wash the tomatoes. Lightly rub the surface with oil. Place on the grill and grill for 10-15 minutes or until soft. Remove with a large spoon to a side dish. Cool and peel. Scoop eggplant pulp from the shell and chop coarsely. Chop the peppers and onions. Add to the eggplant. Chop the tomatoes and add to mixture. Place the raisins and brown sugar in a measuring cup and add the vinegar. Heat in microwave until vinegar is boiling. Remove and allow to sit for 20 minutes. Add to eggplant mixture.

Add the chopped roasted garlic cloves, capers, parsley, basil, salt, and Tabasco. Stir in the raisin mixture. Cover and chill for several hours. Taste and correct the seasonings. Serve as a side dish with grilled fish, chicken or lamb, or serve with thinly sliced bread or toast as an appetizer. Makes about 6 cups caponata. Keeps for 2 weeks or longer, covered, in the refrigerator.

More Cooking with Marilyn Harris

Parsnips with Snow Peas

1 pound fresh parsnips
3 green onions, chopped
1/2 pound fresh snow peas

1 tablespoon sesame seed,
toasted

Peel parsnips and cut into lengthwise strips about 3 inches long. Sauté in a well-sprayed nonstick skillet until parsnips are tender. Add onions and snow peas. Sauté for another 2 minutes. Sprinkle sesame seed over vegetables. Yields 4 (1/2 cup) servings. Exchange: 1/2 bread. Cal 50.

Tried and True Volume II: Diabetic Cookbook

Escalloped Mushrooms

2 cups cracker crumbs
1/2 cup butter
1 pint milk
1 egg yolk

2 tablespoons cornstarch
1 can mushroom soup
1 can mushroom pieces,
drained

Brown 2 cups cracker crumbs in 1/2 cup butter. Make a sauce of milk, egg yolk and cornstarch. Stir in soup and mushrooms. Alternate sauce and crumbs in baking dish, finishing with crumbs on top. Bake in 350° oven until brown.

Affolter-Heritage Reunion Cookbook & More

Artichokes Genovese

A delicious party casserole!

1 raw onion, sliced paper-thin	2 tablespoons butter
3 cloves garlic, minced, divided	1/3 cup wine
	1 cup fresh bread crumbs
2 packages frozen artichokes, or 2 cans water-packed artichokes	Parsley
	Oil
	3/4 cup hot water
1 pound mushrooms, sliced	1 Knorr chicken cube

In a 9x13-inch glass baking dish, put sliced onion, 2 of the minced garlic cloves, and then the artichokes. Fry the mushrooms in butter and wine and place over the artichokes. Sprinkle with bread crumbs, parsley, and other clove of garlic. Drizzle with oil and hot water in which chicken cube has been dissolved. Bake for 45 minutes at 350°. Serves 8.

Angels and Friends Cookbook I

Summer Vegetable Medley

1/4 cup butter	1/4 cup chopped green pepper
1/2 cup chopped green onions	1/2 teaspoon salt
5 ears fresh corn, cut from cob to make 3 cups	1/8 teaspoon pepper
	1/4 teaspoon sugar
2 cups chopped cabbage	Dash of Tabasco
1/4 cup slivered carrots	

In large skillet, melt butter. Add green onions and sauté 3 minutes. Stir in remaining ingredients. Cook, stirring constantly 5 minutes until corn and cabbage are tender crisp. Makes 6 servings.

Per serving: Cal 148; Prot 3g; Fat 9g; Chol 18g.

Wadsworth-Rittman Hospital Cookbook

 More Presidents have come from Ohio than any other state, hence its nickname "The Mother of Presidents." William McKinley 25th, Niles; Rutherford B. Hayes 19th, Fremont; Warren G. Harding 29th, Marion; Ulysses S. Grant 18th, Pt. Pleasant; William Howard Taft 27th (also a Supreme Court Justice), Cincinnati; James A. Garfield 20th, Mentor.

Horseradish

1 horseradish root (about 1
   pound)
1 cup white vinegar
1/2 teaspoon sugar

1 teaspoon salt
1 small turnip, peeled and
   cubed, optional

Vigorously scrub the horseradish root (or peel), cutting away dark parts. (The whiter and cleaner the root, the whiter is the finished product.) Cut into cubes—you should have about 3 cups. It is important that you use a blender, covered, to protect your eyes from the hot fumes that rise from the fresh root. Add vinegar, sugar, salt and gradually add the horseradish cubes. Blend until smooth. Can be refrigerated up to 3 months or frozen. Yields about 3 cups.

Note: If you wish to make it milder, add the turnip.

Herbs: From Cultivation to Cooking

Poultry

Castle Mac-o-Chee. East of West Liberty.

Chicken with Lime Butter

3 whole chicken breasts,
  boned, skinned and halved
1/2 teaspoon salt
1/2 teaspoon pepper
1/3 cup vegetable oil

Juice of 1 lime
1/2 cup butter
1 teaspoon minced chives
1/2 teaspoon dill

Sprinkle chicken with salt and pepper. Heat oil in large skillet over medium heat. Sauté chicken until light brown, about 3 minutes per side. Cover; reduce heat to low. Cook 10 minutes or until chicken is tender. Remove chicken to serving platter. Drain oil from skillet. Add lime juice. Cook over low heat until juice begins to boil, about one minute. Add butter, one tablespoon at a time, until butter becomes opaque and forms a thick sauce. Remove from heat. Stir in chives and dill. Spoon sauce over chicken. Serve immediately. Serves 4-6.

A Cleveland Collection

Chicken Breasts with Red Grapes

2 tablespoons unsalted butter
1 tablespoon olive oil
6 chicken breast halves,
  boned and skinned
1/3 cup white zinfandel or
  other blush wine
1 cup heavy cream

1 tablespoon fresh whole lemon
  thyme leaves or 1 teaspoon
  dried thyme, finely crumbled
Salt
Black pepper, freshly ground
1/2 pound seedless red
  grapes

Heat butter and oil in a sauté pan or skillet over medium-high heat; add chicken and sauté until meat is lightly browned on all sides, about 5 minutes. Add the wine to the pan and bring to a boil, loosening browned bits from bottom of pan with wooden spoon. Stir in the cream, thyme, and salt and pepper to taste. Reduce the heat to a simmer, cover, and cook until the sauce thickens slightly, about 5 minutes. Stir in the grapes and simmer until the grapes are heated through and the chicken is tender but still moist inside, about 5 minutes.

Angels and Friends Cookbook II

Chicken with Green Grapes

¹/₄ cup flour
1¹/₄ teaspoons celery salt
¹/₈ teaspoon pepper
3 chicken breasts, boned,
  skinned, split in half
1 (10¹/₂-ounce) can cream of
  chicken soup, undiluted
¹/₄ teaspoon rosemary,
  crushed

¹/₈ teaspoon tarragon leaves,
  crushed
Flour and dry white wine or
  water for thickening sauce
¹/₂ pound seedless green
  grapes
1¹/₂ cups hot buttered rice,
  optional

Heat oven to 350°. Combine flour, celery salt, and pepper in paper bag; shake each chicken breast in flour mixture to coat well. Brown chicken on top of stove. Combine soup and other ingredients, except grapes, flour, and wine; pour over chicken; and bring to boil. Cover; bake in oven 40-45 minutes or until chicken is tender. Remove chicken; thicken sauce with flour and wine or water mixture, if desired. Stir in grapes and let stand 5 minutes. Arrange chicken on bed of rice; glaze with sauce. Serves 6.

Herbs: From Cultivation to Cooking

Chicken Tarragon

4 (8-ounce) boneless chicken
  breasts
Salt and pepper
2 ounces sweet butter
2 fresh shallots, chopped
1 glass dry white wine

1 pint heavy cream
2 tablespoons tarragon,
  chopped
1 tablespoon fresh parsley,
  chopped

Season the chicken breasts with salt and pepper. Sauté the breasts in butter until golden brown on both sides. Cook in oven for 10 minutes at 400°. Remove the chicken breasts; keep warm.

Remove the butter from the skillet. Add the chopped shallots; do not brown. Swirl in the white wine. Bring to a boil until reduced by one-half.

Add the cream, one tablespoon of tarragon, and reduce the sauce until it thickens slightly. Correct seasoning. Add the rest of the tarragon and the parsley. Pour on the chicken breasts and serve hot. The dish may be accompanied by rice or noodles in butter. Serves 4.

Herbs: From Cultivation to Cooking

Chicken with Raspberry Salsa

2/3 cup bread crumbs
1/4 cup minced fresh parsley
1/4 teaspoon salt
Fresh pepper to taste
6 skinless, boneless chicken
   breast halves

1/3 cup garlic-flavored olive
   oil
1 jar Robert Rothschild
   Raspberry Salsa
1 1/2 cups grated Monterey
   Jack cheese

In shallow bowl, blend together bread crumbs, parsley, salt and pepper. Brush chicken with garlic-flavored olive oil and roll in bread crumb mixture. Place chicken in greased 9x13-inch pan. Bake uncovered at 350° for 20-25 minutes. Pour raspberry salsa over chicken and sprinkle with Jack cheese. Return to oven 5-7 minutes or until heated and chicken is done. Yield: 6 servings.

Robert Rothschild Recipes

Stuffed Chicken Breasts

10 boneless, split chicken
   breasts
3 sticks butter or margarine,
   melted

2 cups seasoned bread
   crumbs
2 cups shredded Cheddar
   cheese

Dip chicken in melted butter, then into bread crumbs. Lay flat and put cheese on top.

Roll like you would an egg roll. Fasten with a toothpick. Bake at 350° for approximately 45 minutes. Place on cookie sheet covered with foil for baking. (You can then throw the foil away and not have to wash your pan.)

MDA Favorite Recipes

Quick Chick Trick

4 chicken breasts or 1 whole
  chicken
1 can cream of chicken soup

8 ounces sour cream
40 Ritz crackers, crushed
1 stick margarine

Boil and debone chicken; tear into small pieces and line bottom of baking dish. Mix together soup and sour cream. Pour over chicken. Put cracker crumbs on top; pour melted margarine over crumbs. Bake 30 minutes until bubbles. May be reheated in microwave.

Heavenly Food II

Herbed Chicken Sauté

2 tablespoons lemon juice
2 tablespoons olive oil
1 tablespoon water
1 1/2 teaspoons onion powder
1/2 teaspoon garlic powder

1 teaspoon basil leaves
1/4 teaspoon black pepper
1 pound boneless, skinless
  chicken breasts

Combine lemon juice, olive oil, and water. Add onion powder, garlic powder, basil leaves, and black pepper. Mix well. Brush over chicken breasts. Sauté in non-stick skillet or lightly oiled skillet until lightly browned and thoroughly cooked (10-12 minutes). Servings: 3-4.

Cooking with TLC

Chicken Parmesan

4 boneless skinless chicken
  breast halves
2 (14 1/2-ounce) cans Italian-
  style stewed tomatoes
1/2 teaspoon oregano or basil,
  crushed

2 tablespoons cornstarch
1/4 teaspoon hot pepper
  sauce (optional)
1/4 cup grated Parmesan
  cheese

Place chicken in baking dish. Bake covered for 15 minutes in pre-heated 425° oven; drain. Combine next 4 ingredients in a sauce-pan, cook, stirring constantly until sauce is thickened. Pour heated sauce over chicken; top with cheese. Bake 5 minutes uncovered. May garnish with fresh parsley.

Tried and True by Mothers of 2's

Packo's Parmesan Chicken Rolls

4 whole chicken breasts,
  boned and skinned (8 halves)
1 stick butter, melted
1 cup bread crumbs

1 cup grated Parmesan
  cheese
1/2 cup slivered almonds

Dip each chicken breast in melted butter. Combine crumbs and cheese. Dip each breast in crumb and cheese mixture; coat well. Roll up tightly and pin with toothpick, if necessary. Line up in a baking dish so that they touch. Sprinkle with remaining butter and almonds. Bake at 350° for one hour. Serves 8.

Tumm Yummies

Parmesan Chicken Sauté

2 1/2 - 3 1/2 pounds chicken
  pieces
Salt and pepper to taste
4 1/2 tablespoons butter,
  divided
1 1/2 tablespoons flour
3/4 cup milk
1/4 cup heavy cream or 1 cup
  milk instead of milk and
  cream

1/4 teaspoon nutmeg
1/2 cup Swiss or Gruyère
  cheese, grated
1/2 cup Parmesan cheese,
  grated
2 tablespoons fresh bread
  crumbs

Brown seasoned chicken pieces for 20 minutes in 3 tablespoons butter. In a small pan, melt remaining butter and add flour; add milk and cream. Boil until thickened and smooth. Stir in nutmeg and Swiss cheese. Sprinkle a 9x13-inch baking dish with 1/2 the Parmesan cheese. Place browned chicken pieces in pan and spoon sauce over the chicken. Cover with the remaining Parmesan and bread crumbs, mixed together. Bake for 1/2 hour in 350° oven. Serves 4-6.

25th Anniversary Cookbook

Chicken With Plum Sauce

8 small, whole chicken
  breasts, split, skinned and
  boned
Salt
Pepper

2 cups ground walnuts
$1/2$ cup bread crumbs
3 tablespoons margarine
3 tablespoons cooking oil
2 eggs, beaten

Place chicken breasts between sheets of wax paper; pound lightly to flatten. Sprinkle with salt and pepper. Combine walnuts and bread crumbs. Melt margarine and oil in skillet. Dip chicken in beaten egg; coat with nut mixture and brown in margarine, turning once. Refrigerate if desired. Heat in 400° oven for 15 minutes before serving.

SHERRIED PLUM SAUCE:

$1 1/2$ cups canned, pitted
  plums with syrup
$3/4$ cup plum preserves
$1/4$ cup dry sherry
2 tablespoons butter or
  margarine

$3/4$ cup chicken broth
$1 1/2$ teaspoons lemon juice
1 tablespoon cornstarch
  (optional)
3 tablespoons water (optional)

Combine all ingredients and bring to a boil. Reduce heat and simmer for 30 minutes. For a thicker sauce, add cornstarch dissolved in water and heat to boiling. Serve with chicken. Makes 6 servings.

Generation to Generation

Party Chicken Pineapple Cakes

Elegant for a bridal luncheon

FILLING:

2 whole chicken breasts,
cooked and cubed
2 stalks celery, chopped fine

2 hard boiled eggs, chopped
Mayonnaise
Salt and pepper to taste

Mix cooked chicken, celery and chopped hard-boiled eggs; add enough mayonnaise to moisten and season with salt and pepper to taste.

SANDWICH:

6 ounces cream cheese
2 tablespoons pineapple juice
20-24 slices white bread

Butter
10-14 pineapple slices,
reserve juice

Mix cream cheese with enough pineapple juice to make a smooth consistency. To assemble cake: Cut two slices of bread, using pineapple can. Butter both pieces on one side. Layer in this order: one slice of bread, buttered side up, one slice pineapple, one scoop of chicken filling and topped with a slice of bread with buttered sides down. Frost top and side of sandwich with frosting mixture. Can make the sandwiches the night before. Place sandwiches on a tray, cover with plastic wrap and a damp tea towel, and frost the next day. Yield: 10-12.

Angels and Friends Cookbook II

Chicken Nuggets

4 chicken breasts

1/2 cup melted butter

CRUMB MIXTURE:

1/2 cup bread crumbs
1/4 cup grated Parmesan
cheese
1/4 teaspoon pepper

1/4 cup grated Cheddar
cheese
1 teaspoon basil
1/2 teaspoon salt

Cut chicken into 1 1/2-inch pieces or smaller. Dip chicken in melted butter, then roll in crumb mixture. Place on a cookie sheet covered with lightly greased aluminum foil. Bake in 400° oven for 10-15 minutes.

175th Anniversary Quilt Cookbook

Grilled Breast of Chicken
with Fresh Basil Tomato Sauce

4 chicken breasts, boned and halved	3 garlic cloves
	16 large, fresh basil leaves

Slice 1/8 of the minced garlic and 2 fresh basil leaves under the skin of each chicken breast. Place breasts in a non-reactive pan.

MARINADE:

1/2 cup white wine vinegar	1/4 teaspoon pepper
5 tablespoons olive oil	1 1/2 teaspoons minced garlic
1/2 teaspoon salt	

Combine the marinade ingredients and pour over the chicken breasts. Marinate 4-6 hours or overnight.

Remove chicken breasts from marinade. Grill over hot coals 8-10 minutes on each side. Serve with the Tomato Basil Sauce.

TOMATO BASIL SAUCE:

1/4 cup chopped onion	1/2 teaspoon salt
1/4 cup chopped green pepper	1/4 teaspoon pepper
1/2 teaspoon minced garlic	1/2 cup chopped fresh basil
2 tablespoons butter	leaves
2 (8-ounce) cans tomato sauce	

Sauté the onion, green pepper, and garlic in the butter until the onion is tender. Stir in tomato sauce. Add the salt and pepper. Simmer for 10 minutes. Add the chopped basil right before serving. Yield: 8 servings.

From The Heritage Restaurant, Cincinnati.

Best Recipes of Ohio Inns and Restaurants

Chicken Divan

2¹/₂ pounds boneless
  skinless chicken breasts,
  cooked and cut-up
2 packages frozen broccoli,
  thawed and drained
2 cans cream of mushroom
  soup

1 cup Cheddar cheese,
  shredded
2 teaspoons prepared mustard
2 small packages sliced
  almonds

Cook chicken one of two ways, either by boiling for 40 minutes or in microwave (12 minutes for 4 pieces). Cut into bite-size pieces. Layer thawed broccoli in a 9x13-inch pan, add the chicken pieces over the top; salt and pepper the chicken to taste. Mix soup, cheese, and mustard together, spread over the chicken. Cook at 350° for 30 minutes; add almond slices to the top and continue to bake for an additional 10-15 minutes.

Tried and True by Mothers of 2's

Provolone Chicken

An impressive dish for a buffet dinner

5 whole chicken breasts,
  deboned, cut in medium bite-
  size pieces, and flattened
3 eggs, beaten
Seasoned bread crumbs
Butter

8 ounces fresh or canned
  mushrooms, sliced
1 cup chicken broth
6 ounces white wine
¹/₂ pound Provolone cheese,
  grated

Marinate chicken in eggs while getting the rest of recipe together; drain each piece of chicken and roll in bread crumbs. Brown in butter until lightly brown on both sides. Transfer into a 9x13-inch casserole, layering in rows, overlapping pieces. Sauté mushrooms and arrange over chicken. Add chicken broth and wine. Cover with grated cheese. Bake, covered, at 350°, for 30 minutes. Uncover and bake 15 minutes longer. Serve immediately. You can freeze, but add chicken broth, wine and cheese just before baking.

Angels and Friends Cookbook II

Swiss Chicken Bake

This is great for company! Men love it!

WHITE SAUCE:

3 tablespoons butter
1/4 cup flour
1/2 cup white wine

1 1/2 cups milk
1 cup shredded Swiss cheese

Melt butter, add flour, and stir; gradually add milk and cook until thickened, then add wine.

CHICKEN:

5 whole chicken breasts
  (deboned)
1/2 teaspoon salt
1/8 teaspoon pepper
2 eggs, beaten

1 cup bread crumbs
1/4 cup oil
1 tablespoon butter
Avocado and tomato slices

Pound out chicken 1/4-inch thick; sprinkle with salt and pepper. Dip in beaten eggs, then crumbs. Brown in 2 tablespoons oil and one tablespoon butter, 2 minutes on each side, adding additional oil as needed. Arrange chicken in 9x13-inch pan. Pour white sauce over. Cover and chill several hours or overnight. Bake covered 50 minutes at 350°—sprinkle with cheese and arrange avocado and tomato slices on top. Bake 10 minutes more uncovered. Serves 10.

Angels and Friends Cookbook I

Elegant Chicken

A wonderful change-of-pace chicken dish.

5 boneless chicken breast
  halves, skinned and cut into
  1-inch pieces
Salt and freshly ground
  pepper
3 tablespoons butter
1 medium onion, sliced

1/2 pound mushrooms, sliced
1 tablespoon flour
1 cup chicken broth, heated
1/2 cup sour cream
1 tablespoon Dijon mustard
Chopped fresh parsley
Freshly cooked rice

Season chicken with salt and pepper. Melt 2 tablespoons butter in heavy large skillet over medium-high heat. Add chicken and cook until opaque, stirring occasionally, about 5 minutes.

Transfer to serving dish. Cover and keep warm. Add onions and mushrooms to skillet and cook until light brown, stirring frequently, 6-8 minutes. Add to chicken in dish, keep warm.

Melt remaining butter in small saucepan over medium-low heat. Add flour and stir 3 minutes. Whisk in broth and stir vigorously until sauce is thickened and smooth, about 5 minutes. Stir in sour cream and mustard. Heat sauce until warmed through, about 3 minutes; do not boil. Pour over chicken. Top with parsley. Serve over rice. Makes 4-6 servings.

Touches of the Hands & Heart

Hawaiian Chicken
(Diabetic)

3 pounds chicken, broiler or
  fryer, cut up
1 1/2 teaspoons salt (optional)
1 (20-ounce) can chunk
  pineapple (unsweetened juice)
1 cup fresh sliced mushrooms

1/2 green pepper, chopped
1/2 cup water
1 tablespoon soy sauce
2 teaspoons instant
  granulated chicken bouillon
1/2 teaspoon ginger

Sprinkle salt on chicken parts and broil. Turn and brown other side. Combine the remaining ingredients, including pineapple juice, and pour over chicken. Bake uncovered 45 minutes at 375° or until chicken is browned. Serves 8.

Per serving (approx 3 ounces; one chicken breast, or one wing, one thigh, and one leg) equals 3 lean meat exchanges; 1 starch/bread exchange; Cal 250; Carb 14g; Prot 12; Fat 12g; Chol 75mg; Sod 353mg.

Recipes from "The Little Switzerland of Ohio"

Down Home Fried Chicken

1 (3-pound) chicken, cut up	Salt and pepper to taste
1 cup buttermilk	1 teaspoon dried thyme
1/2 cup flour	1/8 cup olive or vegetable oil
2 tablespoons chopped	1/8 cup margarine
parsley	1/4 cup chicken broth

Place chicken pieces into bowl. Pour buttermilk over and marinate 2 hours. In another bowl, combine flour, parsley, salt, pepper, and thyme. Drain buttermilk into shallow baking dish. Roll chicken pieces in flour mixture.

Heat oil and butter in skillet. Brown chicken, a few pieces at a time on medium heat. Place chicken on top of buttermilk in baking dish. Add chicken broth to skillet. Scrape up brownings. Pour around chicken. Bake, uncovered, at 375° until crisp and tender, about 50 minutes.

Down Home Cooking from Hocking County

Shaker Fried Chicken

2 frying chickens, 2 1/2	2 tablespoons flour
pounds each	2 tablespoons butter
1 tablespoon parsley, minced	4 tablespoons bacon drippings
1/4 teaspoon dried marjoram	or lard
6 tablespoons butter, melted	1 cup light cream
Salt and pepper	

Wash and dry chickens. Cut them into 16 pieces. Mix herbs with melted butter and coat chicken thoroughly. Let stand at room temperature for one hour. Mix salt and pepper with flour and dredge chicken in this to coat thoroughly. In a Dutch oven, over moderate heat, melt 2 tablespoons butter, add bacon drippings. Add coated chicken and cook to brown well. Pour cream over and let simmer, covered, for 20 minutes. Garnish with watercress and serve with a green salad. Serves 6-8.

The Shaker Cookbook

Founded in 1817, Zoar Village was named for Lot's biblical town of refuse, and represented a haven from persecution for the German Separatists who settled there. The town still retains much of its nineteenth-century character.

Polish Poultry

1 medium onion, chopped
1 garlic clove, minced
1 teaspoon caraway seeds
1 (27-ounce) can sauerkraut,
  undrained
3/4 pound smoked Polish
  sausage, cut into 1-inch
  pieces

1 broiler-fryer chicken (2-3
  pounds), cut up
1/2 teaspoon salt
1/4 teaspoon pepper
1/4 - 1/2 teaspoon dried thyme

In a mixing bowl, combine onion, garlic, caraway seeds, and sauerkraut. Place on the bottom of a 13x9-inch baking dish. Top with sausage and chicken. Sprinkle with salt, pepper, and thyme. Bake at 350° for 60 minutes or until chicken is tender, basting occasionally with pan juices.

Cooking with Class

Swedish Chicken

3 cups cooked, boned chicken
1 cup cream of celery soup
1 cup sour cream
1 tablespoon chopped onion

1 package seasoned dressing
  mix
1 cup hot water
2 sticks margarine

Mix together first 4 ingredients and place in an oblong casserole. Mix dressing mix, hot water, and margarine; place this mixture over top of mixture in casserole. Bake, uncovered, at 350° for one hour.

St. Gerard's 75th Jubilee Cookbook

Awesome Chicken

1 (16-ounce) bottle French
  Catalina dressing
1 can cranberry sauce with
  whole cranberries

1 package Lipton Onion Soup
  Mix
8-12 pieces of chicken

Mix ingredients together. Dip each piece of chicken in mixture and place in baking dish. Pour remaining sauce over chicken. If sauce does not cover chicken, keep basting. Bake uncovered for 2 hours at 275°.

A Sprinkling of Favorite Recipes

No Peek Chicken

1 box Uncle Ben's Long
Grain Wild Rice
4-5 chicken breasts or thighs
1 can cream of celery soup
1 can cream of mushroom
soup

1 envelope Lipton Onion
Soup Mix
2 cups water

Pour wild rice into baking dish. Sprinkle with enclosed seasonings. Place chicken over rice. Mix together can soups and onion soup mix, then spoon over each piece of chicken. Pour water over all. Cover with foil. Bake at 300° for 2-2¼ hours.

Sharing Our Best (Ashland Church of God)

Chicken Curry

Katzinger's Deli's traditional house recipe. A simply fabulous lunch idea!

½ pound raisins
½ cup coconut
¼ Spanish onion, cut into
julienne strips
3 pounds cooked chicken,
skinned and cut into ½-inch
cubes
1 green apple (Granny Smith
if available), cut into ½-inch
cubes

1 red apple, cut into ½-inch
cubes
1 pear, cut into ½-inch cubes
4 stalks celery, bias cut
7 ounces pineapple chunks,
drained
1½ cups mayonnaise
¼ cup honey
2 tablespoons curry powder

Place raisins in hot water for 5 minutes to plump. Drain well. Spread coconut on a cookie sheet and broil until golden brown. Deep fry onion until golden brown. Drain on paper towel.

Toss together raisins, coconut, and onion with all but last 3 ingredients. Combine mayonnaise, honey, and curry powder. Mix thoroughly with rest of ingredients. Refrigerate until chilled. Serves 8-10.

A Taste of Columbus Vol III

Chicken Curry

1 cup butter
4 cups minced onion
4 cloves garlic, minced
4 cups diced tart apple
2 jalapeño chilies, seeded and
   minced
1/2 - 3/4 cup curry powder
2 teaspoons dried thyme

2 cups chicken broth
1 cup dry white wine
1/2 cup dry sherry
1 quart light cream
1/2 cup mango chutney
2 tablespoons cornstarch
4 cups cooked, shredded
   chicken or turkey*

Melt butter in heavy non-aluminum pot. Sauté onions, garlic, apples, and chilies until soft, but not brown. Stir in curry powder and thyme and cook another 10 minutes. Add broth, wine, and sherry and simmer another 15 minutes. Add cream slowly while stirring with wire whisk. Add chutney. Simmer another 15 minutes. Thicken with cornstarch dissolved in 1/4 cup of water. Add chicken and heat through. May be made ahead. May be frozen, but do not add cornstarch or chicken until sauce is deforsted and reheated. Serve with cooked rice and an assortment of side dishes.

SIDE DISHES:
Shredded coconut
Diced pineapple
Assorted nuts

Assorted dried fruit
Watermelon pickles
Chopped cucumber

Note: *For vegetarian curry, substitute 2 (16-ounce) bags of frozen cauliflower, broccoli, and carrot mix, thawed and drained and vegetable broth for chicken broth. Serves 18-20.

Saturday Night Suppers

Grilled Lemonade Chicken

1 (6-ounce) can (²/₃ cup)
  frozen lemonade concentrate,
  thawed
¹/₃ cup low-sodium soy sauce
¹/₂ teaspoon celery salt
¹/₈ teaspoon garlic powder
1 teaspoon low-sodiun
  seasoned salt
2 (2 - 3-pound) broiler-fryers,
  cut up, skin removed

In screw-top jar, combine lemonade concentrate, soy sauce, and seasonings. Cover; shake vigorously to blend. Pour into small bowl. Dip chicken pieces in lemonade mixture. Grill over medium coals for 45-50 minutes, brushing with lemonade mixture and turning frequently. Garnish with lemon twists and parsley, if desired. Serves 8.

Note: Can also be baked in shallow baking pan, 350° oven for 60-70 minutes, turning occasionally in lemonade mixture.

Kinder Kuisine

Chicken Stroganoff or Beef Stroganoff

1 pound chicken breasts,
  boneless, skin removed,
  sliced into strips
1 cup defatted chicken broth
1 medium onion, cut into thin
  slices
2 cups sliced mushrooms
¹/₄ cup dry white wine
  (optional)
1 tablespoon cornstarch
¹/₂ teaspoon salt (optional)
¹/₄ teaspoon black pepper
1 cup low-fat plain yogurt

In skillet sprayed with nonstick spray, sauté chicken, turning to insure cooking on all sides. Cook until chicken is done. Remove chicken from skillet. Add ¹/₄ cup of broth and onions to skillet. Cook until soft. Add mushrooms. Cook, covered, 5 minutes. Remove cover and continue cooking until all liquid is absorbed. Add wine. Bring to boil, then reduce to simmer. Mix cornstarch with remainder of broth and add to skillet. Stir until thickened. Add chicken and salt and pepper. Heat until bubbly. Remove from stove and gently stir in yogurt. Serve immediately. Yields 6 servings. Exchange: 2 meats, 1 vegetable. Cal 161.

Note: For Beef Stroganoff, replace chicken with equal amounts of beef sirloin. Yield, exchanges and calories will remain the same.

Tried and True Volume II: Diabetic Cookbook

Easy Chicken à la King

An easy ladies luncheon.

2 tablespoons butter
1/2 cup onion, chopped
1/4 cup green pepper,
  chopped
1 (10¹/₂-ounce) can cream of
  mushroom soup
1 (8-ounce) package cream
  cheese, softened
Dash of pepper
1¹/₂ cups chicken, cooked
  and cubed

1 (3-ounce) can mushrooms,
  sliced, undrained
2 tablespoons canned
  pimento, chopped
2 tablespoons dry sherry
Pepperidge Farm frozen Patty
  Shells (baked according to
  directions)

In saucepan, cook onion and green pepper in butter until tender. Blend in soup, cheese, and pepper. Stir in chicken and mushrooms. Heat to boiling. Add pimento and sherry. Serve immediately in prepared patty shells. Garnish with fresh parsley. Serves 6.

Angels and Friends Cookbook I

Chicken Casserole

3 cups cooked chicken, cut-up
3-4 cups soft bread cubes
3/4 cup diced celery
1 onion, chopped
1/2 cup chicken broth
1/2 teaspoon salt
1/4 teaspoon pepper

1/4 teaspoon poultry
  seasoning
1/2 teaspoon baking powder
1 egg
3/4 cup milk
1 can celery soup

Arrange cooked chicken in 2x6x10-inch casserole. Sauté bread cubes, celery, and onion in chicken broth; add seasonings, and baking powder. Beat egg slightly; add milk and mix well. Add to bread mixture; pour over chicken. Spread celery soup over top. Sprinkle buttered crumbs on top and bake at 350° for 45 minutes.

Ottoville Sesquicentennial Cookbook

Chicken Casserole

4 cups chicken, cooked and in
  pieces
2¹/₂ cups uncooked
  spaghetti broken in 2-inch
  pieces*
¹/₂ cup chopped pimento
¹/₂ cup chopped green pepper

1 onion, diced
1 can cream of mushroom
  soup
1 can cream of celery soup
1 cup chicken broth
3¹/₂ cups sharp cheese,
  grated

Mix and let stand at least 12 hours in refrigerator. Bake uncovered one hour at 350°. You can substitute cream of chicken for one of the soups. Mushrooms may be added if desired.

Note: *Break spaghetti in brown paper bag to control spillage.

Gardener's Delight

Barbecued Chicken Stew

ORANGE BBQ SAUCE:

4 tablespoons unsalted butter
1 large onion, chopped
6 garlic cloves
2 tablespoons molasses
2 tablespoons fresh lemon
   juice
2 teaspoons salt
2 cups chicken stock
1/2 cup tomato paste

3 tablespoons hot pepper
   sauce
1 cup honey
1 1/2 teaspoons black pepper
1/2 teaspoon white pepper
1/2 teaspoon cayenne pepper
1/2 teaspoon ground cumin
1/2 cup orange juice

Combine all ingredients and simmer. Yield: 3 cups.

CHICKEN STEW:

2 pounds boneless skinless
   chicken breast
2 cups Orange BBQ Sauce
4 tablespoons unsalted butter
1 medium Spanish onion,
   thinly sliced
3 medium diced green
   peppers

2 tablespoons flour
4 cups chicken stock
2 pounds sweet potatoes,
   peeled and cut into 1-inch
   chunks
1 pound plum tomatoes,
   chopped
1 1/2 teaspoons salt

Marinate chicken in Orange BBQ Sauce overnight. Grill chicken breast, cut into cubes. Melt butter in skillet and cook onions and peppers. Sprinkle flour, add chicken stock and sweet potatoes, tomatoes, salt, and remaining BBQ sauce. Bring to boil. Add chicken cubes. Let simmer until potatoes are tender, about 30-35 minutes. Serve over rice with cornbread. Serves 8.

Hats Off to "Real Men Cook" Cookbook

Easy Grilled Chicken

Marinate skinless chicken pieces in Wishbone Italian Dressing for 4 hours or longer. Grill chicken 15 minutes on each side.

Recipes from "The Little Switzerland of Ohio"

Chicken Chow Mein

2 tablespoons butter
1 small onion, cut thin
1 cup diced celery
3 cups cooked chicken
1/2 cup mushrooms, sliced
  (canned or fresh)
1 small can sliced water
  chestnuts
2 envelopes Lipton's Cream
  of Chicken Soup
1 1/2 teaspoons Kitchen
  Bouquet
2 teaspoons soy sauce

Salt and pepper to taste
1 green or red mango, cut up
1 pint tomatoes
2 cups chicken broth and
  mushroom liquid
2 tablespoons cornstarch
1 (No. 2) can mixed La Choy
  vegetables
1 (No. 2) can bean sprouts,
  drained
4 teaspoons red pepper jelly
  or molasses

Brown butter slightly; add onion and celery. Cook 5 minutes, then add chicken, mushrooms, water chestnuts, soup, all seasonings, mango, and tomatoes. Simmer 25 minutes; add 2 cups liquid (broth) as needed. Taste and add more seasoning if desired. Add cornstarch mixed with some of the broth. Stir and cook until thick. Add Chinese vegetables, bean sprouts, and pepper jelly or molasses. Mix well and put in casserole and cover. Bake at 325-350° for 1-1 1/2 hours. Can be served over browned rice, noodles, or Chinese noodles.

Note: The secret in dishes like this, soups, and potato salads, is to season as you go—don't wait until done. Don't be afraid to taste as you go.

The Fifth Generation Cookbook

Chicken Enchiladas

2 small carrots, finely diced
1 green pepper, finely diced
1 garlic clove, minced
1 tablespoon butter
1 tablespoon olive oil
1 (8-ounce) package cream
 cheese
1 (4-ounce) can chopped
 green chilies

4 cups shredded cooked
 chicken
2 cups mild salsa
16-20 soft flour tortillas
1 cup shredded Monterey
 Jack cheese
1/4 cup chopped cilantro

Sauté carrots, pepper, and garlic in butter and oil until softened. Add cream cheese, heat until melted; stir in green chilies and shredded chicken. Set aside. Pour one cup salsa into 9x12-bakiing pan. Heat tortillas (1 or 2 at a time) for 20 seconds in microwave oven or in hot skillet. Using about 1/2 cup, spread chicken/cream cheese mixture down center of each tortilla. Roll up carefully and place on salsa in baking dish. Repeat until all tortillas are filled. Spread with second cup of salsa and sprinkle cheese on top. Bake at 350° for 20-25 minutes until heated through and cheese is melted. Sprinkle with cilantro before servings. Serves 8.

Saturday Night Suppers

Mary Alice's Hot Chicken Salad

4 cups cooked chicken
2/3 cup toasted slivered
 almonds
1 cup grated Cheddar cheese
2 cups sliced celery
4 hard-boiled eggs, sliced
1/4 cup chopped onion

1 (4-ounce) can pimentos,
 well drained
1 (6 - 7-ounce) can water
 chestnuts, sliced
2 tablespoons lemon juice
3/4 cup mayonnaise
1 1/2 cups crushed potato chips

Toss first 8 ingredients together with lemon juice mixed with mayonnaise. Cover with crushed potato chips. Bake at 400° for 25 minutes. Serves 8-12. Prepare one day before use.

Treasured Recipes

Chicken with Spanish Rice

1 tablespoon plus 1 teaspoon oil
2 pounds skinless, boneless chicken breasts
1 teaspoon paprika
8 ounces uncooked rice
1/2 cup sliced scallions
1 1/2 cups chicken broth
1 cup canned whole tomatoes with liquid
2 tablespoons chopped parsley
1/8 teaspoon ground black pepper
1 1/2 cups green beans, halved

In a large skillet, heat oil. Cut chicken in squares. Season with paprika on both sides. Cook until golden brown on both sides, 7-8 minutes. Remove chicken and put in covered dish to keep warm. Add rice and scallions to skillet. Cook; stir frequently until rice is golden, 2-3 minutes. Stir in broth, tomatoes with liquid, parsley, and pepper. Crush tomatoes with spoon. Bring to boil. Return chicken and any liquid in bowl. Cover; cook over low heat 15 minutes. Add green beans and cover; cook an additional 15 minutes.

The PTA Pantry

Savory Crescent Chicken Squares

1 (3-ounce) package cream cheese, softened
3 tablespoons margarine, melted, divided
2 cups cubed cooked chicken or 2 (5-ounce) cans boned chicken
1/4 teaspoon salt
1/8 teaspoon pepper
2 tablespoons milk
1 tablespoon chopped chives or onion
1 tablespoon chopped pimiento (if desired)
1 (8-ounce) can Pillsbury Refrigerated Quick Crescent Dinner Rolls
3/4 cup seasoned croutons, crushed

Heat oven to 350°. In medium bowl, blend cream cheese and 2 tablespoons margarine until smooth. Add next 6 ingredients; mix well. Separate dough into 4 rectangles; firmly press perforations around edges together to seal. Spoon 1/2 cup meat mixture onto center of each rectangle. Pull 4 corners of dough to top center of chicken mixture; twist slightly and seal edges. Place on ungreased cookie sheet. Brush tops with reserved tablespoon of margarine; sprinkle with seasoned crouton crumbs. Bake at 350° for 20-25 minutes or until golden brown. Serves 4.

Firebells Cookbook

Chicken Pot Pie With Cornbread Crust

1 (10-ounce) package frozen
  peas and carrots
1/2 cup chopped onion
1/2 cup chopped fresh
  mushrooms (canned works
  just as well)
1/4 cup margarine or butter
1/3 cup all-purpose flour
1/2 teaspoon salt
1/2 teaspoon dried sage,
  marjoram, or thyme, crushed
1/8 teaspoon pepper
2 cups chicken broth
3/4 cup milk
3 cups cubed cooked chicken
  or turkey
1/4 cup snipped parsley
1/4 cup chopped pimiento,
  optional
1 (7 1/2-ounce) package corn
  muffin mix

Cook peas and carrots according to package directions; drain. In a saucepan cook onion and mushrooms in margarine or butter until tender. Stir in flour, salt, sage, marjoram, or thyme, and pepper. Add chicken broth and milk all at once. Cook and stir until thickened and bubbly. Stir in drained peas and carrots, chicken or turkey, parsley, and pimiento. Heat until bubbly. Pour chicken mixture into 6 round 10-ounce casseroles (or use a 12x7 1/2x2-inch baking dish). Mix corn muffin mix according to package. Spoon mixture atop the casserole. Bake in a 450° oven for 12-15 minutes or until muffin mix appears done.

Recipes & Remembrances

Ohio Chicken Pot Pie

Chicken pot pies in the Midwest tend to be meaty, with just a few vegetables for color, and served with a gravy on top. They are substantial, heartwarming dishes, so it's no wonder they're making a comeback.

3 pounds chicken pieces,
  white and dark meat
1 large carrot, quartered
1 bay leaf
1/2 cup (1 stick) butter,
  divided
1/4 cup chopped celery
1/4 cup chopped onion
7 tablespoons all-purpose
  flour, divided
1 teaspoon poultry seasoning
2 cups milk, divided
1/2 teaspoon salt, or to taste
1/2 teaspoon freshly ground
  pepper, or to taste
1/4 cup chopped parsley
Pastry for 2-crust pie
1 tablespoon fresh lemon
  juice

CONTINUED

In a deep kettle, cover the chicken with water (or chicken broth). Add the carrot and bay leaf, bring to a boil, then reduce heat and simmer until very tender, about 30 minutes. When the chicken is cool enough to handle, discard the skin and bones and bay leaf and cut the meat into bite-size pieces—you should have 3½ - 4 cups of chicken. Chop 2 of the carrot pieces very finely and combine with the chicken in a greased 9x13-inch flat pan. Cover with plastic wrap and refrigerate. Chill the broth until the fat rises and can be discarded.

Preheat oven to 375°. In a large saucepan, melt ¼ cup of the butter over medium heat; add the celery and the onion and cook until tender, but not brown, about 4-5 minutes. Stir in 3 tablespoons of the flour and the poultry seasoning and cook and stir until the mixture bubbles up in the middle of the pan. Add 1 cup of the milk and one cup of the broth and whisk and cook over medium heat until the mixture thickens; season with ¼ teaspoon salt, ¼ teaspoon pepper, and the parsley.

Pour the sauce over the chicken and set aside. Roll out the pastry to fit the top of the dish, crimping the edges to the top of the dish; slash the top so the steam can escape. Bake for 45 minutes, or until the top is golden brown and bubbling up in the center.

While the pot pie bakes, make the gravy. In a medium saucepan, melt the remaining ¼ cup butter and add the remaining 4 tablespoons flour and ¼ teaspoon salt and pepper. Cook and stir until the mixture bubbles in the pan, about 2 minutes; do not allow it to brown. Whisk in one cup of the broth, the remaining one cup of milk, and the lemon juice; cook and whisk the gravy over medium heat until thickened, about 3 minutes. Serve with the baked pot pie. Makes 10-12 servings.

Heartland

Cornish Hens Italiano

2-3 Cornish hens, halved	2 tablespoons butter
1 1/2 teaspoons sage	2 tablespoons olive oil
1 teaspoon rosemary	1 cup dry white wine
1 teaspoon garlic powder	1 tablespoon flour
1 teaspoon salt	1/2 cup warm water
1/8 teaspoon pepper	

Mix dry seasonings and rub on hens inside and out. In Dutch oven, melt butter and oil and brown hens on all sides. Add wine; cover and simmer until tender (approximately 45 minutes). Remove hens to platter; cover and keep warm. Mix flour with warm water and add to pan juices for Cornish sauce. Serve with noodles mixed with sour cream and Parmesan cheese.

What's Cooking at Holden School

Dressing (or Stuffing)

1 loaf of bread, diced and toasted	2 tablespoons butter
2 cups cooked and deboned chicken, diced	1 tablespoon chicken base
	1/2 teaspoon black pepper
1 cup diced celery	1 teaspoon salt
1/2 cup diced carrots	6 eggs, beaten
2 cups chicken broth	5-6 cups milk
	1/2 teaspoon seasoned salt

Mix all ingredients well. Fry in skillet. (Can mix together and put in refrigerator overnight. Fry next day.)

Tasty Recipes

Ham and Cheese Potato Salad with Shallot-Herb Dressing

2 pounds small red new
  potatoes, well scrubbed
3 cups cubed cooked ham
2 cups coarsely shredded
  Swiss cheese
1/2 cup sun-dried tomatoes
  packed in oil, drained and cut
  into small strips
1/2 cup thinly sliced green
  onions

3 tablespoons chopped fresh
  parsley
1 tablespoon chopped fresh
  dill
1 small head romaine lettuce,
  washed and dried
Extra sprigs of parsley, for
  garnish

Slice the potatoes into thin slices—about 1/4 inch thickness. (Leave peel on.) Place in a steamer and steam for 8 minutes or just until fork-tender. Remove potatoes to a side dish and lightly toss with 1/2 cup of the Tangy Shallot-Herb Dressing. Allow to sit for 30 minutes.

In a large bowl, gently toss together the potatoes, ham, cheese, tomatoes, onions, parsley, and dill. Toss the remaining dressing into the salad. Taste and correct the seasonings.

At serving time coarsely shred the romaine. Make a bed of the lettuce on a platter and spoon the ham salad over the top. Garnish with parsley sprigs. Serve at room temperature or chilled. Makes 8 servings.

TANGY SHALLOT-HERB DRESSING:
2 shallots, peeled and minced
1/2 cup dry white wine
1/4 cup white wine vinegar
1 cup mayonnaise
1/4 cup chopped fresh parsley

3 tablespoons chopped fresh
  tarragon
1/4 cup chopped fresh dill
Generous dash Tabasco sauce
1 teaspoon Dijon mustard

In a small non-corrosive saucepan, boil together the shallots, wine, and vinegar until the liquid is reduced to 1/4 cup. Cool. Whisk into the mayonnaise along with the herbs, Tabasco and mustard. Chill until ready to serve. Makes about 1 1/4 cups.

More Cooking with Marilyn Harris

Kits Marinated Turkey

2 cups sauterne	1 clove garlic, chopped
1 cup oil	8 turkey breast filets
1 cup soy sauce	

Combine wine, oil, soy sauce and garlic in bowl. Mix well. Rinse turkey and pat dry. Add to marinade. Marinate, covered, 24-26 hours. Place turkey on grill over low coals. Grill with cover closed, for 45 minutes, turning occasionally. Makes 8 servings.

Affolter-Heritage Reunion Cookbook & More

Almost Homemade Dressing

The slight crunchiness of the corn mixed with the turkey, onion, mushrooms, and seasoning make this taste homemade—to be honest—it's just as good as homemade!

1 medium onion chopped	2 boxes chicken stuffing
2 (4-ounce) cans sliced	(Stove Top)
mushrooms	1 (16-ounce) can corn
1 packet Butter Buds	2 cups chopped turkey or
3 1/3 cups water plus 1/2 cup	chicken breast
water	1/8 teaspoon ground pepper

Put chopped onion, mushrooms, Butter Buds, water, and seasoning packets (from stuffing mixes) into medium saucepan over high heat. Bring to a boil. Reduce heat. Add corn. Simmer 4 minutes. Add bread crumbs from stuffing boxes. Remove from heat. Let sit 5 minutes. Heat turkey in microwave until warm (about 40 seconds). Season turkey with pepper. Stir turkey into stuffing. Serve immediately. Yield: 12 servings. Cal 199; Fat 3.5 grams.

Down Home Cookin' Without the Down Home Fat

Meats

Glamorgan Castle, built by the inventor of the overhead traveling crane, is now the property of the Alliance School District. Alliance.

Cincinnati Chili

The first chili parlor opened its doors next to the Empress Burlesque (later named the Gaiety) in downtown Cincinnati in 1922, naming itself The Empress Chili Parlor. This establishment was owned by Greek Tom Kiradjieff who banked on the city sharing his taste for the unusual blend of spices. The rest is history. The original recipe which has always been mixed secretly at home, was never revealed. Yet chili restaurants sprang up all over town, including Skyline and Gold Star. Local chili aficionados developed preferences for their favorites. Al Heitz, a Camp Washington devotee, liked the old recipe best because it left his lips numb; old timers say that the chilies have indeed "cooled off" through the years. Inevitably, various chili recipes were published in cookbooks. Recently, a packaged Cincinnati Chili Mix has appeared on supermarket shelves. Whether the chili is hot or not, Cincinnati prides itself on being a true chili capital.

2-3 pounds ground beef	2 cayenne peppers (more to
1 quart cold water	taste)
1 (6-ounce) can tomato paste	1½ tablespoons
2 large onions, chopped	unsweetened cocoa
(about 1½ cups)	Salt and pepper to taste
1½ tablespoons vinegar	1½ pounds cooked
1 teaspoon Worcestershire	spaghetti
sauce	1 pound Cheddar cheese,
1 garlic clove, chopped fine	grated
2 tablespoons chili powder	1 box oyster crackers
5 bay leaves	1 (16-ounce) can kidney beans
2 teaspoons cinnamon	1 onion, chopped fine
1 teaspoon allspice	(optional)

Crumble the raw ground beef into the water. Add all of the ingredients except the spaghetti, cheese, crackers, beans, and onions and bring to a boil. Stir well, breaking all the meat up before it cooks. Cover and simmer 2 or more hours, stirring occasionally. Yield: 8-10 servings.

The proper way to serve this chili is over spaghetti on an oval dish. (There should be a piece of pepper for every serving for absolute authenticity.) For a "3-Way," top it off with a pile of grated cheese with a dish of crackers on the side. To make a "4-Way," add a spoonful of onions before the cheese is placed on top. For a "5-Way," add warmed beans in addition to onions and cheese.

Cincinnati Recipe Treasury

Baked Hamburger Steak

1 pound hamburger	Salt and pepper to taste
1/2 cup bread crumbs	1/2 teaspoon Gravy Master or
1/2 cup milk	Kitchen Bouquet
1 small onion, chopped fine	Flour and water
2 cups beef broth	

Mix and shape first 4 ingredients into 4 patties. Brown in skillet, then put into roaster pan. Add beef broth to drippings in skillet; stir well. Heat to boiling, scraping bottom of skillet; add salt and pepper to taste and Gravy Master or Kitchen Bouquet. Thicken with flour and water to make a gravy. Pour gravy over hamburger steaks, cover and bake at 350° for one hour. To make 20 servings, use 5 pounds hamburger and 5 times other ingredients.

Heirloom Recipes and By Gone Days

Brown Beef Over Pasta

1 pound ground beef	1/4 head cabbage, shredded
2 bay leaves	1 stalk celery, diced
1 small carrot, diced	1 small onion, diced
1 teaspoon parsley flakes, crushed	1 (16-ounce) can bean sprouts, drained and cut
1 teaspoon dried chives, crushed	2 cups tomato juice, no salt added
1 tablespoon minced garlic	

Brown beef in skillet with bay leaves; wash with hot water, and drain well. Grind herbs in a pestle and mortar. Combine all ingredients in a wide ovenproof dish. Bake in 350° oven until vegetables are tender, about one hour. Serve over cooked pasta. Serves 4.

Heartline Cookbook

 Canton is the boyhood home of W. H. Hoover, whose name became a household word after he began manufacturing vacuum cleaners.

Dolmas
(Stuffed Grape Leaves)

1 (16-ounce) jar imported
  grape leaves
1 - 1¹/2 pounds ground beef
¹/2 - ³/4 cup long grain rice,
  washed and drained
2 medium onions, finely
  chopped
¹/2 teaspoon salt

¹/4 teaspoon pepper
3 tablespoons lemon juice,
  concentrate
2 tablespoons cooking oil
¹/4 teaspoon salt
¹/8 teaspoon pepper
Water enough to cover all
  dolmas

Rinse brine water from grape leaves and remove stems. Combine beef, rice, onions, salt, and pepper. Place a small amount of meat mixture in center of leaf and roll up by tucking in the sides and roll end to end. Do not overstuff as rice needs room to expand as it cooks.

Arrange all the rolls in a heavy-bottomed pot lined with several flat grape leaves. Add lemon juice, oil, water, salt and pepper. Simmer for approximately 1¹/2 hours until rice is done and leaves are tender.

Note: The dolmas may be reheated by placing in a covered baking pan with a little liquid. Place in 250° oven for about 20-30 minutes until dolmas are heated through.

Now That Mom's Not Around

Hamburg Stroganoff

Noodles or rice
¹/2 cup chopped onions
¹/2 cup chopped peppers
Garlic salt (optional)
2 tablespoons butter or oleo
1 pound hamburg
2 teaspoons flour

2 teaspoons salt
¹/2 teaspoon pepper
1 (4-ounce) can mushrooms
1 (10³/4-ounce) can cream of
  mushroom soup
1 cup sour cream

Cook noodles or rice for family's size and set aside. Mix together onions, peppers, and garlic salt; brown in butter or oleo. Add hamburg, flour, salt and pepper to first mixture and brown. Add mushrooms and cream of mushroom soup and simmer. Add sour cream (can add ¹/2 - ³/4 cup milk to stretch it). Serve over noodles or rice.

Our Collection of Heavenly Recipes

Mini Meat Loaves

2 pounds ground beef
1 pound pork sausage
1 medium onion, chopped
4 eggs, slightly beaten
1 can chicken rice soup,
  undiluted
1 teaspoon salt

1 1/2 teaspoons poultry
  seasoning
4 cups cornflake crumbs,
  divided
1 can mushroom soup,
  undiluted

In large deep bowl, break up beef and sausage. Add chopped onion, eggs, chicken rice soup, salt, poultry seasoning, and 2 cups of the cornflake crumbs. Mix thoroughly. Shape into 18 rolls, approximately 1/3 cup of mix each, about 4 inches long and 1 1/2 inches thick. Then roll in remaining cornflake crumbs, coating all sides. Place in 9x13-inch pan, slightly separated so they brown on all sides. Spread mushroom soup on the rolls; bake at 325° for one hour.

Tried and True by Mothers of 2's

Indian Meat Loaf

1 pound ground beef
1 cup creamed-style corn
1/2 green pepper
1/2 chopped onion
1 egg

1 (No. 2) can tomatoes
1 teaspoon salt
Pepper as you like
1/2 cup cornmeal

Mix together well. Bake about one hour at 350°.

Sharing Our Best (Elizabeth House)

German Meat Loaf

With Ohio having such a high percentage of citizens with a German heritage, you can expect all sorts of good dishes made with sauerkraut. This meat loaf is seasoned with both kraut and rye bread crumbs—an inspired combination. Serve the moist and sassy meat loaf with mashed potatoes and a glass of beer. Meat loaf has never been so good!

2 cups soft unseeded rye
   bread crumbs
1 (16-ounce) can sauerkraut,
   drained
2 eggs, lightly beaten
1/2 cup milk

1/2 cup chopped onion
1 teaspoon caraway seed
1/2 teaspoon ground pepper
2 tablespoons catsup or chili
   sauce
2 pounds lean ground beef

Preheat the oven to 350°. In a large bowl combine all the ingredients except the meat and mix well. Add the ground beef and mix thoroughly. Pat into a thick, flat loaf approximately 10 inches long and 8 inches wide and place on a rack in a greased or foil-lined 9x13-inch pan. Bake for 1 1/4 hours, or until nicely browned. Let stand 10 minutes before slicing.

Heartland

Swedish Meat Balls

1 pound ground beef
1/2 cup bread or cracker
   crumbs, soaked in 2/3 cup
   milk
1 egg
2 tablespoons grated onion

1 teaspoon salt
1/8 teaspoon pepper
1/8 teaspoon nutmeg
1/2 cup flour
6 beef bouillon cubes
Kitchen Bouquet

Mix all ingredients except flour, bouillon cubes, and Kitchen Bouquet. Form into small balls. Brown in one teaspoon Crisco. Take balls out of grease. Mix 4 cups cold water and 1/2 cup flour in saucepan with wire whisk. Add bouillon cubes. Bring to a boil, mixing to avoid lumps. Add Kitchen Bouquet for color. Strain into meat balls. Simmer slowly for about 1/2 hour.

Seasoned with Love

Barbecued Meatballs

3 pounds ground beef
1 (12-ounce) can evaporated
   milk
1 cup oatmeal
1 cup cracker crumbs
2 eggs

$^1/_2$ cup chopped onion
$^1/_2$ teaspoon garlic salt
$^1/_2$ teaspoon pepper
2 teaspoons salt
1 teaspoon chili powder

Combine all ingredients (mixture will be soft); shape into walnut-size balls. Place meatballs in single layer on waxed paper-lined cookie sheets; freeze until solid. Store frozen meatballs in freezer bags until ready to cook.

SAUCE:

2 cups catsup
1 cup brown sugar
$^1/_2$ teaspoon garlic powder

$^1/_4$ cup onion
$^1/_2$ teaspoon liquid smoke, or
   to taste

Combine all ingredients and stir until sugar is dissolved. Place frozen meatballs in a 13x9x2-inch baking pan. Pour on the sauce. Bake at 350° for one hour. Yield: 80 meatballs.

Tasty Recipes

Sloppy Joes

2$^1/_2$ pounds hamburger
1 medium onion, chopped
2$^1/_2$ tablespoons
   Worcestershire sauce
$^1/_3$ cup brown sugar

$^1/_2$ cup catsup
1 tablespoon mustard
1 (10$^3/_4$-ounce) can cream of
   mushroom soup

Brown meat; drain. Add rest of ingredients and cook slowly until thick.

Recipes & Remembrances

 Festivals celebrate Ohio's differences and common bonds: the Swiss in Tuscarawas County; the Welsh in Jackson; the Poles in Youngstown; the Hungarians in Toledo; the Germans in Columbus and Cincinnati; and Cleveland covers all the bases with an all-nations festival each summer.

Jackpots

This is a favorite with teenagers.

1 pound ground beef	1 tablespoon onion, minced
1/2 cup ketchup	15-18 buttermilk biscuits
2 tablespoons brown sugar	(Hungry Jack)
1 tablespoon prepared	Cheese, shredded
mustard	
1 1/2 teaspoons	
Worcestershire sauce	

Brown meat. Drain. Mix meat with ketchup, brown sugar, prepared mustard, Worcestershire sauce and onion. Simmer for 5 minutes. Separate biscuits. Place one biscuit in each ungreased cupcake cup. Press dough up sides. Spoon mixture into shaped biscuit. Sprinkle with cheese. Bake at 400° for 8-10 minutes. (Until lightly browned.) Serves 5-6 people.

Note: Can use 2 (10-ounce) cans of biscuits and make 1 1/2 recipes of mix.

Cooking with TLC

Shipwreck

2 medium onions, sliced	1 cup sliced carrots
2 medium potatoes, sliced	Salt and pepper
1 pound ground beef or	Paprika
turkey	1 creamed soup (any flavor)
1/2 cup uncooked rice	1 cup boiling water
1 cup diced celery	

Layer first 6 ingredients, seasoning with salt, pepper, and paprika. Mix creamed soup of your choice with boiling water and pour over top of vegetables. Bake at 300° for 3-4 hours or could be placed in a crockpot and cooked per your crockpot method.

Gardener's Delight

Hamburger-Corn Casserole

This casserole really fooled our husbands. When we tested it, they couldn't tell any difference between our rehab and the original. Served with a green salad, it's a complete meal.

2 cups nonfat plain yogurt, drained to equal 1 cup (see below)

1 1/2 pounds ground round or sirloin (90% lean or better)

1 cup chopped onion

1 (12-ounce) can whole kernel corn, drained

1 (10 3/4-ounce) can lowfat cream of chicken soup, such as Campbell's Healthy Request

1 (10 3/4-ounce) can lowfat cream of mushroom soup, such as Campbell's Healthy Request

1/4 cup chopped pimento

3/4 teaspoon salt

1/4 teaspoon black pepper

3 cups cooked, drained cholesterol-free noodles (6 ounces dry)

1 cup (2 slices bread) soft bread crumbs

1 1/2 tablespoons margarine, melted

Four to six hours ahead: Line colander with coffee filter or 2 layers of paper towels; pour 2 cups of yogurt into colander. Put colander in bowl. Place in refrigerator for 4-6 hours. Discard liquid. This should yield one cup or 8 ounces of thickened yogurt.

Preheat oven to 350°. Spray 2-quart casserole with vegetable oil spray. In medium skillet, over medium-high heat, brown ground beef; drain and blot with paper towels. Add onion to skillet and cook until tender but not brown. Add corn, soups, pimento, salt, pepper, and drained yogurt; mix well. Stir in cooked noodles. Pour into prepared casserole. Mix bread crumbs and margarine; sprinkle over top. Bake at 350° for 30 minutes or until heated through. Yield: 8-10 servings.

Nutrients per serving: Cal 281; Fat 9g (29%); Carbo 31g; Chol 42mg; Sod 643mg; Prot 19g.

Recipe Rehab

Husband's Delight

1 1/2 pounds ground chuck
2 (8-ounce) cans tomato sauce
3 tablespoons ketchup
1 teaspoon salt
1 tablespoon sugar
1/4 teaspoon garlic salt
1/2 pint sour cream

1 (3-ounce) package cream
  cheese
1/2 medium onion, chopped
  fine
1 (10-ounce) package egg
  noodles
1 cup grated cheese

Brown ground chuck; drain off fat. Add tomato sauce, ketchup, salt, sugar, and garlic salt; simmer 15 minutes. Blend in bowl the sour cream, cream cheese, and onion. Cook noodles until done and drain. Grease 9x13-inch dish with oleo. Add half noodles. Spread all the meat sauce over the noodles. Spread on cream cheese mixture; add remaining noodles. Top with grated cheese. Bake at 350° for 25 minutes.

Incredible Edibles

Corned Beef Casserole

1 can chicken soup
1 soup can filled with milk
1/2 cup chopped onion
1/2 pound grated sharp
  Cheddar cheese

1 can corned beef, flaked
1 small can mushroom pieces
1 (8-ounce) package wide
  noodles

Heat soup, milk and onions; add half of the cheese, half of the beef and also the can of mushrooms. When hot, add the noodles. When the noodles have softened, pour into a buttered casserole. Top with remainder of the cheese and beef. Bake for 45 minutes at 350°.

Heavenly Dishes

Ohio Caverns in Logan County is the largest cavern in Ohio and has been acclaimed as one of America's most colorful caverns.

Enchiladas Acapulco

1 pound ground beef
1 (8-ounce) can tomato sauce
3/4 cup chopped bell pepper,
  divided
1 can kidney beans, drained
1/2 pound Velveeta Mexican
  Process Cheese, cubed,
  divided

8 (6-inch) corn tortillas
Oil
1/2 cup chopped tomato

Brown meat and drain. Add tomato sauce and 1/2 cup bell pepper. Cook over medium heat 5 minutes, stirring. Add beans and 1/4 pound cheese. Continue cooking until cheese is melted.

Dip tortillas in hot oil; drain. Fill each tortilla with 1/4 cup meat mixture; roll up. Place seam-side-down in baking dish. Top with remaining meat mixture. Cover. Bake at 350° for 20 minutes. Top with remaining cheese. Bake, uncovered, 5-8 minutes, until cheese is melted. Top with remaining pepper and tomatoes to serve.

Down Home Cooking from Hocking County

Easy Empanadas

1 1/4 pounds ground meat,
  cooked and drained
1/2 cup chopped Spanish
  olives
2/3 cup raisins
2/3 cup salsa, commercial or
  homemade

1 tablespoon taco seasoning
2 (17.3-ounce) cans large-size
  buttermilk biscuits
1 egg plus 1 tablespoon water

Combine cooked meat with olives, raisins, salsa and taco seasoning and stir until well mixed. Roll each biscuit into a 6-inch circle. Place a scant 1/4 cup of meat mixture on bottom half of each rolled-out biscuit. With finger or brush, moisten edge of biscuit with water, fold in half and press edges together with fork. Pierce top of each empanada with fork tines 2-3 times. Place on ungreased baking sheet and brush with egg mixed with water. Bake at 400° for 20-25 minutes. Can be made up to baking as much as 3-4 hours ahead, well wrapped with plastic wrap and refrigerated. Serves 8.

Saturday Night Suppers

Bean Burrito Bake

1 pound ground beef	1 cup salsa
1 (16-ounce) can refried beans	1 1/2 cups shredded Cheddar
1 cup Bisquick	cheese
1/4 cup water	Sour cream (if desired)
1 avocado, sliced (if desired)	

Heat oven to 400°. Grease pie plate, 10x1 1/2 inches. Brown ground beef and drain. Mix beans, baking mix, and water. Spread mixture in bottom and halfway up side of pie plate. Layer with beef, avocado, and salsa.

Bake 20-30 minutes or until knife inserted in center comes out clean. Sprinkle with cheese. Bake 2-3 minutes longer or until cheese is melted. Serve with sour cream. Makes 8 servings.

The Fifth Generation Cookbook

Truckers' Beans

Very good cooked a day ahead and then just heated through.

1 pound ground beef	1 tablespoon prepared
1 package dry onion soup mix	mustard
2 (16-ounce) cans pork and	1 cup brown sugar
beans	1 (16-ounce) can tomato sauce
2 (16-ounce) cans kidney	
beans	

Sauté the ground beef until it loses red color. Put in large casserole. Add remaining ingredients. Do not drain pork and beans or kidney beans. Mix well. Bake at 350° for 1 - 1 1/2 hours until brown on top. Serves 15 or more.

Saturday Night Suppers

Fromage Beef Pie

1 pound extra lean ground beef	2 eggs, beaten
1 (6-ounce) box beef Stove Top Dressing	1/2 cup fresh or canned sliced mushrooms
1 (4-ounce) tomato sauce	1 green pepper, chopped
2 teaspoons instant minced onion	1 cup shredded Cheddar cheese
1/2 teaspoon salt	1 tomato, sliced

Combine beef, one cup croutons and some of the seasoning from package of dressing, tomato sauce, onion, salt, and one egg. Press into sides and bottom of 9-inch pie pan. Mix remaining ingredients except tomato (croutons, egg, mushrooms, green pepper, and cheese). Arrange this and tomato slices over beef crust. Bake at 375° for 30 minutes. Serves 6. Tastes like pizza without a crust.

Treasured Recipes

Shepherd's Pie

1 tablespoon vegetable oil	1 cup canned tomatoes, chopped
1 medium-size onion, chopped	
1 pound ground beef (lean)	2 medium-size potatoes, cooked until tender
1 teaspoon basil, dried	
1/2 pound green beans (fresh), steamed until tender	1 egg, beaten
	1/2 cup water

Heat oil in large skillet and sauté onion until golden. Add beef and basil and cook until browned. Stir in green beans and tomatoes, then turn mixture into casserole. Preheat oven to 350°. Mash potatoes together with egg and water; spoon evenly over meat mixture and bake for 15 minutes.

Down Home Cooking from Hocking County

Beautiful waterfalls, caves, cliffs, hollows, gorges, and rock formations make Hocking Hills a hiker and camper's dream place.

Cranberry Beef Stew

Give this unusual combination of flavors a try. This is one of the best stews you'll ever taste.

2-2¹/₂ pounds stew meat
2 tablespoons oil
3 cups water
2 beef bouillon cubes
1 teaspoon Worcestershire
   sauce
1 garlic clove, minced
2 teaspoons salt
¹/₂ teaspoon paprika

¹/₂ teaspoon pepper
6 small carrots, cut in chunks
1 (16-ounce) jar pearl onions
1 (16-ounce) can whole berry
   cranberry sauce
¹/₄ cup cold water
2 teaspoons cornstarch
¹/₂ teaspoon Kitchen
   Bouquet

In a Dutch oven, brown meat in oil. Add water, bouillon cubes, Worcestershire sauce, garlic, salt, paprika, and pepper. Cover and simmer for 1¹/₄ hours. Add more water to cover beef if necessary. Add carrots, onions with liquid, and cranberry sauce; simmer for 45 minutes. In small bowl mix together cornstarch and water. Add to stew; stir until thickened. Add Kitchen Bouquet and heat for 5 minutes. Yield: 6-8 servings.

Cooking on the Wild Side

Sandy's Roast Beef Supreme

1 (5 - 7-pound) tip roast
2 cans golden mushroom soup
3 large cloves garlic

1 large onion, sliced
1 package onion soup mix
1 brown gravy mix

Layer sliced onions on bottom of crock pot. Wash roast off with cold water. Dry and make small slits. Insert garlic cloves. Place in crockpot, then sprinkle soup mix (dry) over roast. Prepare mushroom soup and add brown gravy mix and pour over all. Top with remaining onion slices. Cook on low heat. If put on to cook Saturday night, by noon Sunday it is tender and succulent. This is a very rich dish and a family favorite.

Home Cookin' with 4-H

Grandma Myers' Barbecued Beef

2¹/₂ - 3 pounds roast beef
1 bottle chili sauce
1 bottle catsup
2 tablespoons sugar
³/₄ teaspoon dry mustard

3 teaspoons pickling spice
1 teaspoon pepper
1 medium green pepper,
  chopped
1 large onion, chopped

Roast beef (or pressure cook) until well done. Shred beef. Combine all other ingredients and cook approximately 1 hour. (Make a garni bag with cheesecloth for pickling spice; don't dump pickling spice directly into beef.) Add beef to barbecue sauce; cook together 1-2 hours or more. Freezes well (if it lasts that long).

MDA Favorite Recipes

Sirloin Supreme

1 large sweet onion
1 large green pepper
2 pounds sirloin steak

2 tablespoons cooking oil
1 (8-ounce) can sliced
  mushrooms, drained

SAUCE:
³/₄ cup catsup
³/₄ cup beef broth
3 tablespoons flour

4 tablespoons soy sauce
Freshly ground pepper

Cut onion and green pepper into ¹/₄-inch rings; set aside. Cut steak into strips 2 inches long and ¹/₂-inch wide. Brown meat in hot oil in heavy saucepan or Dutch oven; set aside.

In saucepan, blend catsup and beef broth. Blend flour, soy sauce, and pepper, and stir into catsup and broth mixture. Heat until bubbling, stirring constantly.

Return meat to heat and add sauce and onion rings. Cover and simmer ¹/₂ hour, stirring occasionally to prevent sticking. Add green pepper rings and mushrooms and simmer an additional 10 minutes. Serve with hot, fluffy rice. Serves 6-8.

Note: If a lesser cut of meat is used, such as round steak, increase cooking time to allow meat to become tender.

Plain & Fancy Favorites

Bourbon-Marinated Flank Steak

You don't have to grill this steak on an outdoor grill. It has a great flavor when broiled under a very hot, preheated broiler. The time would be approximately the same as the grilling time.

1 large flank steak
(approximately 2 pounds)
1/2 cup light soy sauce
3 tablespoons vegetable oil
2 medium onions, sliced
3 large cloves garlic, chopped
2 tablespoons minced fresh
gingerroot

2 tablespoons dark brown
sugar
1/4 teaspoon hot pepper
sauce
1/2 cup bourbon

Trim all visible fat from the flank steak. In a heavy-duty, gallon-sized plastic bag with a zip top, mix together all of the marinade ingredients. Add steak. Refrigerate for at least 8 hours or as long as 24 hours.

Cook on a hot grill for 8 minutes on the first side and 5 minutes on the second side for a medium-rare steak. Increase the cooking time if a more well-done steak is desired. To serve, cut across the grain into 1-inch-wide strips. Serves 4-6.

Cooking with Marilyn

Beef with Broccoli

MARINADE:

1 tablespoon water
1 tablespoon wine
1¹/₂ tablespoons soy sauce
¹/₂ teaspoon garlic powder

¹/₂ teaspoon sugar
³/₄ pound flank steak, cut in
 strips

Marinate steak in above ingredients.

1 tablespoon Mazola corn oil
1 slice gingerroot
1 green onion
1 clove garlic

1 bunch broccoli
¹/₂ teaspoon sugar
1¹/₂ teaspoons cornstarch

Heat oil until hot. Add ginger and green onion. Cook until light brown. Add meat and stir-fry until meat turns brown. Take out of wok. Crush garlic and add to oil in wok, then add broccoli. Stir-fry quickly, then add sugar and cornstarch and mix well. Arrange broccoli on platter—flowers out—then place meat in middle of platter. Serves 6.

Favorite Recipes from Poland Women's Club

Slovak Goulash

1 pound beef, cut up in cubes
2 medium onions, chopped
3 tablespoons Worcestershire
 sauce
³/₄ teaspoon vinegar
6 tablespoons catsup
1¹/₄ teaspoons paprika

1¹/₄ teaspoons salt
1¹/₂ cups hot water
3 tablespoons flour
¹/₂ cup cold water
1 (16-ounce) package broad
 noodles, cooked

Brown meat in large heavy pan. Add onions, Worcestershire sauce, vinegar, catsup, paprika, and salt. Mix well and add water, stir and cover. Let cook slowly about 2 hours or until meat is tender. Blend flour with ¹/₂ cup cold water and add to meat. Let cook 15 minutes. Serve over hot buttered noodles. (You may add more hot water if gravy is too thick.)

Seasoned with Love

Easy Swiss Steak

2¹/₂ pounds round steak,
  ¹/₂-inch thick
1 medium onion, cut into rings
2-3 cloves garlic, minced or
  sliced
2 tablespoons butter

1 (8-ounce) can cream of
  celery soup
1 (8-ounce) can cream of
  mushroom soup
1 soup can water

In frying pan, brown meat, onion, and garlic in butter. Place meat in a casserole dish. Salt and pepper lightly. Mix soups and water; pour over the steak. Cover and bake in the oven for 2¹/₂ hours at 350°. Serve over mashed potatoes. Makes 4-6 servings.

The PTA Pantry

Sautéed Veal Macadamia

Elegant but easy.

12 ounces sliced veal,
  defatted and pounded
  between plastic wrap until
  properly tenderized, then cut
  crosswise into 6 pieces
6 tablespoons flour
2 tablespoons clarified butter
Garlic powder to taste
Seasoning salt to taste

¹/₄ teaspoon lime juice
¹/₄ cup white wine
¹/₂ cup undiluted cream of
  mushroom soup
8 macadamia nuts, chopped
6 sliced peeled avocados,
  ¹/₂-inch thick
1 teaspoon minced parsley

Dust veal with flour. Melt butter in pan until bubbly. Sauté veal until lightly browned, about 2 minutes. Turn veal and season to taste with garlic powder and salt. Dribble lime juice and wine on top and continue sautéing until veal has been cooked (about 2 minutes) on second side. Remove from heat and add mushroom soup and nuts. Stir until all ingredients are hot.

Layer 3 pieces of veal on each plate. Spoon sauce on top. Top with avocado slices and sprinkle with parsley. Serves 2.

Chef Dwight M. Drake, Country Club at Muirfield Village.

A Taste of Columbus Vol III

Mushroom Steak

1/2 tablespoon butter or oleo
2 pounds round steak, cut in
chunks and sprinkled with
meat tenderizer
1 envelope onion soup
1/2 green pepper, sliced
1 pound fresh mushrooms
1 (No. 2) can whole tomatoes,
drained (save 1/2 cup juice)

1/4 teaspoon salt
Dash of pepper
1 tablespoon parsley (dried or
fresh)
1 tablespoon A-1 Sauce or
Worcestershire sauce
1 tablespoon cornstarch

Use butter to grease bottom of 10x15-inch pan. Put meat in pan and sprinkle with tenderizer. Sprinkle with soup mix. Arrange pepper slices, mushrooms, and tomatoes in pan. Salt, pepper, and sprinkle with parsley. To the 1/2 cup reserved juice, add A-1 Sauce and cornstarch. Pour over ingredients in pan. Cover pan tightly with foil. Bake 2 hours at 350°. Serve over noodles.

Ottoville Sesquicentennial Cookbook

Veal Française

Try this for your next dinner party.

11/2 pounds veal, cut in
medallions and pounded flat
1 cup flour

1 egg, beaten
1/4 pound butter

Dip veal in flour, next in egg, then in flour again; shake off excess flour. Sauté in butter turning once, until cooked (about 5 minutes) over medium heat. Remove meat to platter and keep warm.

SAUCE:

1/2 cup chicken broth
1/4 cup white wine
1/8 cup lemon juice
1/4 cup butter

1 cup whipping cream
1 tablespoon fresh parsley,
chopped
Lemon slices

Mix all sauce ingredients together in fry pan and bring to a boil. Add veal and heat for 5 minutes. Arrange veal on a serving platter and garnish with thin slices of lemon. Serves 4.

Angels and Friends Cookbook II

Italian Veal Stew with Dumplings

A wonderful one-dish dinner.

1 pound veal, cut in cubes
Flour
2 cups hot water
1/2 cup diced carrots (not too
  thick)
1/2 cup diced potatoes
1/4 cup chopped celery
1/4 cup chopped onion

1 teaspoon Worcestershire
  sauce
1/2 teaspoon salt
Dash of pepper
1/2 cup Great Northern beans
1/2 cup frozen peas
1 (8-ounce) can tomato sauce

DUMPLINGS:

1 cup sifted flour
1/2 teaspoon salt
1 1/2 teaspoons baking
  powder

1/2 cup milk
2 tablespoons salad oil (to
  make a soft dough)

Roll meat in flour and brown in fat. Add hot water and cook for one hour. Add vegetables and all other ingredients except tomato sauce. Cook for 30 more minutes. Add tomato sauce and bring to a boil. Combine all ingredients for dumplings and stir. Drop dumplings from spoon into veal stew. Cover tightly and steam without lifting the cover for 12-15 minutes. Serves 4-6.

Angels and Friends Cookbook I

City Chicken

It is believed this is strictly a Cincinnati recipe that came about because "some butcher probably had a pile of pork and veal scraps left over one day," according to Russ Gibbs, Findlay Market's "oldest" proprietor with 40 years at Butter and Egg Stand #28. City chickens are available ready-made at most of the meat stands, which number over half of the 32 stands inside the market building.

1 pound lean pork	**1/4 cup cornmeal**
1/2 pound veal	**Salt and pepper to taste**
6 wooden skewers	**Frying oil**
1/2 cup flour	

Cut the meat into bite-sized cubes. Thread the pork and veal onto the wooden skewers, two pieces of pork and one of veal, until all the meat is gone and each skewer has an equal amount. Place the flour, cornmeal, and seasonings into a bag and toss in the city chickens. Shake until the meat is well covered with the mixture. Fry at a medium heat, turning occasionally, until browned on all sides. This should take approximately 20-30 minutes so that the pork will be cooked through. Drain on absorbent paper. Afterward, wash the skewers and use them again. Yield: 2-3 servings.

Note: The city chicken can be floured and dipped in an egg batter if so desired. Of course, Russ recommends this alternative.

Cincinnati Recipe Treasury

Barbecued Sausage Balls

1 pound bulk pork sausage	**2 tablespoons brown sugar**
1 egg, slightly beaten	**1 tablespoon vinegar**
1/3 cup fine dry bread crumbs	**1 tablespoon soy sauce**
1/2 teaspoon sage (optional)	**(optional)**
1/2 cup catsup	

Mix sausage, egg, bread crumbs, and sage. Shape into 24 (1 1/2-inch) balls. Brown slowly on all sides, about 15 minutes. Pour off excess fat. Combine remaining ingredients; pour over meat. Cover and simmer 30 minutes, stirring occasionally to coat meatballs. Makes 4-5 servings.

Women's Centennial Cookbook

BBQ Spareribs Aloha

3 pounds lean spareribs
1 (14½-ounce) can
  pineapple slices, drained with
  syrup reserved
1 (15-ounce) can tomato sauce

½ cup minced onion
¼ cup minced green pepper
¼ cup vinegar
1 tablespoon Worcestershire

Cut ribs into pieces and grill 4 inches from coals for 30 minutes. Meanwhile, combine reserved pineapple syrup with remaining ingredients, except pineapple. Simmer 20 minutes. Baste ribs with sauce and cook 20 more minutes. Add pineapple to grill the last 5 minutes of cooking time. Reheat rest of sauce and serve over pineapple-topped ribs. Makes 5 servings.

Per serving: Cal 490; Prot 34g; Fat 22g; Chol 40g.

Wadsworth-Rittman Hospital Cookbook

BBQ Pork Chop Casserole

4 loin pork chops
¼ cup diced onion
¾ cup chili sauce
¼ cup ketchup
1 teaspoon dry mustard
¼ teaspoon garlic powder

2 tablespoons brown sugar
½ cup water
3 tablespoons cider vinegar
1 beef bouillon cube
Salt to taste
Pepper to taste

Brown pork chops. Place in 1½-quart casserole. Sauté onion until soft in pan drippings. Add remaining ingredients and bring to boil. Pour over chops. Bake at 350° for 1½ hours, covered.

Firebells Cookbook

Apple-Stuffed Pork Loin with Raspberry Sauce

Nearly 180 years ago, stagecoach drivers pulled up at The Buxton Inn in Granville, Ohio. Today, former school teachers, Ralph and Audrey Orr, are busy restoring not just the Inn, but a whole block in this town amid Ohio's Welsh Mountains. It is a treat to stay at the Buxton, as each room is furnished in period antiques. The food served in the dining room is well known, prompting diners to drive many miles. This recipe is a favorite at the Inn. It combines pork and apples, two Ohio favorites.

1 cup chopped onion
1¹/₂ cups chopped celery
¹/₂ cup butter or margarine
3 cups cored and chopped tart
  red apples
¹/₂ teaspoon ground allspice
¹/₄ teaspoon ground
  cardamom

5 cups dry bread cubes
¹/₂ cup raisins or chopped
  pecans
1 (3-4 pound) boneless single
  pork loin roast
Dash each garlic powder,
  pepper and salt

In large skillet, cook onion and celery in butter until tender. Add apples, allspice and cardamom; cook, uncovered, for 5 minutes, stirring occasionally. In large bowl, combine apple mixture with bread and raisins; toss gently until bread is coated.

Preheat oven to 325°. Trim excess fat from meat; split lengthwise almost through. Spoon about half of stuffing over meat; fold, tie with string to secure. Place remaining stuffing in 1-quart baking dish. Place meat on a rack in 17x12-inch roasting pan. Sprinkle with garlic powder, pepper and salt; insert meat thermometer. Roast meat, uncovered, 60-70 minutes or until thermometer registers 160-170°. Cover and heat remaining stuffing during the last 40 minutes of roasting. To serve, slice pork; serve with additional stuffing and Raspberry Sauce. Makes 8-10 servings.

RASPBERRY SAUCE:

2 cups fresh raspberries, or 2
  cups frozen raspberries,
  thawed and undrained
¹/₂ cup apricot nectar
¹/₂ cup red currant jelly

2 tablespoons brandy
  (optional)
1 tablespoon honey or sugar
4 teaspoons cornstarch
1 tablespoon water

In medium saucepan, combine raspberries, nectar, jelly, brandy and honey. Over low heat, stirring frequently, cook until mixture boils. Strain to remove seeds; return mixture to saucepan. In small bowl, combine cornstarch and water; add to raspberry mixture. Cook and stir until clear and thickened, stirring constantly. Makes 1³/₄ cups.

Bountiful Ohio

Pork Chop Supper for Four

4-5 pork loin chops, medium sliced
1/4 cup flour
1/4 teaspoon salt
1/8 teaspoon pepper
1/4 teaspoon garlic powder
1/8 teaspoon paprika
1/4 cup real butter
1/2 onion, thinly sliced
1 (13³/4-ounce) College Inn chicken broth
1/2 cube Knorr chicken bouillon
1/2 teaspoon sugar
1/8 cup dry white wine (Chardonnay), optional
4 medium potatoes, thinly sliced
1/2 tablespoon flour
6 fresh mushrooms, sliced (optional)

Mix flour, salt, pepper, garlic powder, and paprika in bowl. Coat pork chops with this mixture. Melt butter in pan and slowly brown chops on both sides, adding onion. Add College Inn chicken broth to pan with meat. Add Knorr chicken bouillon, sugar and wine (if desired); simmer on low heat with lid on pan for about 40 minutes. Lift lid and add fresh sliced potatoes and mushrooms (if desired); cook until potatoes are tender. Thicken the juices with flour and water mixture until gravylike consistency. Serve with fresh steamed green beans.

The PTA Pantry

Pork Chops in Dill Gravy

1/2 cup green onions, thinly sliced	1/2 cup Chablis or other dry white wine
1/2 cup fresh mushrooms, sliced	1 teaspoon Worcestershire sauce
3 tablespoons butter or margarine	1 teaspoon dried dill weed
6 (3/4-inch thick) pork chops	1/3 cup water
1 teaspoon salt	2 tablespoons flour
1/4 teaspoon pepper	1 (8-ounce) carton sour cream
	Hot cooked rice

In a large skillet, sauté onions and mushrooms in butter until tender. Remove from skillet; set aside. Sprinkle pork chops with salt and pepper; place in skillet and brown on both sides. Combine sautéed vegetables, wine, Worcestershire sauce, and dill weed; pour over chops. Cover, reduce heat, and simmer 40 minutes or until pork chops are tender. Remove chops from skillet; set aside. Combine water and flour, stirring until smooth; add to pan drippings in skillet. Cook over low heat, stirring constantly, until thickened and bubbly. Stir in sour cream. Cook until thoroughly heated. Serve chops over hot, cooked rice; spoon gravy over chops, as desired. Yield: 6 servings.

Simply Sensational

Grilled Pork Chops

6 pork chops about 1 1/4 inches thick	2 teaspoons seasoned salt
1/2 cup soy sauce	1 teaspoon ginger
1/2 cup cooking sherry	1/2 teaspoon dry mustard

Combine all ingredients except chops. Use this to marinade chops. Cover and refrigerate 4-6 hours or overnight. Turn several times. Remove from marinade and place on grill. Cook 20-30 minutes or until meat is not pink in the center. Remove from grill immediately. Do not overcook.

Women's Centennial Cookbook

Pork Roast with Mustard Sauce and Honey Apples

1 tablespoon rubbed sage	1/2 cup Dijon mustard
1/4 teaspoon dried marjoram	5 pounds rolled boneless
2 tablespoons soy sauce	pork loin roast
2 cloves garlic, minced	

Combine first 5 ingredients in small bowl; mix well. Place roast, fat-side-up, in shallow roasting pan. Spread with mustard mixture. Insert meat thermometer, making sure it does not touch fat. Bake uncovered at 325° for 2 - 2 1/2 hours or until thermometer registers 160°. Serve roast with Honey Apples.

HONEY APPLES:

4 Granny Smith apples	1/4 teaspoon ground
1/2 cup honey	cinnamon
1/4 teaspoon salt	2 tablespoons vinegar

Peel, core and slice apples into 1/2-inch thick slices; set aside. Combine remaining ingredients in large saucepan; bring to boil. Add apples; reduce heat and simmer 10 minutes. Serves 10-12.

MDA Favorite Recipes

Luau Pork Ambrosia

1 (5-pound) pork roast	1/8 teaspoon ginger
4 jars baby food strained	1/8 teaspoon pepper
apricots	1 (1-pound, 13-ounce) can
1/3 cup honey	whole unpeeled apricots
1/4 cup fresh lemon juice	1 tablespoon grated lemon
1/4 cup soy sauce	rind
1/2 clove garlic, minced	1/4 cup freshly grated coconut
1 small onion, minced	Parsley sprigs
1 cup ginger ale	

Remove chine bone from roast; tie roast. Place roast in marinating dish. Combine 2 jars strained apricots, honey, lemon juice, soy sauce, garlic, onion, ginger ale, ginger, and pepper; pour over pork. Marinate for 4-5 hours, turning occasionally.

Line grill with quilted aluminum foil; let coals burn down until covered with gray ash. Remove pork from marinade; reserve mari-

CONTINUED

nade. Place roast on spit; cook over low coals for about 3 hours. Cook for 25 minutes longer, basting frequently with marinade. Spread one jar strained apricots over roast. Cook for 5 minutes longer. Heat reserved marinade with remaining strained apricots; serve as sauce over roast. Heat whole apricots and lemon rind together. Remove roast to hot serving platter. Garnish with whole apricots; sprinkle with coconut and parsley. Yield: 6 servings.

Treasured Recipes from Mason, Ohio

Roast Pork with Orange Sauce

If you enjoy roast pork, you may find yourself using this recipe.

1 (4- to 6-pound) loin of pork (if over 6 pounds double the recipe)
Freshly ground pepper
1 small onion, sliced
1 orange, peeled and cut into segments
1/2 cup chopped celery
1 teaspoon oregano (or 1/4 cup fresh)
1 cup orange juice
2 tablespoons balsamic or wine vinegar

Sprinkle the meat with freshly ground pepper. Put it in a roasting pan, fat-side-up. (I use parchment paper, wrapping the meat in it and putting the sauce inside the paper.) Mix the onion, orange, celery, oregano, orange juice, and vinegar; pour over the meat. Baste often with pan juices. Roast at 350° for 25-30 minutes per pound until done. You can also put the meat into aluminum foil and put sauce inside it. Serves 4-6.

Note: I'll bet you did not know that oregano is so easy to grow. Plant a small pot of it and it will outlive you. It is perennial and is wonderful to grow since it requires so little care. You can use it all year round.

Viva Italia

Herb and Onion Pork Tenderloin

1 pound pork tenderloin,
  well-trimmed
2 cups sliced onions,
  separated into rings
2 cloves garlic, minced

1 tablespoon water
1/2 teaspoon rosemary
1/4 teaspoon thyme
1/4 teaspoon salt
1/8 teaspoon pepper

Heat oven to 375°. Spray rack from broiling pan with vegetable oil spray. Cut a lengthwise slit down the center of tenderloin, almost to, but not through the bottom of tenderloin. Open tenderloin so it lies flat (cut-side-down); place on prepared rack. In a medium saucepan, over medium-high heat, sauté onions and garlic in one tablespoon water until tender; stir in seasonings. Spread onion mixture over tenderloin. Bake at 375° for 40 minutes or until meat is done. Yield: 4 servings.

Lifetime Warranty

Glazed Ham Loaves

2 pounds ground fresh pork
2 pounds ground cured ham
2 cups graham cracker
  crumbs
3 eggs
1 cup milk

1 (10-ounce) can tomato soup
1 cup packed brown sugar
1/2 cup vinegar
Dry mustard and cloves to
  taste

Combine ground pork, ground ham, cracker crumbs, eggs, and milk in bowl; mix well. Shape into individual loaves or meatballs. Place in baking pan. Combine soup, brown sugar, vinegar, dry mustard, and cloves in saucepan. Simmer for 5 minutes. Pour over ham loaves. Bake at 350° for 1 1/4 hours. Yield: 12 servings.

The Ohio State Grange Cookbook

Spiced Roast Pork

1 tablespoon spicy brown mustard	3 tablespoons lime juice
1 tablespoon Cajun seasoning	1 (4- to 5-pound) pork loin, tied
2 tablespoons fresh minced sage	4 cloves garlic
	¹/₄ cup hot pepper sauce
	¹/₄ cup Worcestershire sauce

In a bowl, combine the first 4 ingredients. With a sharp, pointed knife, make 4 deep slashes in pork loin and insert garlic cloves. Rub combined mixture all over pork loin. Place in large glass bowl. Add hot pepper sauce and Worcestershire sauce. Cover and marinate in refrigerator overnight.

Preheat oven to 425°. Remove pork from marinade. Reserve marinade. Place pork, fat-side-up, on rack of roasting pan. Roast for 25 minutes. Reduce heat to 350°. Roast for 1¹/₂ - 2 hours or until juices run clear when pierced with fork, basting occasionally with reserved marinade. Remove from oven, cover and let stand 10 minutes before carving.

SAUCE:

¹/₂ cup wine	1 tablespoon paprika
¹/₂ cup water	1 bay leaf
1 tablespoon cornstarch	

In saucepan, add all ingredients. Add 3 tablespoons of pan juices. On medium heat, cook until Sauce is thick, stirring constantly. Remove from heat and discard bay leaf. Set aside. Transfer roast to cutting board. Slice roast. Transfer to flat platter, pour sauce over and serve.

Easy Cooking with Herbs & Spices

Ham Loaf

²/₃ pound ground ham	1 cup milk
1¹/₃ pounds ground pork	¹/₄ teaspoon black pepper
1 cup bread crumbs	2 eggs, unbeaten

Mix together well. Form into one large or 2 smaller loaves. Bake one hour at 350°. Baste frequently with the following glaze.

GLAZE:

¹/₃ cup brown sugar	¹/₄ cup vinegar
1 tablespoon mustard	

A Taste of Toronto—Ohio, that is

Mini Ham Loaves

Your guests will enjoy these.

3 pounds ground ham	2 cups cornflakes, crushed
2 pounds lean ground pork	2 cups milk
4-5 eggs	

RAISIN SAUCE:

2 tablespoons cornstarch	1 1/2 cups brown sugar
1/4 cup cold water	1 tablespoon dry mustard
6 ounce can frozen orange	2 tablespoons cider vinegar
juice concentrate, thawed	1 1/2 cups golden raisins

Mix ham, pork, eggs, cornflake crumbs and milk; shape into small loaves, using about a rounded 1/2 cup of meat mixture. Bake, uncovered, on a greased jelly roll pan at 325° for 30 minutes. Meanwhile, prepare sauce. Dissolve cornstarch in cold water. Combine with the remaining sauce ingredients in a saucepan. Bring to a boil and cook several minutes. Baste ham loaves with raisin sauce; reduce heat to 300° and continue baking for an additional 30 minutes. (For a family-size ham loaf, use half of ingredients. Bake at 300° for 1 1/2 - 2 hours.) You can prepare ahead and bake just before serving.

Angels and Friends Cookbook II

Ham Puff

7 eggs	2 tablespoons minced parsley
4 cups milk	2 1/2 cups grated sharp
1 teaspoon dry mustard	Cheddar
1 (7-ounce) package	3 cups cubed ham
Pepperidge Farm Herb cubed	
stuffing	

Beat eggs, milk, and dry mustard. Stir in stuffing, parsley, cheese, and ham. Pour into oblong glass baking dish. Bake at 325° for one hour, uncovered. Serves 8.

MDA Favorite Recipes

Aunt Effie's Ham on the Grill

1 ham slice, 1-inch thick
1/2 cup ginger ale
1/2 cup orange juice
1/4 cup brown sugar
1 tablespoon salad oil

1 1/2 teaspoons wine vinegar
1 teaspoon dry mustard
1/4 teaspoon ground ginger
1/8 teaspoon ground cloves

Slash fat edge of ham. Combine ingredients and pour over ham in shallow dish. Marinade overnight, spooning over ham several times. Cook over low coals about 15 minutes on each side. Brush frequently with marinade.

A Sprinkling of Favorite Recipes

Canadian Bacon Stack-Ups

1 cup whole cranberry sauce	1 tablespoon butter, melted
2 tablespoons light corn syrup	1 tablespoon brown sugar
1 (1-pound) can sweet	$1/4$ teaspoon ginger
potatoes, drained	1 pound Canadian-style bacon

Combine the cranberry sauce and light corn syrup in a bowl. With electric mixer, beat potatoes with butter, sugar, and ginger till light. Slice bacon into 12 pieces.

In a 10x6-inch baking dish, spread half of potatoes over half of bacon slices. Cover with remaining 6 bacon slices and top each with mound of potatoes. Drizzle cranberry sauce over stacks. Bake at 350° for 45 minutes, basting with sauce. Serves 6.

The Fifth Generation Cookbook

Cakes

Ohio's State Capitol, affectionately called the "Hat Box Capitol" because of its distinctive rotunda. Columbus.

Tom's Palate Pleasing Praline Cheesecake

CRUMB NUT CRUST:

1 cup graham cracker crumbs
1/3 cup finely chopped pecans

6 tablespoons melted butter
1/4 cup granulated sugar

Press into a 9-inch springform pan and bake 10 minutes in a 350°
oven. Cool before filling.

FILLING:

1 1/3 pounds cream cheese
1 cup dark brown sugar
2 tablespoons all-purpose
  flour

3 large eggs
1 teaspoon vanilla extract
1/2 teaspoon dark rum
1/3 cup chopped pecans

Preheat oven to 350°. In a large mixing bowl, beat together cream
cheese, sugar, and flour until smooth. Add eggs, one at a time,
beating thoroughly after each. Add vanilla, rum, and pecans and
blend in. Pour the mixture into the prepared crust and bake for 60
minutes. Turn oven off, open the door, and allow the cake to cool
to room temperature. Chill. Delicioso!

Hats Off to "Real Men Cook" Cookbook

Raspberry Cheesecake

1 1/2 cups vanilla wafer
  crumbs
1/4 cup sugar
1/3 cup butter, melted
1 envelope unflavored gelatin
1/2 cup cold water
1/2 cup boiling water
2 (8-ounce) packages cream
  cheese, softened

1/2 cup sugar
1 teaspoon vanilla
1 jar Robert Rothschild
  Gourmet Red Raspberry
  Sauce
1/4 cup Robert Rothschild
  Seedless Raspberry
  Preserves

Combine crumbs, sugar, and butter. Press into bottom and 1 1/2
inches up side of a 9-inch springform pan. Bake at 350° for 10
minutes; cool. In small bowl sprinkle gelatin over cold water; let
stand 5 minutes. Add boiling water; stir until gelatin dissolves. In
bowl of electric mixer, beat cream cheese, sugar, and vanilla. Gradually add gourmet sauce and gelatin, mixing thoroughly; pour into
crust. Refrigerate overnight. Remove sides of pan. Spread seedless preserves over top. Garnish with whipped cream if desired.
Yield: 10-12 servings.

Robert Rothschild Recipes

Mon Ami Oreo Cookie Cheesecake

CRUST:

1 1/4 cups Oreo cookie   1/4 cup melted butter
crumbs

Mix cookie crumbs with melted butter; press in bottom of 9-inch springform pan and refrigerate 1/2 hour.

FILLING:

2 pounds cream cheese, at   1/3 cup whipping cream
room temperature   2 teaspoons vanilla, divided
1 1/2 cups sugar, divided   1 1/2 cups Oreo cookie
2 tablespoons flour   crumbs
4 extra-large eggs   2 cups sour cream
2 large egg yolks

In large mixer bowl, beat cream cheese until fluffy. Add 1 1/4 cups sugar and flour, then blend in eggs and yolks until smooth. Stir in cream and one teaspoon vanilla. Pour half this mixture into prepared pan, sprinkle with crumbs, and pour in remaining batter. Bake 15 minutes at 425°; reduce temperature to 225° and bake 50 minutes. Cover loosely with foil if browning too quickly. Increase temperature to 350°; blend sour cream, 1/4 cup sugar, and one teaspoon vanilla. Spread over cheesecake and bake 7 minutes. Refrigerate overnight. Top with Glaze and garnish.

GLAZE:

1 cup whipping cream, scalded   1 teaspoon vanilla
8 ounces semi-sweet
chocolate

Combine scalded whipping cream with chocolate and vanilla, and stir one minute. Refrigerate 15 minutes before pouring over chilled cheesecake.

Mon Ami Restaurant and Historic Winery, Port Clinton, Ohio.

Dining in Historic Ohio

Wapakoneta was home to Neil Armstrong, the first man to walk on the moon (July 20, 1969). The Neil Armstrong Air & Space Museum tells the entire thrilling saga through models, real aircraft, photos, film footage and eerie radio transmissions.

Orange Chiffon Cheese Cake

CRUST:

1 cup graham cracker crumbs   ¹/₄ cup melted margarine

Spray a 9-inch spring-form pan with vegetable spray. Blend crust ingredients and press onto bottom of pan. Bake in a 350° oven for 8-10 minutes. Cool.

ORANGE FILLING:

1 cup orange juice
1 envelope unflavored gelatin
12 ounces low-fat cream
  cheese or cream cheese
  alternative
1 cup part skim Ricotta
  cheese
12 packets Equal

1 packet sugar-free dessert
  topping
¹/₂ cup water
2 medium oranges, peeled,
  seeded and chopped
1 orange, peeled and
  sectioned for garnish

Pour orange juice into small pan. Sprinkle gelatin over juice and let soften. Heat, stirring until gelatin dissolves. Blend cream cheese and Ricotta in a large bowl until smooth. Prepare topping according to package directions, using ¹/₂ cup water. Add gelatin to cheese mixture, stirring in Equal. Fold whipped topping into cheese mixture. Stir in chopped oranges. Spoon into prepared crust. Chill 6 hours or overnight. Garnish with orange sections at serving time. Yields 16 servings.

Exchanges: ¹/₂ milk, ¹/₂ fruit, 1¹/₂ fat. Cal 149.

Tried and True Volume II: Diabetic Cookbook

Sauerkraut Chocolate Cake

Yes, you read correctly—sauerkraut cake. This recipe is very old and very wonderful. It probably came into being because some frugal housewife had some extra kraut to use up and tossed it in a cake she was stirring up at the time. The kraut creates a very moist cake, though you will not be able to taste it. If you refrigerate it, be sure to bring it to room temperature before serving.

1 (16-ounce) can sauerkraut, rinsed and well drained
2/3 cup margarine
1 1/2 cups sugar
3 eggs
2 teaspoons vanilla extract
1/2 cup unsweetened cocoa powder

1 teaspoon baking powder
1 teaspoon salt
1 teaspoon baking soda
2 1/4 cups all-purpose flour
1 cup cold water
Quick Chocolate Frosting

Squeeze all excess moisture from the kraut with your hands. Chop it finely with a knife or pulse 4 or 5 times in a food processor bowl; set aside. Preheat the oven to 350°.

In a large mixer bowl, beat the margarine and sugar until fluffy, about 3 minutes. Add the eggs one at a time, mixing well after each addition. Add the vanilla, cocoa, baking powder, salt, and baking soda; blend. Add the flour alternately with the water, beginning and ending with the flour. Fold in the sauerkraut. Pour into a greased 13x9-inch pan and bake for 30 minutes or until the center of the cake springs back when you touch it with your finger. Cool and frost with chocolate frosting. Makes 12-16 servings.

QUICK CHOCOLATE FROSTING:

1/2 cup (1 stick) butter or margarine, softened
4 cups confectioners' sugar
1 egg white
1 teaspoon vanilla extract

Pinch of salt
3 packets premelted unsweetened chocolate, or 3 ounces (3 squares), melted

In a large mixer bowl, combine all the ingredients and beat until thoroughly blended. If the mixture is too thick, add a bit of hot water.

Heartland

Anita's Surprise Chocolate Cake

Dense, dark and delicious.

FILLING:

¹/₄ cup sugar
1 teaspoon vanilla
1 (8-ounce) package cream
  cheese, softened

1 egg
¹/₂ cup shredded coconut
6 ounces chocolate morsels

Preheat oven to 350°. Grease and lightly flour a Bundt or tube pan. Beat sugar, vanilla, cream cheese, and egg until smooth. Stir in coconut and chocolate morsels. Set aside.

CAKE:

2 cups sugar
1 cup corn oil
2 eggs
2 teaspoons baking powder
2 teaspoons baking soda
2 cups all-purpose flour

³/₄ cup unsweetened cocoa
2 teaspoons salt
1 teaspoon vanilla
1 cup buttermilk
1 cup strong coffee
¹/₂ cup chopped walnuts

Beat sugar, oil, and eggs at high speed for one minute. Add remaining cake ingredients, except nuts, and continue beating at medium speed for 3 minutes. Stir in nuts. Batter will be thin. Pour two-thirds of the batter into prepared pan. Spoon the filling mixture over the batter, being careful to keep it away from the walls of the pan.

Pour remaining batter over filling and bake for 55 minutes. Turn oven temperature down to 325° and continue baking an additional 15 minutes. Cool in pan, upright, for approximately 30-45 minutes. Remove from pan and cool on a wire rack.

GLAZE:

1 cup confectioners' sugar
3 tablespoons unsweetened
  cocoa

2 tablespoons butter, softened
2 teaspoons vanilla
1-3 tablespoons hot water

Stir all ingredients to blend and beat at high speed for one minute. Drizzle over cake and serve. Cake can also be frosted. Prepare frosting by doubling the glaze ingredients and using 2-3 tablespoons hot water. Yield: 16 servings.

Five Star Sensations

Passover Chocolate Pudding Cake

CRUST:

1/3 cup unsalted butter	1 1/3 cups matzo crumbs
2 ounces semi-sweet chocolate	1/3 cup sugar

Preheat oven to 350°. Melt butter and chocolate in double boiler stirring until smooth. Mix in crumbs and sugar. Press mixture on bottom and sides of 9-inch spring-form pan. Bake 8 minutes until firm. Refrigerate until well chilled.

FILLING:

9 ounces semi-sweet chocolate, coarsely chopped	6 eggs
11 ounces cream cheese	4 teaspoons vanilla
2/3 cup sugar	1/3 cup whipping cream

Preheat oven to 375°. Melt chocolate in a double boiler, stirring until smooth. Cool slightly. Beat cream cheese and sugar until light and fluffy. Beat in eggs, one at a time. Add vanilla and cream. Beat in chocolate and cream mixture. Pour into crust. Bake until outside is firm and lightly browned but center is still soft when pan is shaken, 30-35 minutes. Refrigerate until well chilled.

TOPPING:

1 1/2 cups whipping cream	1/2 teaspoon vanilla
1/4 cup powdered sugar	

Beat whipping cream, powdered sugar, and vanilla to soft peaks. To serve remove cake from spring-form pan. Spread whipped cream evenly over top. Can be made a day in advance and refrigerated. Don't put on the whipped cream until several hours before serving.

Generation to Generation

Crumb Cake

2 cups flour	1 cup sour milk
1/2 cup shortening	1 teaspoon soda
2 cups brown sugar	1 teaspoon vanilla
1 egg	

Crumb first 3 ingredients as for pie crust. Take out one cup of mixture. Use this for the top of cake. Mix remaining ingredients in bowl. Add to crumb mixture and stir well. Put in a greased and floured cake pan and top with reserved crumbs. Bake at 350° for 30-40 minutes.

Salem Mennonite Cookbook

Wacky Cocoa Cake

3 cups unsifted all-purpose flour	1 teaspoon salt
	2 cups water
2 cups sugar	3/4 cup vegetable oil
1/2 cup Hershey's cocoa	2 tablespoons vinegar
2 teaspoons baking soda	2 teaspoons vanilla extract

Combine flour, sugar, cocoa, baking soda, and salt in large mixer bowl. Add water, oil, vinegar, and vanilla; beat 3 minutes at medium speed until thoroughly blended. Pour batter into a greased and floured 9x13-inch pan. Bake at 350° for 35-40 minutes or until cake tester inserted in center comes out clean. Cool; frost with Smooth'n' Creamy Frosting.

SMOOTH 'N' CREAMY FROSTING:

2 small packages pistachio Jell-O instant pudding	1 cup cold milk
1/4 cup confectioners' sugar	1 (8-ounce) tub Cool Whip, thawed

Combine pudding mix, sugar, and milk in a small bowl. Beat slowly with rotary beater or lowest speed of electric mixer until well blended, about one minute. Fold in whipped topping. Spread on cake at once. Store cake in refrigerator.

Tried and True by Mothers of 2's

A Very Special Rum Cake

A rich, wonderful cake that will make discernible waves. Try it and see.

CAKE:

1 cup chopped walnuts	1/2 cup cold water
1 (18 1/2-ounce) package	1/2 cup vegetable oil
yellow cake mix with pudding	1/2 cup any 80-proof dark rum
3 large eggs	

This cake does well in a (12-cup) Bundt pan, but you can also bake it in a 10-inch tube pan. Grease the pan well, sprinkle flour over it. Spread the chopped nuts over the bottom of pan. Preheat oven to 325°.

Put remaining ingredients in mixing bowl. Beat on medium speed for about 5 minutes or until well blended. Pour the batter over the nuts. Bake for one hour or until a fork comes out dry when cake is pierced near the center. When cake is cool, invert it on a large plate. Prick as many holes in top as you can without ruining the cake.

GLAZE AND TOPPING:

1 stick unsalted butter	1 cup heavy cream
1/4 cup water	3 tablespoons chopped
1 cup sugar	walnuts
1/2 cup 80-proof rum	

Melt butter in small pan, put in water and sugar. Boil for 5 minutes, stirring often. Remove from heat source and stir in rum.

Using a pastry brush, brush tops and sides of cake with mixture. Pour some into the holes you have made in cake. Repeat the procedure, using the liquid that has collected on bottom of plate. Repeat again and again until all the liquid is absorbed by the cake. This cake will taste better if you leave it for some hours to absorb the rum. You can do the next step at the last minute.

Whip the cream. Add sugar if desired, or a bit of rum flavoring. Put it on top of the cake, also in the hole in center. Do this immediately before serving. Put walnuts on top of whipped cream. Serves 8 elegantly.

Viva Italia

Cola Cake

2 cups all-purpose flour
2 cups sugar
2 tablespoons cocoa
1 cup margarine
1 cup cola
1/4 teaspoon salt

1/2 cup buttermilk
1 teaspoon baking soda
1 1/2 cups miniature
   marshmallows
2 eggs
1 teaspoon vanilla

FROSTING:

2 tablespoons cocoa
1/2 cup margarine
6 tablespoons cola

1 pound confectioners' sugar
1 teaspoon vanilla
1 cup chopped nuts

Sift together flour, sugar, and cocoa. Heat margarine and cola to boiling. Pour over dry ingredients and mix well. Do not use mixer. Add salt, buttermilk, soda, marshmallows, eggs, and vanilla; mix well. Pour batter into greased 9x13x2-inch pan. Bake in preheated 350° oven for 30-35 minutes. In small saucepan, combine cocoa, margarine, and cola. Heat to boiling. Pour over confectioners' sugar and mix well. Add vanilla and nuts; blend well. Spread over hot cake.

Treasured Recipes from Mason, Ohio

Lemon Gold Cake

2 1/4 cups sifted cake flour
1 1/2 cups sugar
2 teaspoons baking powder
1 teaspoon salt
1/2 cup salad oil

6 eggs, separated
3/4 cup cold water
2 teaspoons fresh lemon juice
1 teaspoon grated lemon rind
1/2 teaspoon cream of tartar

Sift dry ingredients in large bowl. Add salad oil, egg yolks, water, lemon juice and rind. Beat with spoon until smooth. Add cream of tartar to egg whites and beat until very very stiff. Pour egg yolk mixture gradually over the whipped egg whites, carefully folding with rubber scraper just until blended. Pour into ungreased 10x14-inch tube pan. Bake in moderate oven, 325°, for 70 minutes or until the top springs back when lightly touched. Invert pan to cool. Ice or sprinkle confectioners' sugar over top.

Affolter-Heritage Reunion Cookbook & More

Potica Cake

1 cup oleo
1/2 cup milk
2 packages dry yeast
1/4 cup lukewarm water

2 1/2 cups flour
1/4 teaspoon salt
2 tablespoons sugar
3 egg yolks

Melt and cool oleo and milk. Mix yeast in lukewarm water. Sift flour, salt, and sugar. Stir the egg yolks into the milk mixture. Add this mixture into sifted flour mixture. Add the yeast mixture. Beat well and cover and refrigerate overnight. This dough will be very sticky.

FILLING:

1/2 cup ground nuts
1/2 cup chopped dates or
   raisins
3 tablespoons sugar

1 teaspoon cinnamon
1/4 cup milk
3 egg whites, stiffly beaten
1 cup sugar

Mix to a paste over heat the nuts, dates or raisins, 3 tablespoons sugar, cinnamon, and milk. Cool this mixture. Beat the egg whites until stiff gradually adding one cup sugar. Fold in the filling paste. Roll out 1/2 of the dough into a 20-inch square on well-floured cloth. Spread 1/2 of the filling over dough and roll up as for jelly roll. Put this into a greased angel food cake pan. Roll other half and proceed in same method as above. Place over other roll in pan. You will have 2 layers but the cake becomes one during baking. Bake one hour and 5 minutes at 350°. Sprinkle with powdered sugar or glaze with confectioners' frosting if desired.

Seasoned with Love

Ricotta Cake

1 box yellow cake mix
1 pound ricotta cheese
3/4 cup sugar

2 teaspoons vanilla
3 whole eggs

Mix cake mix as directed on box. Pour into a 9x13-inch pan. Beat in a mixer the ricotta cheese, sugar, vanilla and eggs. Pour over cake mix in pan. Bake at 350° for 30-35 minutes. Sprinkle with powdered sugar. Cool and refrigerate.

Note: Cake bakes and makes a layer of cheese at bottom of cake.

Seasoned with Love

Twinkie Cake

1 box yellow cake mix	1 can Eagle Brand Condensed Milk
1 can cream of coconut	1 (8-ounce) carton Cool Whip

Mix cake and bake as directed in a 9x13-inch baking pan. Remove from oven and while still warm, poke holes (lot of holes) with a fork. Mix together cream of coconut, and Eagle Brand Condensed Milk. Beat well. Pour all over the warm cake and allow to soak in until all mixture is gone. Refrigerate for a few hours until good and cold. Frost with Cool Whip.

A Sprinkling of Favorite Recipes

Aunt Bessie's Oatmeal Cake

1 1/2 cups boiling water	1 teaspoon vanilla
1 cup quick oatmeal	1 1/2 cups flour
1 stick oleo	1 teaspoon cinnamon
1 cup brown sugar	1 teaspoon soda
1 cup white sugar	1/2 teaspoon salt
2 eggs	

Pour boiling water over oatmeal and let stand 20 minutes. In another bowl cream oleo, sugars, vanilla, and eggs. Add flour, soda, cinnamon, and salt. Stir in oats. Spread batter in a greased and floured 9x13-inch pan and bake 45 minutes in a preheated 350° oven.

TOPPING:

1 stick oleo	1/2 cup evaporated milk
1 teaspoon vanilla	1 cup flaked coconut
1 cup brown sugar	1 cup chopped pecans

Melt oleo and add remaining ingredients. Spread over baked cake and return to oven for 10 minutes.

A Matter of Taste

238

Pumpkin Roll

3 eggs
1 cup sugar
2/3 cup unspiced pumpkin
1 teaspoon lemon juice
3/4 cup flour
1 teaspoon baking powder

2 teaspoons cinnamon
1 teaspoon ginger
1/2 teaspoon salt
1/2 teaspoon nutmeg
Chopped nuts (optional)

Beat eggs at high speed for 5 minutes. Gradually add sugar. Stir in pumpkin and lemon juice. Set aside. In separate bowl, stir together flour, baking powder, cinnamon, ginger, salt, and nutmeg. Fold in pumpkin mixture. Line jellyroll pan or 1-inch-deep cookie sheet with waxed paper (or grease and flour it). Spread mixture in this pan, and sprinkle with nuts, if desired. Bake at 375° for 15 minutes. Turn out onto towel sprinkled with powdered sugar; roll up and let cool.

FILLING:
1 cup powdered sugar
4 tablespoons butter
1 (8-ounce) package cream
   cheese

1/2 teaspoon vanilla

Beat ingredients until smooth. Unroll cake, spread on the filling, and roll back up. Chill.

What's Cooking at Holden School

Pumpkin Crunch

1 (29-ounce) can pumpkin
3 eggs
1 cup sugar
1/2 teaspoon salt
1/2 teaspoon lemon juice

1 teaspoon pumpkin pie spice
1 box yellow cake mix
1 cup chopped pecans
3/4 cup melted butter
Cool Whip

Mix until smooth with mixer, pumpkin, eggs, sugar, salt, juice, and spice. Spread in well-greased 13x9x2-inch pan. Spread cake mix evenly over top of pumpkin mixture. Sprinkle with chopped nuts and drizzle melted butter on top. Bake at 350° for 50 minutes. Cut in squares and serve with Cool Whip.

Oeder Family & Friends Cookbook

Moravian Sugar Cake

1 small potato, peeled and cubed	3 - 3½ cups all-purpose flour
1 package active dry yeast	2 tablespoons butter
⅓ cup granulated sugar	½ cup brown sugar
⅓ cup lard, melted	½ teaspoon cinnamom
1½ teaspoons salt	1 tablespoon cream or milk

Cook potato in one cup of water until tender. Set aside ¼ cup cooking liquid. Mash potato in remaining water, adding water, if needed, to make one cup potato mixture. Soften yeast in reserved cooking liquid. Combine potato mixture, yeast mixture, sugar, lard and salt. Mix well. Stir in one cup flour, beat well. Let rise in warm place until spongy, 30-45 minutes. Stir down. Add enough remaining flour to make a soft dough. Turn out on floured surface, knead lightly about 4 minutes. Shape into a ball.

Place in lightly greased bowl. Turn once. Cover, let rise in warm place until double (about 45 minutes). Punch down. Turn out on floured surface. Divide in half. Cover, let rest 10 minutes. Roll into 2 (8-inch) squares. Pat into 2 (8x8x2-inch) baking pans. Cover, let rise in warm place until double (about 45 minutes). With finger make indentations in top at 1½-inch intervals. Dot with butter. Top with mixture of brown sugar and cinnamon. Drizzle with about one tablespoon of cream or milk. Bake at 375° till golden brown, 20-25 minutes.

NOTE: Can use Crisco instead of lard.

Affolter-Heritage Reunion Cookbook & More

Spice Cake with Cream Cheese Frosting

2 cups sifted flour
1 tablespoon cinnamon
1/2 teaspoon baking powder
2 teaspoons baking soda
1/2 teaspoon salt
1 cup granulated sugar

1 cup packed brown sugar
1 cup vegetable oil
1 teaspoon vanilla
3 eggs
2 cups shredded zucchini
1 cup chopped walnuts

Into a large bowl, sift first 5 ingredients; set aside. In another large bowl, using mixer at high speed, beat sugars, oil, vanilla, and eggs until well blended. Reduce speed to low and beat in dry ingredients and zucchini. Add walnuts. Bake in a greased 13x9x2-inch pan at 350° for 45 minutes or until center is fully cooked. Cool completely in pan on rack. Frost top of cake with Cream Cheese Frosting. Serves 16.

CREAM CHEESE FROSTING:

1/2 (8-ounce) package cream
  cheese softened
1/3 cup butter, softened

3 cups sifted confectioners'
  sugar
1 teaspoon vanilla

In bowl, using mixer at low speed, beat until creamy. Makes 1 1/2 cups.

500 Recipes Using Zucchini

Apricot Nectar Cake

CAKE:

1 (18 1/2-ounce) box yellow
  cake mix
4 eggs

3/4 cup oil
3/4 cup apricot nectar
3 teaspoons lemon extract

LEMON GLAZE:

1 1/2 cups powdered sugar

2 lemons, juiced, rind grated

Preheat oven to 325°. In a medium mixing bowl, combine cake mix, eggs, oil, apricot nectar, and lemon extract. Beat with electric mixer at medium speed for 4 minutes. Pour into a greased and floured 9-inch tube or Bundt pan. Bake for 55 minutes. Let stand 5 minutes. Turn out onto a serving dish. Prick holes in cake with an ice pick or skewer. Prepare Lemon Glaze and spread over warm cake. Yield: 14 servings.

Cooking on the Wild Side

Coconut-Nut-Wafer Cake

2 sticks butter or oleo
2 cups sugar
6 whole eggs
1 (12-ounce) box vanilla
   wafers, crushed

1/2 cup milk
7 ounces flaked coconut
1 cup chopped nuts (pecans)

Cream butter and sugar. Add eggs, one at a time. Beat after each egg. Add crushed wafers alternately with milk. Add coconut and nuts. Bake in greased and floured tube pan one hour 15 minutes at 325°. Let cake cool before removal from pan. Very moist.

Gardener's Delight

Janet's Honey Cake

1 stick margarine or butter
1 cup sugar
3 eggs
1 cup honey
3 cups flour
2 teaspoons baking soda

1 cup orange juice
1 peeled apple, grated
1/2 cup chopped dates
1/2 cup chopped nuts
1/2 cup apricot preserves

Cream margarine, sugar, and eggs, add honey. Mix well. Add dry ingredients, alternating with orange juice. Fold in the apple, dates, nuts, and preserves. Pour into a greased Bundt pan and bake at 350° for one hour.

Generation to Generation

Rhubarb Crunch Cake

This moist cake is delicious as is or can be served with a topping of whipped cream or ice cream. If fresh rhubarb is not available, frozen works well too.

CAKE:

2 cups rhubarb, cut into
  1/2-inch pieces
2 tablespoons flour
1 1/2 cups sugar
1/2 cup solid vegetable
  shortening

1 egg
2 cups flour
1 teaspoon baking soda
1/2 teaspoon salt
1 cup buttermilk
1 teaspoon vanilla

Preheat oven to 350°. In medium bowl, combine rhubarb and 2 tablespoons flour; toss gently until rhubarb is lightly coated. In large mixer bowl, combine sugar and shortening; beat well. Add egg; beat well. Sift together 2 cups flour, baking soda, and salt; add alternately with buttermilk, stir well. Add vanilla and rhubarb. Turn into greased 13x9-inch pan.

TOPPING:

3/4 cup sugar
1 teaspoon ground cinnamon

1/4 cup butter or margarine,
  softened

In small bowl, combine topping ingredients; mix until crumbly. Sprinkle evenly over cake. Bake 35-40 minutes or until cake springs back when touched lightly with finger.

Bountiful Ohio

Rhubarb Surprise

8 cups rhubarb, chopped
1/2 cup butter
3 cups sugar, divided
1 1/2 cups flour
1/2 teaspoon salt

1 1/2 teaspoons baking
  powder
1/2 cup milk
2 tablespoons cornstarch
1 cup boiling water

Spread 8 cups chopped rhubarb evenly in a 9x13-inch greased pan. Cream the butter, 1 1/2 cups of the sugar, flour, salt, and baking powder alternately with milk. Spread mixture over rhubarb. Combine remaining sugar (1 1/2 cups) and cornstarch. Sprinkle evenly over batter. Pour one cup boiling water evenly over all. Bake for one hour at 375°.

Heavenly Dishes

Pineapple Cheese Torte

PAT-IN-THE-PAN-CRUST:

1/3 cup butter or margarine
1 cup flour
1 1/4 cups powdered sugar

1/4 cup finely chopped
  almonds

Combine crust ingredients; pat into the bottom of a 12x8x2-inch baking dish. Bake at 350° for 20 minutes.

FILLING:

2 (8-ounce) packages cream
  cheese
1/2 cup sugar

2 eggs
2/3 cup unsweetened
  pineapple juice

Beat cream cheese in bowl until fluffy. Beat in sugar and eggs. Stir in juice. Pour filling over crust. Bake at 350° for 20 minutes or until center is set. Cool.

PINEAPPLE TOPPING:

1/4 cup flour
1/4 cup sugar
1 (20-ounce) can crushed
  pineapple, drained, save juice

1/2 cup whipping cream

Combine flour and sugar in a saucepan. Stir in one cup of reserved pineapple juice. Bring to boil, stirring constantly. Boil and stir one minute. Remove from heat; fold in pineapple. Cool. Whip cream until stiff peaks form; fold into topping. Spread carefully over dessert. Refrigerate 6 hours or overnight. Garnish with strawberries if desired. Yield: 12-16 servings.

Favorite Recipes

The most accurate representation of Christopher Columbus's flagship, the Santa Maria, can be seen at its mooring on the Scioto River in downtown Columbus. Costumed guides explain the life and hardships of the 15th-century sailors who explored uncharted waters half a world away from home.

Pineapple Delight Cake

1 box yellow cake mix
1/2 cup oil
4 eggs
1 can mandarin oranges
1 large can crushed pineapple
2 tablespoons cornstarch
1/4 cup sugar
2 boxes instant vanilla
  pudding

1 cup whipping cream
1 cup water
2 cups granulated sugar
1 1/2 cups Crisco
2 sticks butter or margarine
Coconut (optional)

Mix cake mix, oil, eggs, and mandarin oranges together and bake in 2 (10-inch) pans at 350° for 30 minutes. Remove from oven and cool, then split and make 4 layers.

Combine crushed pineapple, cornstarch, and 1/4 cup sugar and cook on medium heat until thickened. Cool.

Mix pudding, cream, and water until thick. Mix sugar, Crisco, and butter until smooth, then add to pudding mixture.

Put pineapple mixture on all 4 layers of cake. Top with pudding mixture. Garnish with coconut if desired.

Home Cookin' with 4-H

Carrot Cake

The pineapple makes it moist.

4 large eggs	2 cups sugar
1½ cups salad oil	1 (8⅓-ounce) can crushed
2 cups flour	pineapple in juice, drained
2 teaspoons baking soda	2 cups (packed) peeled and
2 teaspoons baking powder	shredded carrots
1½ teaspoons salt	½ cup chopped nuts
2 teaspoons cinnamon	

Place eggs and oil in mixing bowl and blend well. Sift together flour, soda, baking powder, salt, cinnamon, and sugar. Add to egg mixture and blend thoroughly. Add pineapple, carrots, and nuts. Mix well. Pour into greased 13x9-inch pan. Bake at 350° for 35-40 minutes. Allow to cool.

FROSTING:

½ cup margarine	1 teaspoon vanilla
1 (8-ounce) package cream	1 (1-pound) box
cheese, softened	confectioners' sugar

Cream together margarine, cream cheese, and vanilla. Add sugar and beat well. Frost cake and refrigerate for 2 days before serving. Serves 24.

Chef Jim Girvis, French Loaf.

A Taste of Columbus Vol IV

Orange Carrot Cake

1 cup soft butter
2 cups sugar
1 teaspoon cinnamon
1/2 teaspoon nutmeg
1 tablespoon grated orange
   rind
4 eggs

1 1/2 cups grated carrots
2/3 cup chopped walnuts or
   pecans
3 cups sifted all-purpose flour
3 teaspoons baking powder
1/2 teaspoon salt
1/3 cup orange juice

In large bowl cream butter and sugar. Add cinnamon, nutmeg, and orange rind. Beat in eggs, one at a time. Add carrots and nuts. Sift together flour, baking powder and salt; add alternately with the orange juice. Turn into a greased and floured 10-inch tube pan. Bake at 350° for 60-65 minutes, until tester comes out clean. Cool in pan 15 minutes. Turn out and cool completely on wire rack.

ORANGE GLAZE:

1 1/2 cups sifted
   confectioners' sugar
1 tablespoon soft butter

1/2 teaspoon grated orange
   rind
2-3 tablespoons orange juice

In small bowl, mix above ingredients and add enough juice to make a slightly runny glaze. Pour over cake.

Women's Centennial Cookbook

Microwave Pineapple and Apple Dump Cake

1 (20-ounce) can crushed
   pineapple, drained
1 (20-ounce) can apple pie
   filling

1 (18.5-ounce) box yellow
   pudding cake mix
1 cup chopped nuts
2 sticks melted margarine

Grease 9x13-inch dish. Spread pineapple in bottom and top with apple filling. Sprinkle with cake mix and level. Sprinkle with nuts. Pour melted margarine over all. Microwave uncovered at HIGH 15-16 minutes. Oven method: Bake at 350° for 40-45 minutes. A lemon mix also tastes good in this recipe.

Appletizers

Bavarian Apple Torte

1/2 cup softened butter or
  margarine
1/3 cup sugar
1/4 teaspoon vanilla

1 cup flour
Cream Cheese Filling and
  Apple Topping
1/2 cup chopped pecans

CREAM CHEESE FILLING:
1 (8-ounce) package cream
  cheese
1/4 cup sugar

1 egg
1/2 teaspoon vanilla

APPLE TOPPING:
4 cups peeled, cored and
  sliced apples
1/2 cup sugar

1/2 teaspoon ground
  cinnamon

Cream butter and sugar in a small mixing bowl. Stir in vanilla. Add flour and mix well. Spread in bottom and 2 inches up the sides of a greased 9-inch spring-form pan. Spread Cream Cheese Filling evenly over pastry. Spoon Apple Topping over filling. Sprinkle with nuts (may be added during last 10 minutes to avoid burning). Bake at 450° for 10 minutes. Reduce temperature to 400° and bake for 25 minutes. Cool before removing from pan.

25th Anniversary Cookbook

Apricot Rum Torte

A dessert that's worth the extra effort.

1 cup flour, sifted
1 teaspoon baking powder,
  sifted
1/4 teaspoon salt, sifted
1/2 cup milk

1 tablespoon butter
2 eggs
1 cup sugar
1 teaspoon rum

Sift together flour, baking powder, and salt. Set aside. In a small saucepan, heat milk and butter until melted. Beat eggs in medium bowl with mixer until light and fluffy. Beat in sugar and rum until well blended. Stir in milk mixture, then fold in dry ingredients. Generously grease and flour 2 (8- or 9-inch) cake pans. Pour batter into pans, dividing evenly. Bake in a preheated 350° oven for 35 minutes or until top springs back. Loosen cake around edges. Turn onto racks to cool slightly. Meanwhile, prepare Coffee Rum Syrup.

CONTINUED

COFFEE RUM SYRUP:

1 cup sugar
1 cup extra-strong black
  coffee

¹/₄ cup rum

Combine sugar and coffee in a saucepan over low heat. Stir. Once sugar is dissolved, raise heat and bring to boil for 3 minutes. Add rum. Spoon warm syrup slowly over tops of warm cakes until most is absorbed. (Put cakes on plates or wax paper as some syrup will gather under cakes.) Chill cakes and prepare Pastry Cream.

PASTRY CREAM:

¹/₃ cup sugar
¹/₄ cup flour
¹/₈ teaspoon salt
1 cup milk
2 egg yolks

1 tablespoon rum
¹/₂ cup apricot preserves
1 cup whipping cream,
  whipped stiff
Chopped pecans (optional)

Combine sugar, flour, and salt in small saucepan. Gradually stir in one cup milk. Cook, stirring constantly, over low heat until mixture thickens. Lightly beat 2 egg yolks in a small bowl. Pour small amount of hot mixture into yolks, blend well; pour yolk mixture into saucepan with milk and flour mixture. Cook 3 minutes, stirring constantly. Add rum. Press a piece of wax paper over cream surface and chill thoroughly in refrigerator. When cream mixture is chilled, split each cake layer in half horizontally. Makes 4 cake layers. Place layer on serving plate. Add layer of pastry cream and continue to alternate cake and cream ending with final cake layer.

Spread apricot preserves over top of cake. Frost sides with whipped cream and pipe a whipped cream lattice over top. Press chopped pecans on side, if desired. Chill well before serving. Yield: 10 servings.

Note: May be prepared early in the day and assembled except for whipped cream topping. Refrigerate covered until time to frost.

Simply Sensational

Ohio has some strange laws: In Columbus, it is illegal for stores to sell cornflakes on Sunday. In Cleveland, women are forbidden to wear patent leather shoes, lest men see reflections of their underwear. In Oxford, it is illegal for a woman to disrobe in front of a man's picture. In Youngstown, it is illegal to run out of gas.

Chocolate Raspberry Torte

1 (18-ounce) package devil's food cake mix with pudding	1 cup Robert Rothschild Seedless Raspberry Preserves, divided
1 (8-ounce) package cream cheese, softened	
1 (7-ounce) jar marshmallow cream	

Prepare cake according to package directions. Pour into greased and floured 15x10-inch jelly roll pan; bake for 18-20 minutes. Cool. Remove from pan and cut into thirds. Combine cream cheese, marshmallow cream and 3/4 cup raspberry preserves. Place one 1/3 of cake on serving platter, spread with 1/3 of filling. Repeat with remaining cake and filling. Heat remaining 1/4 cup raspberry jam and drizzle over top. Chill for at least 4 hours.

Robert Rothschild Recipes

Mary Yoder's Date Pudding or Amish Wedding Cake

1 cup sugar	1 teaspoon baking powder
2 tablespoons butter or oleo	1 teaspoon vanilla
1 egg	1 cup dates, chopped
1/2 cup milk	1 cup walnuts, chopped
1 cup flour	

SAUCE:

1 cup brown sugar	1 cup water
1 stick oleo	1 tablespoon cornstarch
1 egg	

Mix the cake ingredients and bake in a 13x9x2-inch baking pan at 350° for 35 minutes. Cook the sauce ingredients until thick. Pour over cake.

Mary Yoder's Amish Kitchen Cookbook

 Before and during the Civil War, Ohioans successfully conducted 50,000 to 75,000 fugitive slaves through Ohio on the Underground Railroad guiding them to Canada. In Northern Ohio, the town of Oberlin was a haven for fugitive slaves. Abolitionist Rev. John Bardwell's home has sliding panels behind closet walls opening into passageways which hid fugitives. At Monteith Hall in Elyria, there's a tunnel extending from the basement floor to the Black River.

Ice Cream Cake Roll

1/2 cup cake flour	2 squares unsweetened
1/2 teaspoon baking powder	chocolate
1/4 teaspoon salt	2 tablespoons sugar
4 eggs, room temperature	1/4 teaspoon baking soda
3/4 cup sugar	3 tablespoons cold water
1 teaspoon vanilla	1 quart ice cream

Sift flour, baking powder, and salt 3 times. Place eggs in deep bowl and gradually add 3/4 cup sugar while beating mixture. Continue beating until thick and lemon-colored. Add flour mixture all at once; stir until well blended, and add vanilla.

Melt chocolate, remove from heat and immediately add 2 tablespoons sugar, soda, and water. Stir until thick and light. Fold quickly into batter. Blend well. Turn into a greased, oblong 15x10x1-inch pan that has been lined with wax paper and greased again. Bake at 375° for 15 minutes. Remove immediately and turn out on a clean towel sprinkled with powdered sugar. Roll up cake gently in towel and let cool on cake rack. When cool, unroll and spread with ice cream which has been softened. Roll as for a jelly roll. Package and freeze until ready to serve.

Salem Mennonite Cookbook

Mother's Birthday Torte

A real beauty! This torte can be made with any seasonal fruit.

9 egg whites
³/₄ teaspoon cream of tartar
¹/₈ teaspoon salt
3 cups sugar
2¹/₂ teaspoons vanilla,
  divided

1¹/₂ teaspoons white vinegar
4 cups (2 pints) heavy cream
1 pint strawberries

Preheat oven to 325°. Lightly grease 2 (9-inch) cake pans with cutters or line pan with parchment paper.

Beat egg whites, cream of tartar, and salt until very stiff. Slowly add sugar, 1¹/₂ teaspoons vanilla, and vinegar and continue beating. Divide batter into cake pans. Bake for 60 minutes. Let cool in pans for 5 minutes; remove and cool completely.

To assemble torte, whip cream and one teaspoon vanilla. Slice one-third of the strawberries. Place one cooled meringue on a serving plate, trimming, if necessary, to fit. Cover with about 1¹/₂ cups whipped cream and sliced strawberries. Invert second meringue, place on top of first and trim. Ice the top and sides with the remaining whipped cream, arrange whole strawberries on top and refrigerate. Yield: 8-10 servings.

Note: To avoid crystallizing, leave meringue in cool oven for 2-3 hours after baking.

Five Star Sensations

With an incredible 56 rides, Cedar Point, on the tip of Sandusky Bay, is the nation's largest amusement ride park. It includes four vintage carousels and eleven roller coasters—the largest array anywhere in the world. "The Raptor" took roller coaster technology to new heights. This inverted roller coaster is the tallest, fastest and steepest scream machine in the world. Cedar Point is aptly nicknamed "The Thrill Capitol."

Cookies and Candies

"The Magnum XL200," one of the many innovative roller coasters at Cedar Point. Sandusky Bay.

Kahlua-Filled Cookie Cups

1/3 cup sugar
1/2 cup butter, softened
1/2 teaspoon vanilla extract
1/8 teaspoon almond extract

1 egg yolk
1 cup flour
Dash of salt

FILLING:

2 tablespoons unsweetened
    cocoa
1/2 cup butter, softened
1 cup powdered sugar

2 tablespoons coffee liqueur
    (Kahlua)
Grated chocolate

Heat oven to 350°. Grease 24 miniature muffin cups. Beat sugar and butter until fluffy. Add vanilla, almond and egg yolk. Blend well. Stir in flour and salt. Mix well. Chill one hour. Place 2 teaspoons dough into muffin cups and press up sides to form shell. Bake 10-15 minutes.

Carefully remove from cups. Cool. In small bowl, beat cocoa and butter until fluffy. Add powdered sugar and liqueur. Blend well. Spoon filling into pastry bag and pipe into cookie cups. Sprinkle with grated chocolate.

A Sprinkling of Favorite Recipes

Dynamite Chocolate Chip Cookies

1 cup butter, unsalted
1 cup granulated sugar
1/2 cup brown sugar
2 eggs
2 teaspoons vanilla
2 cups flour

1 1/2 teaspoons salt
1 teaspoon soda
1 (12-ounce) package
    semi-sweet chocolate bits
1 cup raisins
1/2 cup coconut

Cream together butter, sugars, eggs, and vanilla until light and fluffy. Stir in dry ingredients. Blend well.

Add chocolate chips, raisins, and coconut. Grease cookie sheet, drop by teaspoon and bake at 325° for 8 minutes. Yield: 3 dozen medium cookies.

The Kettle Cookbook

Chocolate-Covered Cherry Cookies

1 1/2 cups flour
1/2 cup cocoa
1/4 teaspoon salt
1/4 teaspoon baking powder
1/4 teaspoon baking soda
1/2 cup softened oleo
1 cup sugar

1 egg
1 1/2 teaspoons vanilla
10 ounces maraschino
 cherries
1 (6-ounce) package
 semi-sweet chocolate chips
1/2 cup Eagle Brand Milk

Sift together flour, cocoa, salt, baking powder, and baking soda. Beat together oleo and sugar until fluffy. Add egg and vanilla; beat well. Add dry ingredients and beat until well blended. Shape dough into 1-inch balls. Place on ungreased cookie sheet. Press down center of dough with thumb. Drain cherries; reserve juice. Place a cherry in the center of each cookie.

In a small saucepan combine chocolate chip pieces and Eagle Brand Milk. On very low heat, heat until chocolate is melted. Stir in 4 teaspoons cherry juice. Spoon about one teaspoon frosting over each cherry, spreading to cover cherry (frosting may be thinned with more juice).

Bake in 350° oven about 10 minutes or until done. Remove to wire rack to cool. Makes about 4 dozen.

Treasures and Pleasures

Millionaire's Shortbread

BASE:

1 1/2 sticks butter, NOT
   margarine, softened
3/4 cup sugar

1 2/3 cups all-purpose flour
1/2 cup cornstarch
1 teaspoon baking powder

Preheat oven to 350°. Cream together butter and sugar till light and fluffy. Sift together flour, cornstarch and baking powder; beat into the butter mixture. Spread in a 13x9x2-inch baking pan and smooth top. Bake for 20 minutes or until golden brown. Cool for 10 minutes while you make caramel.

CARAMEL:

3/4 cup sugar
1 1/2 sticks butter, NOT
   margarine
1 tablespoon corn syrup or
   honey

1 (14-ounce) can condensed
   milk
Few drops vanilla

Put all caramel ingredients, except vanilla, into a heavy-bottomed saucepan. Over medium heat, stir until butter melts and sugar is dissolved completely. Bring to boil and boil for 5-7 minutes, watching carefully, stirring constantly. Remove pan from heat, stir in vanilla and continue stirring 2-3 minutes to cool slightly. Pour over shortbread layer; leave to cool completely.

TOP LAYER:

6 squares semi-sweet
   chocolate or

6 ounces semi-sweet
   chocolate chips

Melt chocolate, pour over cooled caramel layer; move pan from side to side to completely cover area. Leave to cool then cut into squares with a sharp knife. Store, covered, in refrigerator.

Plain & Fancy Favorites

Nut Squares

1 stick butter
2 cups Oreo crumbs (NOT
  ready-made crumbs)
1/2-1 cup coconut
2 cups (or more) chocolate
  chips
1 package brickle chips

1 can sweetened condensed
  milk
2-3 cups coarsely chopped
  mixed nuts (any combination
  of pecans, walnuts, almonds,
  hazelnuts or macadamia nuts)

Preheat oven to 350°. Line a 9x13-inch pan with foil. Melt butter in lined pan, swirl butter evenly in pan and brush on sides. Sprinkle Oreo crumbs evenly in pan and press down. Layer coconut, chocolate chips, and brickle chips one at a time evenly over crumbs. Pour on condensed milk. Completely cover top with nuts to make one even layer. Press down lightly. Bake 10 minutes and while still in oven, press down with spatula. Continue baking for another 20-30 minutes or until caramel between nuts is golden in color. Remove from oven and allow to cool. When very cool, unmold from pan onto cutting board. Cover and let sit overnight. Cut in small squares. Wrap well to keep at room temperature for serving, or cover with plastic wrap or foil to freeze.

Plain & Fancy Favorites

Triple Treat Cookies

1 cup white sugar
1 cup oleo, softened
2 eggs
1 teaspoon vanilla
3 cups flour

1 cup brown sugar
1 cup peanut butter
2 teaspoons soda
1 1/2 teaspoons salt
1 1/2 cups chocolate chips

Combine ingredients and roll dough into balls. Bake on greased cookie sheets about 10 minutes at 350°. Combine filling ingredients and put between 2 cookies.

FILLING:
1/2 cup peanut butter
1/3 cup milk

1 teaspoon vanilla
3 cups powdered sugar

Favorite Recipes from the Heart of Amish Country

Maple Creams

1 cup shortening	2 eggs
1 teaspoon vanilla	3³/4 cups flour
1/2 teaspoon maple flavoring	2 teaspoons baking soda
2 cups brown sugar	1 cup sour cream

Cream together shortening, vanilla, maple flavoring, brown sugar, and eggs. In a separate bowl, stir flour and soda together; add to creamed mixture, alternately with sour cream. Drop onto greased cookie sheets and bake at 350° until brown; do not underbake.

ICING:

6 tablespoons butter	1/2 cup evaporated milk
1 teaspoon maple flavoring	Confectioners' sugar

Melt butter and cool to room temperature; stir in maple flavoring and milk. Stir in confectioners' sugar until icing is thick enough. Frost cooled cookies with a thick layer of icing.

The Fifth Generation Cookbook

Rain Forest Cookies
(Gingersnaps)

1 cup granulated sugar	1/2 teaspoon salt
3/4 cup shortening	1 teaspoon cinnamon
1/4 cup molasses	1/2 teaspoon cloves
1 egg	1/4 teaspoon nutmeg
2 cups flour	1 1/2 teaspoons ginger
1 1/2 teaspoons soda	1/2 cup sugar

Cream one cup granulated sugar and shortening together until light and fluffy. Add molasses and beaten egg. Beat thoroughly. Sift flour with soda, salt, and spices. Add creamed mixture. Blend together carefully so that all ingredients are well-mixed.

Roll small portions of dough between palms of hands into small balls, about the size of walnuts. Roll balls in 1/2 cup sugar. Place 2 inches apart on greased cookie sheet. Bake at 375° for 15 minutes. The cookies flatten out as they bake.

When they are baked, remove at once from cookie sheet. Makes 5 dozen.

Our Collection of Heavenly Recipes

Old-Fashioned Sugar Cookies

As tender as love, and that's what they are made of, along with the essentials that make a rich cookie. Eight dozen? You'll make a double batch of these the next time. Grace Robinson often brought these mouth-watering cookies for office birthday celebrations at The Blade.

1 cup butter	2 eggs
1 cup vegetable oil	1 teaspoon baking soda
1 cup granulated sugar	4 cups flour
1 cup powdered sugar	1 teaspoon cream of tartar
1 teaspoon vanilla	1 teaspoon salt

Thoroughly cream butter, vegetable oil, and both sugars. Add vanilla and eggs; beat well. Sift dry ingredients; stir in and blend.

Roll a teaspoon of dough into a small ball. Place on a lightly greased cookie sheet and press down with the bottom of a glass tumbler which has been dipped in sugar. Repeat with remaining dough. Bake 12 minutes in 375° oven.

Aren't You Going to Taste It, Honey?

Golden Sugar Cookies

Of all the cookies we made, this sugar cookie was the most popular. It is a handsome cookie and stays soft.

2¹/₂ cups flour	¹/₂ teaspoon vanilla
1 teaspoon baking soda	¹/₂ teaspoon lemon flavoring
1 teaspoon cream of tartar	2 cups sugar
¹/₄ teaspoon salt	3 egg yolks
1 cup butter	

Sift the first 4 ingredients together and set aside. Cream butter and extracts; gradually add the sugar, creaming until fluffy after each addition. Add the egg yolks, one at a time. Add the dry ingredients in fourths to the creamed mixture; beat just until blended after each addition. Form dough into 1-inch balls and place 2 inches apart on cookie sheet. Bake at 350° for 10 minutes.

Heirloom Recipes and By Gone Days

Vinegar Cookies

2 sticks (1 cup) margarine, softened	2 cups flour
	1/2 teaspoon baking soda
1 cup sugar	1 teaspoon vinegar

Cream margarine and sugar; mix in flour, soda, and vinegar. Make small balls out of dough, place onto greased cookie sheets and flatten with a fork or small wooden mallet. Bake 8-10 minutes at 350°. Makes 3 1/2 dozen.

Cooking with Class

Biscotti Regina/The Twice-Baked Queen

Despite the name, these cookies are baked only once.

3 cups flour	3/4 cup sugar
3 teaspoons baking powder	3 eggs
1/2 teaspoon salt	1 teaspoon vanilla
1 stick sweet butter (or margarine)	1/2 pound sesame seeds

Combine flour, baking powder, and salt; set aside. Cream the butter and sugar. Add eggs and vanilla to creamed mixture. Mix with flour until a soft dough is formed. Take small pieces of dough and shape to size of small fingers. Dampen the palm of your hand with milk and roll shaped dough on your palm just enough to moisten. Roll the dough into a bowl in which you have put the sesame seeds. Bake on an ungreased cookie sheet about 1/2-inch apart at 400° for 20 minutes or until golden brown. Makes about 65-75 cookies.

Viva Italia

Lemon Drop Cookies

1 box lemon supreme cake mix	1 small carton Cool Whip, soft
	Powdered sugar
2 eggs	

Mix above together. Drop by teaspoon into powdered sugar. Make into small balls. Place on greased cookie sheet. Bake 10-12 minutes at 350°. (Try strawberry or chocolate cake mix.) M-M-M good!

Recipes & Remembrances

Raisin-Filled Cookies

DOUGH:

2 cups sugar
1 cup shortening
2 eggs
5-5½ cups flour
1 teaspoon soda

4 teaspoons baking powder
Pinch of salt
1 cup sweet milk
1 teaspoon vanilla

Cream sugar and shortening; add unbeaten eggs. Sift flour, soda, baking powder and salt together. Add to creamed mixture alternately with milk. Add vanilla. Roll out and cut. Place teaspoon of filling on circle of dough. Cover with another circle of dough. Pinch edges together. Place on cookie sheet, and bake at 350° for 10-15 minutes or until lightly brown.

FILLING:

1 box raisins (ground)
1 cup sugar
3 tablespoons cornstarch

1 cup water
Pinch of salt

Combine, and cook until thick. Cool before using.

A Taste of Toronto—Ohio, that is

Orange Pecan Delights

¾ cup butter
1 cup brown sugar, packed
½ cup sugar
2 eggs, unbeaten
1 tablespoon grated orange
   rind

½ cup sour cream
3 cups flour
2 teaspoons baking powder
½ teaspoon soda
1 cup chopped pecans

Cream butter and sugars. Add eggs and rind and beat well. Stir in the sour cream and blend in the sifted dry ingredients gradually. Add the nuts and drop in rounded teaspoonfuls on greased baking sheet. Bake at 375° for 12 minutes. Ice with following Orange Icing.

ORANGE ICING:

2 cups sifted powdered sugar
2 teaspoons grated orange
   rind

⅛ teaspoon salt
2-3 tablespoons orange juice

Mix until of spreading consistency.

Women's Centennial Cookbook

Pineapple-Apricot Cookies

1 can crushed pineapple	6 cups flour
1 can apricots	1 teaspoon salt
1 cup sugar	1 cake yeast, crumbled
1 cup shortening	2 cups sour cream
1 cup butter or margarine	3 egg yolks

Combine pineapple, apricots, and sugar in saucepan. Cook until thickened, stirring frequently; cool. Cut shortening and butter into flour and salt in bowl. Combine yeast with sour cream and egg yolks in bowl; mix well. Add to crumb mixture; mix well. Chill for 3 hours to overnight. Roll on sugared surface; cut into 3-inch squares. Spoon fruit filling into centers of squares; bring up edges to enclose filling and seal. Place on cookie sheet. Bake at 350° for 10-12 minutes or until golden brown. Remove to wire rack to cool. Yield: 5 dozen.

The Ohio State Grange Cookbook

Whoopie Pies

COOKIE:

1/2 cup salad oil	2 cups flour
1 cup sugar	1 1/2 teaspoons baking soda
1/2 cup cocoa	1/2 teaspoon salt
1 cup milk	1 teaspoon vanilla
1 egg	

Mix ingredients in order given and beat until well mixed. Drop on ungreased cookie sheet from a tablespoon. Bake for 7-10 minutes in a 375° oven or until done. Yield: 40 cookies. Spread filling between 2 cookies.

FILLING:

1 cup milk	1 cup Crisco
4 tablespoons flour or 2	1 cup sugar
tablespoons cornstarch	1 teaspoon vanilla
1/2 cup oleo	1/4 teaspoon salt

Cook milk and flour (cornstarch) together. This will be very thick. Cool completely. Cream together the oleo, Crisco, and sugar. Add vanilla and salt. Add cooled, cooked mixture and beat with electric mixer on high speed for at least 5 minutes. Will be very creamy.

By Our Cookstove

Bravo Brownies

1/2 cup vegetable oil
6 tablespoons cocoa
1 beaten egg
1 cup sugar
1 1/4 cups flour

1/2 teaspoon baking soda
1/2 teaspoon salt
1 teaspoon vanilla
3/4 cup orange juice
1 cup chocolate chips

Combine all ingredients except chocolate chips and beat until smooth. Stir in chocolate chips. Bake at 350° in greased 9x9-inch pan for 30 minutes. Done when toothpick inserted in center comes out clean. Cut after cool. Serves 9-12.

Heavenly Food II

Hershey's Syrup Brownies

1/2 cup oleo
1 cup sugar
4 eggs
1 (1-pound) can Hershey's
   syrup

1 cup plus 1 heaping
   tablespoon flour
Chopped nuts (optional)

Beat oleo and sugar until light and fluffy. Add eggs, syrup, and flour. Mix and add chopped nuts if desired. Bake in 9x13-inch pan for 25 minutes at 350°. Can be iced also. Freezes well.

Incredible Edibles

Sour Cream Apple Squares

2 cups flour
2 cups brown sugar
1/2 cup butter or margarine,
  softened
1 cup chopped nuts
1-2 teaspoons cinnamon
1 teaspoon soda

1/2 teaspoon salt
1 cup dairy sour cream
1 teaspoon vanilla
1 egg
2 cups peeled, cored, finely
  chopped apples.

Combine first 3 ingredients in large bowl. Beat at low speed until fine crumbs form. Stir in nuts. Press 2³/4 cups mixture into ungreased 9x13-inch or 10x15-inch pan. To remaining crumb mixture add next 6 ingredients. Blend well. Stir in chopped apples. Spoon mixture evenly over crumb base. Bake 9x13-inch pan for 30-40 minutes or 10x15-inch pan for 25-35 minutes at 350°. Cool before cutting. Makes 12-15 squares or 3-4 dozen bars. Store loosely covered. To serve, may top with whipped cream or powdered sugar.

Appletizers

Sour Cream Raisin Fingerpies

1 1/4 cups flour
1/2 cup sugar
1/2 cup butter, softened
3/4 cup sugar, part brown
1 cup milk
1 cup sour cream

3 eggs
1/2 teaspoon cinnamon
1/4 teaspoon nutmeg
1/4 teaspoon salt
1 teaspoon vanilla
1 cup raisins

In small mixing bowl, combine the first 3 ingredients. Combine well with fingers or a low speed of electric mixer to blend. Press evenly into baking pan, 9-inch square or 8x10 inches. Bake at 350° for 12-17 minutes or until edges are lightly browned.

Meanwhile, prepare filling. In same mixing bowl, beat together the remaining ingredients except for the raisins. Fold in raisins. Pour over crust and return to oven. Bake 30-40 minutes or until custard has set and knife inserted in center comes out clean. (The filling may puff during baking, but it settles back down during cooling.) Cool and cut into bars. Keep in refrigerator with airtight cover.

Share with Love

Frosted Raisin Bars

2 cups seedless raisins
1 teaspoon soda
1 1/2 cups sugar
3 1/2 cups flour
1 cup butter

2 teaspoons cinnamon
1/8 teaspoon salt
1 teaspoon vanilla
2 eggs

Cover raisins with water; bring to a boil. Let cool for 20 minutes. Add enough water to raisin juice to equal one cup. Add soda. Add remaining ingredients all at once; stir until blended well. Spread very thin on 2 large, greased and floured cookie sheets. Bake at 350° for 15-18 minutes. Frost while hot with following frosting.

FROSTING:

2 cups powdered sugar
1/4 cup melted butter

1/2 teaspoon salt

Mix all ingredients well with enough water for spreading consistency. Spread over raisin bars while they are hot.

Heirloom Recipes and By Gone Days

Apricot Bars

2/3 cup dried apricots
1/4 pound (1 stick) butter or
    margarine, softened
1/4 cup sugar
1 1/3 cups sifted all-purpose
    flour, divided
1/2 teaspoon baking powder

1/4 teaspoon salt
1 cup packed brown sugar
2 eggs, well beaten
1/2 teaspoon vanilla
1/2 cup chopped nuts
Confectioners' sugar (optional

Preheat oven to 350°. Lightly grease an 8x8x2-inch pan. Rinse apricots, place in saucepan, cover with water and boil 10 minutes; drain, cool and chop. Mix butter, sugar, and one cup flour until crumbly. Pack into pan. Bake approximately 25 minutes until lightly brown.

Sift remaining 1/3 cup flour, baking powder, and salt; set aside. Gradually beat brown sugar into eggs, add sifted flour mixture and blend well. Add vanilla, nuts, and apricots. Spread over baked layer.

Bake approximately 30 minutes or until done. Cool in pan, cut into bars and roll in confectioners' sugar. Yield: 16 bars.

Five Star Sensations

Fat-Free Granola Bars

This homemade version will save you bundles of money!

1/4 cup Ultra Fat-Free Promise Margarine	3 1/2 cups fat-free granola
1 (10.5-ounce) bag of miniature marshmallows	1/2 cup raisins
	2 cups Rice Krispies

In a large Dutch oven pan, melt Ultra Fat-Free Promise with marshmallows over low heat, stirring constantly. Once marshmallows are melted, remove from heat. Add granola, raisins and Rice Krispies. Mix well.

Spray a cookie sheet with edges (approximately 15x10 inches with 1/2-inch edge) with a non-fat cooking spray. Pour onto sheet. Spray palm of hand with no-fat spray. With palm of hand press granola mixture firmly down. Let cool.

Cut into 20 bars. Wrap individual bars with plastic wrap. Keep in a cool, dry place. Yield: 20 bars. Cal 126; Fat 0g.

Variations: 1. For tropical fat-free granola bars, substitute 1/4 cup chopped dried pineapple and 1/4 cup chopped dried papaya for raisins. 2. For berry granola bars, substitute 1/2 cup dried cranberries.

Down Home Cookin' Without the Down Home Fat

Chocolate Toffee Crunch Bars

COOKIE BASE:

1/3 cup butter, melted	2 cups finely crushed vanilla wafers
1/4 cup packed brown sugar	

Preheat oven to 350°. In bowl, combine brown sugar and crumbs. Stir in butter. Press in 13x9-inch pan. Bake for 8 minutes.

1/2 cup butter	1 (6-ounce) package chocolate chips
1/2 cup brown sugar	1/2 cup finely chopped nuts

Heat butter and brown sugar in pan over medium heat until boiling. Boil 1 minute. Pour immediately over cookie base and spread to edges. Bake at 350° for 10 minutes. Let stand 2 minutes. Sprinkle with chocolate chips (mini-chips work best). Let stand 2-3 minutes. Then spread chips. Sprinkle with chopped nuts.

25th Anniversary Cookbook

Seven-Layer Cookies

1 stick butter or margarine
1 cup graham cracker crumbs
1 cup chopped pecans
1 cup coconut
1 (6-ounce) package
  butterscotch chips

1 (6-ounce) package
  chocolate chips
1 can Eagle Brand sweetened
  condensed milk

Melt butter in a 9x13-inch pan. Layer crumbs, nuts, coconut, butterscotch, and chocolate chips. Pour milk evenly over all. Bake at 300° until melted and light brown around edges (about 30 minutes). Cool and cut into squares.

Tumm Yummies

Pumpkin Fudge

2 cups sugar
2 tablespoons pumpkin
1/4 teaspoon pumpkin pie
  spice

1/4 teaspoon cornstarch
1/2 cup evaporated milk
1/2 teaspoon vanilla

Cook together sugar, pumpkin spice, cornstarch, and canned milk until it forms a soft ball. Add vanilla and cool. Beat until creamy. Pour onto buttered plate.

St. Gerard's 75th Jubilee Cookbook

Coconut Bonbons

1 cup sugar
1 1/2 cups light corn syrup
1/2 cup water
1 (14-ounce) package flaked
  coconut

1/2 teaspoon vanilla
Chocolate

Combine sugar, syrup, and water in saucepan, cook stirring constantly to dissolve sugar. Cook to 236°, soft-ball stage; remove from heat. Stir in coconut and vanilla. Cool and form into 1-inch balls. May be coated with dark or white chocolate. Balls may be frozen until ready to coat.

Share with Love

Creamy Caramels

1 1/2 cups half and half
1 1/2 cups whipping cream
2 cups sugar
1/4 teaspoon salt

1 1/3 cups light corn syrup
2 teaspoons vanilla
1 cup toasted walnuts

Butter 9-inch square pan. Combine half and half and whipping cream in 4-cup measure. Mix sugar, salt, corn syrup and one cup of the combined cream in heavy saucepan (3 to 4-quart). Cook over medium heat, stirring constantly until syrup reaches 234° (soft ball). Add one more cup of cream and stir until mixture again reaches 234°. Add remaining cream and stir until mixture reaches 250° (hard ball). Remove from heat, add vanilla and nuts. Pour into pan, cool and wrap.

Affolter-Heritage Reunion Cookbook & More

Buckeyes

Ohio is known as the Buckeye State, and these candies are made to resemble the buckeye seed. (The real buckeye is reputedly poisonous.)

1/2 cup (1 stick) butter or
  margarine, at room
  temperature
1 (1-pound) box
  confectioners' sugar

1 1/2 cups peanut butter
1 teaspoon vanilla extract
1 (12-ounce) package real
  chocolate chips
1/4 stick paraffin

Cream the butter, confectioners' sugar, peanut butter, and vanilla. Form into small (buckeye-size) balls and refrigerate overnight. Melt the chocolate chips and paraffin in the top of a double boiler. Stick a toothpick in the candy ball and dip it into the chocolate mixture. Leave part of the ball uncovered so that it resembles a buckeye, but cover the toothpick hole. Place on waxed paper to cool and harden. These candies can be frozen. Yield: 3-4 dozen.

Cincinnati Recipe Treasury

Gelatin Candy Squares

Great make-ahead recipe to mail for Christmas as a "gift from your kitchen."

1⅓ cups applesauce	1¾ cups sugar
2 envelopes gelatin, unflavored	1½ teaspoons lemon juice, concentrate
1 (6-ounce) package fruit-flavored gelatin (your choice)	Sugar (for rolling when dried)

Prepare 9x5-inch loaf pan by filling halfway with cold water and set aside. In a 2-quart saucepan, combine all ingredients, except the sugar for rolling. Heat to boiling and boil for one minute, stirring frequently to prevent sticking and burning. Pour out water in loaf pan and immediately pour cooked gelatin mixture into wet pan. When loaf pan is cool enough to handle, refrigerate about 3 hours or until the candy is firm. You may refrigerate longer, even over-night.

Cut the candy into 1-inch squares with a knife that has been dipped in cold water. This helps to prevent candy from sticking. Remove candy piece by piece from the pan and place on cooling racks. Allow to air dry on racks for at least 8 hours. Do NOT cover candy.

When candy squares have dried, roll each square in a bowl full of granulated sugar until all sides are coated. Store in tin cans. Yield: 45-50 squares.

Note: When using orange or peach gelatin, add one teaspoon cinnamon for an extraordinary great flavor.

Now That Mom's Not Around

 Aboriginal Indians created the world's largest snake—a quarter-mile-long, 5-feet-high, 20-feet-wide serpent with its mouth wide open, its body twisted into seven sharp curves. No one knows why they did it; maybe just a way of expressing themselves artistically. There is a museum near Serpent Mound, 4 miles northwest of Locust Grove.

Cookie Pops

1/2 cup margarine	1 1/2 cups flour
1 1/2 cups brown sugar	1/2 teaspoon baking powder
1/2 cup granulated sugar	1/2 teaspoon baking soda
1/2 cup peanut butter	10 popsicle sticks
1 teaspoon vanilla	10 fun-size Snickers or Milky
1 egg	Way candy bars

Cream margarine and sugars. Add peanut butter; mix well. Add vanilla and egg; mix well. Add flour, baking powder, and baking soda; mix until a nice dough is formed. Put a popsicle stick in each of 10 candy bars. Shape 1/4 cup dough around each candy bar. Place 4 inches apart on ungreased baking sheet. Bake at 350° for 13-16 minutes or until dough is golden brown. Cool completely on baking sheet. Remove carefully.

MDA Favorite Recipes

Caramel Popcorn

2/3 cup popping corn	1/4 cup white corn syrup
1/4 cup oil	1 teaspoon salt
1/2 cup butter or margarine	1 teaspoon baking soda
1 cup firmly packed brown sugar	

Preheat oven to 300°. Spray large roasting pan with nonstick vegetable spray. Pop corn in oil; pour into prepared pan. Melt butter in large saucepan. Add brown sugar, corn syrup, and salt. Boil for 5 minutes. Remove from heat. Add baking soda and stir until frothy. Pour over popcorn and toss to coat. Bake at 300° for 3-5 minutes; toss. Bake additional 3-5 minutes; remove from oven. Toss mixture; allow to set for 3-5 minutes. Break into small pieces. Be prepared to make a second batch—it disappears quickly! Yield: 4 cups.

A Cleveland Collection

Peanut Butter Pop

1/2 cup water

1/4 cup sugar

1/4 cup peanut butter, creamy
  or chunky

1 cup lowfat milk

Bring water and sugar to boil and boil for 3 minutes. Remove from heat and stir in peanut butter, then add milk. Cool for 10-15 minutes. Pour into 6 (5-ounce) paper cups. Add wooden sticks. Freeze until firm. Remove 3 minutes before serving. Peel off paper cups. Makes 6 pops.

Kinder Kuisine

Chocolate Fondant Candy

If you like Almond Joy or Mound bars, you'll like these. Makes a ton of candy.

1 pound semi-sweet Baker's
  chocolate

1/4 pound paraffin

2 pounds confectioners' sugar

1 can condensed milk

4 cups pecans

1 stick oleo

2 cans coconut (7 ounces
  total)

2 tablespoons vanilla

Place chocolate and paraffin in double boiler to soften. Blend all other ingredients together. Chill until firm. Form in small balls and dip in chocolate.

Cooking with TLC

Sugarless Candy

We made this during World War II when sugar was rationed. But it is good now, too!

1 can Eagle Brand sweetened
  condensed milk

3 tablespoons cocoa

3 tablespoons butter

1 teaspoon vanilla

1 3/4 cups graham cracker
  crumbs

1 cup English walnuts

Heat milk in double boiler, add cocoa and stir well. Then add the rest of the ingredients. Pour into 8x8-inch pan and let set about 24 hours, then cut in squares.

Affolter-Heritage Reunion Cookbook & More

Dog Cookies

The recipe for these crunchy treats was canine-tested before it was published for dog lovers everywhere. Neighborhood pets were invited to a tasting set up on a red and white-check-covered table on the lawn. The cookies disappeared in seconds, and the furry tasters looked for more. If ever this food editor puts a product on the retail market, it won't be salsa, jams, or noodles, but these cookies. I joined in the tasting. They were pretty good.

¹/₂ cup all-purpose flour
1 cup whole wheat flour
1 cup dry skim milk
¹/₃ cup quick cooking oats
2 tablespoons wheat germ
¹/₃ cup vegetable oil

1 large egg, beaten
2 beef or chicken bouillon
   cubes, dissolved in 1
   tablespoon hot water
¹/₂ cup water

Combine flours, milk powder, oats, wheat germ, oil, egg, bouillon, and water in food processor or in mixing bowl. Mix well and form into a ball.

Divide ball into 2 parts. Knead one piece for about one minute and roll out on a lightly floured surface to ¹/₂-inch thickness. Cut with a small biscuit cutter. Place 6 biscuits on a 9- or 10-inch microwave-safe plate. Cook on 50% power for about 6 minutes, until firm. Roll out remaining piece of dough and the scraps left from cutting the biscuits, cut, and cook.

Or bake all biscuits at once for 15 minutes in 350° oven. Makes about 24, depending upon the size of the cutter. A small size is suggested. Refrigerate.

Aren't You Going to Taste It, Honey?

Pies and Desserts

Yoder's Amish Home offers a glimpse into the Amish lifestyle. Between Trail and Walnut Creek.

100-Year-Old Old-Fashion Cream Pie

3 eggs, separated
3 tablespoons sugar
1 1/2 tablespoons flour
Pinch of salt
1 large can Carnation (pour in
  pint cup and finish filling with
  milk)

1 1/2 cups brown sugar
1 teaspoon vanilla
1 (10-inch) unbaked pie shell

Beat egg whites stiff; add white sugar, flour, and salt. Add egg yolks and beat again. Add milk and brown sugar. Beat 2 minutes. Add vanilla and mix. Pour into 10-inch unbaked pie shell (glass pie dish preferred). Bake at 400° until light brown. Reduce oven to 325° for 30 minutes. Makes very large pie.

A Matter of Taste

Pink Lemonade Pie

1 (8- or 9-inch) pastry shell,
  baked
1 (8-ounce) package cream
  cheese, softened
1 (14-ounce) can Eagle Brand
  Milk

6 ounces frozen pink
  lemonade, thawed
Red food coloring, optional
4 ounces Cool Whip, thawed
1/2 cup coconut, tinted pink

In a large bowl, beat cream cheese until fluffy, gradually beat in Eagle Brand Milk. Add lemonade and a few drops of red food coloring (if desired). Fold in Cool Whip. Pour in pastry shell and chill for 4 hours or until set. Garnish with pink coconut. This is also very good with frozen orange juice instead of lemonade.

Mary Yoder's Amish Kitchen Cookbook

Kelleys Island is the largest American island in Lake Erie. Its archaeological sites show human occupation from about 12,000 BC to AD 1300. Inscription Rock, the most extensive and best preserved prehistoric Native American pictograph ever found in America, and the 30,000-year-old, 400-foot-long Glacial Grooves, are two of the unique sites. The entire island is on the National Register of Historic Places.

Fort Knox Pie

1 envelope Knox Unflavored
  Gelatin
1/4 cup cold water
2 cups whipping or heavy
  cream, divided
1 (6-ounce) bag semi-sweet
  chocolate chips

2 eggs
1 teaspoon vanilla
22 Kraft Caramels
2 tablespoons butter
Chocolate-Pecan Crust

In small saucepan sprinkle gelatin over water; let stand for one minute. Stir over low heat until completely dissolved. Stir in one cup cream. Bring to boiling point. Add to blender with chocolate chips. Process until chocolate is melted. While processing, add 1/2 cup cream, eggs, and vanilla. Process until blended. Pour into bowl. Chill until thickened (about 15 minutes).

In small pan combine caramels, 1/4 cup cream and butter. Simmer, stirring occasionally until caramels are melted. Pour onto crust. Let cool for 10 minutes. With whisk or spoon, beat gelatin mixture until smooth. Pour into crust. Chill until firm. Garnish with remaining cream (whipped).

CHOCOLATE-PECAN CRUST:

1 box chocolate wafers
3/4 cup pecans, finely chopped

1/2 cup butter or margarine,
  melted

Combine 2 cups chocolate wafer crumbs, pecans, and butter. Press into 10-inch pie pan and up sides to form high rim. Bake at 350° for 10 minutes; cool.

Tumm Yummies

15-Minute Custard Pie

4 slightly beaten eggs
1/2 cup sugar
1/4 teaspoon salt
1 teaspoon vanilla

2 1/2 cups scalded milk
9-inch unbaked pie shell
  (1/8-inch thick)
Nutmeg

Preheat oven to 475°. Thoroughly mix eggs, sugar, salt and vanilla; beat slightly. Slowly stir in hot milk. At once, pour into unbaked pastry shell. To avoid spills, fill at oven. Dash top with nutmeg. Bake in very hot oven for 5 minutes. Reduce heat to 425°. Bake 10 minutes longer or until knife inserted halfway between center and edge comes out clean. Cool on rack. Serve cool or chilled. Keep unused portion refrigerated. This custard does not get watery and is very tasty.

175th Anniversary Quilt Cookbook

Never-Fail Pie Crust

1 cup shortening
2 cups flour
1 teaspoon salt

1 tablespoon vinegar
1/3 cup milk

Cut shortening into flour and salt. Put vinegar into milk and immediately stir into flour mixture. Mixture will be damp; work on a well-floured surface. Makes a double-crust pie.

Recipes & Remembrances

Raisin Cream Pie

1 cup raisins
1 cup water
1 cup sugar
1/2 cup brown sugar
4 tablespoons flour
2 eggs

1/2 cup water
2 tablespoons margarine
3 tablespoons lemon juice
1 tablespoon vanilla
Cool Whip
Baked pie shell

Bring to a boil raisins and water. Beat sugars, flour, eggs, and water together. Mix with hot raisins. Cook until thick. Remove from heat. Add margarine, lemon juice, and vanilla. Cool. Pour into baked shell. Top with Cool Whip.

25th Anniversary Cookbook

Paradise Pumpkin Pie

FIRST MIXTURE:

8 ounces cream cheese
1/4 cup sugar

1/2 teaspoon vanilla
1 egg, beaten

SECOND MIXTURE:

1 1/4 cups pumpkin
1/2 cup sugar
1/4 teaspoon nutmeg

1 teaspoon cinnamon
1 cup evaporated milk
2 eggs, beaten

Pour into a 9-inch unbaked pie shell first mixture, then carefully spoon second mixture on top. Bake at 350° for 65-70 minutes.

Favorite Recipes from Poland Women's Club

Low-Calorie Pumpkin Pie

1 (16-ounce) can solid-pack
  pumpkin
1 (13-ounce) can evaporated
  skim milk
1 egg
2 egg whites
1/2 cup biscuit mix
  (Bisquick-type)

2 tablespoons sugar
8 packets sugar substitute
2 teaspoons pumpkin pie
  spice
2 teaspoons vanilla

Heat oven to 350°. Lightly spray 9-inch pie pan with vegetable spray. Place all ingredients in blender, food processor, or mixing bowl. Blend one minute or beat 2 minutes with mixer. Pour into pie pan and bake for 50 minutes or until center is puffed up. To serve, cut pie into 8 pieces. Makes 8 servings.

Per Serving (1 piece): Equals 1 starch/bread exchange, 1/2 medium-fat meat exchange; Cal 114; Carbo 18g; Prot 6g; Fat 2g; Sod 173mg.

Recipes & Remembrances

Peanut Butter Pie

1/2 cup peanut butter
1 (8-ounce) package cream
   cheese, softened
1 cup powdered sugar

1/2 cup milk
9 ounces Cool Whip, thawed
1 graham cracker crust
Chopped dry roasted peanuts

Beat peanut butter, cream cheese, sugar, and milk until well mixed. Fold in Cool Whip. Pour into pie crust and top with peanuts. Freeze until ready to serve.

Recipes from "The Little Switzerland of Ohio"

Peanut Butter Pie

2/3 cup sugar
1/2 teaspoon salt
1 cup dark corn syrup

1/3 cup creamy peanut butter
3 eggs
1 cup salted peanuts

Beat sugar, salt, corn syrup, peanut butter, and eggs. Stir in peanuts. Pour into unbaked pie shell. Bake in 375° oven for about 45 minutes until crust is golden brown. Cool slightly until center is firm. Chill in refrigerator and serve with whipped cream.

The Amish Way Cookbook

Chocolate Cream Pie

A chocolate pie like no other.

1/2 cup granulated sugar
3 heaping tablespoons
   Nestles Quik (no substitute)
3 heaping tablespoons
   cornstarch
1/4 teaspoon salt

3 egg yolks
2 cups whole milk
1 teaspoon vanilla
2 tablespoons butter or
   margarine
1 (9-inch) baked pie shell

Mix dry ingredients together. Slightly beat egg yolks and add milk. Add to dry ingredients and cook over medium heat until thick. Add vanilla and butter. Cool. Pour into baked pie shell.

Touches of the Hands & Heart

Hershey Bar Pie

17 marshmallows
1/4 pound butter
6 Hershey bars with or
   without almonds

1/2 pint whipped cream
1 graham cracker crust

Melt marshmallows in top of double boiler with butter. Add Hershey bars. Melt all together and stir well. Cool mixture slightly and add whipped cream. Pour into graham cracker crust and chill before serving.

The Amish Way Cookbook

German Sweet Chocolate Pie

A chocoholic's dream.

1 (4-ounce) package
   German's sweet chocolate
1/4 cup butter
1 2/3 cups (12 or 13-ounce
   can) evaporated milk
1 1/2 cups granulated sugar
3 tablespoons cornstarch

1/8 teaspoon salt
2 eggs
1 teaspoon vanilla
1 unbaked (9-inch) pie shell,
   deep dish or highly fluted
1 1/3 cups flaked coconut
1/2 cup chopped pecans

Melt chocolate with butter over low heat, stirring until blended. Remove from heat; gradually blend in milk.

In separate bowl, mix sugar, cornstarch, and salt thoroughly. Beat in eggs and vanilla. Gradually blend in chocolate mixture. Pour into pie shell.

Combine coconut and nuts; sprinkle over filling. Bake in a 350° oven for 60 minutes or until pie is puffed and browned.

Note: For the last 20 minutes of baking, cover with aluminum foil. (Filling will be soft, but will set while cooling.)
Baker Ruth Youngquist, Red Door Tavern.

A Taste of Columbus Vol IV

Bellefontaine is the highest point in Ohio at 1550 feet above sea level, and was home to the inventor of concrete, Pharmacist George Bartholemew, and, therefore, is also home to the first concrete street, Court Street.

Grasshopper Pie

Brookside Golf and Country Club's traditional house recipe. Elegant.

1 1/3 cups fine crumbs of
   chocolate wafer cookies*
1/4 cup softened butter or
   margarine
1 cup whipping cream
1 envelope unflavored gelatin
1/4 cup sugar
1/8 teaspoon salt
1/2 cup cold water

3 egg yolks, slightly beaten,
   reserve whites
1/4 cup crème de menthe
1/4 cup crème de cacao
3 egg whites
1/4 cup sugar
Whipped cream for topping
Chocolate curls**

Thoroughly blend crumbs and butter. Press firmly with back of spoon over bottom and sides of 9-inch pie pan. Bake at 375° for 8 minutes. Allow to cool before filling.

In small mixing bowl, whip cream. Set aside. In small bowl, combine gelatin, sugar, and salt. Add cold water and egg yolks and blend thoroughly. Place mixture in top of double boiler. Bring water to boil and cook mixture, stirring constantly until gelatin dissolves and mixture thickens slightly. Remove from heat. Stir in crème de menthe and crème de cacao. Chill thoroughly.

Beat egg whites until stiff but not dry. Gradually add sugar and continue beating until very stiff. Fold in gelatin mixture. Fold in whipped cream. Pour into chocolate crumb crust. Garnish with additional whipped cream and chocolate curls.

*These are usually found above the dairy case.

**Chocolate curls can be made from a block of unsweetened chocolate by making long thin strokes with a vegetable peeler.

A Taste of Columbus Vol IV

Blueberry-Peach Pie

1 cup sugar
3 tablespoons cornstarch
1 cup water
1/4 cup lemon-flavored gelatin
4 cups sliced fresh or frozen
   peaches, thawed

3/4 cup fresh or frozen
   blueberries, thawed
Pastry shell

CONTINUED

Combine first 3 ingredients in a medium saucepan. Bring to a boil over medium heat, cook 1 minute, stirring constantly. Remove from heat and add gelatin, stirring until gelatin dissolves; cool. Combine peaches and blueberrries in a large bowl. Add gelatin mixture and toss gently. Spoon into prepared pastry shell. Cover and chill 1 hour or until set. Serve with sweetened whipped cream.

PAT IN PIE CRUST:

1½ cups flour	2 tablespoons milk
1 teaspoon salt	1½ tablespoons sugar
½ cup salad oil	

Mix with fork in bowl. Pat into pie pan.

A Matter of Taste

Peaches and Cream Pie

A cake-like crust adds an interesting texture to this popular dessert.

CRUST:

¾ cup flour	3 tablespoons margarine,
1 teaspoon baking powder	softened
½ teaspoon salt	1 egg
1 (3-ounce) package vanilla	½ cup milk
pudding (not instant)	

Combine all ingredients and beat with mixer for 2 minutes. Pour into greased 9-inch pie plate. Set aside.

FILLING:

1 (29-ounce) can peaches,	½ cup sugar
sliced and drained, reserve	3 tablespoons peach juice
juice	
1 (8-ounce) package cream	
cheese, softened	

Place peaches over crust. Combine remaining filling ingredients and spoon over top of fruit to within one inch of edge of dish.

TOPPING:

1 tablespoon sugar	½ teaspoon cinnamon

Mix topping ingredients together and sprinkle over pie. Bake in a preheated 350° oven for 35-40 minutes. Refrigerate and serve cold. Must be prepared several hours ahead. Yields: 8 servings.

Simply Sensational

Blackberry-Raspberry Pie

One of the Columbus Monthly's top ten dishes.

2 cups flour
1 teaspoon salt
2/3 cup Crisco shortening
Approximately 2/3 cup ice
  water
3 cups fresh blackberries*
4 cups fresh red raspberries*

1 3/4 cups sugar
1 tablespoon grated lemon
  peel
6 tablespoons flour
2 tablespoons sugar
2 tablespoons butter

Mix together flour and salt. Add shortening and blend into flour with hands until shortening forms lumps about 1/8-inch in diameter. Add water and press gently with fingertips to form a ball. Do not overwork it. Cover with towel and let it sit at least 5 minutes.

Prepare filling by combining berries, first amount of sugar, lemon peel, and flour. Roll out half of pie dough and fill the bottom of a 10-inch pie pan. Then roll out the rest of the dough and cut into long strips. Place filling on bottom crust, and working quickly, make a lattice-top pie crust.

Sprinkle top with second amount of sugar. Cut butter into small pieces and poke into holes in top crust. Place immediately in pre-heated oven at 350° for about 50 minutes or until it bubbles in center. Serves 8.

Note: *Frozen berries may be used if unsweetened and individually frozen. Do not thaw.
Chef Jean Cork, Shaw's.

A Taste of Columbus Vol III

Raspberry Cream Pie

So good! They'll ask for this recipe every time you serve it.

2 cups graham cracker crumbs	1 (16-ounce) package frozen raspberries
5 tablespoons melted butter	1 tablespoon cornstarch
1/2 pound butter	1 1/2 sliced bananas
2 cups confectioners' sugar	Cool Whip
2 whole eggs	

Mix together crumbs and 5 tablespoons butter and press into 10-inch pie dish. Cream together 1/2 pound butter, sugar, and eggs and beat very well for 10 minutes. Thaw and drain raspberries, reserving liquid. Thicken liquid with cornstarch over low heat till it comes to a boil. Let cool and then add raspberries back into it. Pour filling in pie shell, arrange slices of bananas on top, pour raspberries over bananas (staying away from the edge) and top with Cool Whip. Serve cold. Serves 8-10.

Angels and Friends Cookbook I

Nana's French Strawberry Pie

1 (3-ounce) package cream cheese	1 cup sugar
1 baked (9-inch) pie shell	1 tablespoon butter
1 1/2 quarts strawberries	4 tablespoons flour
	1 cup whipping cream

Blend cream cheese with just enough cream or milk to soften; spread over bottom of pie shell. Place 3 cups of berries in cheese-coated shell. Mash remaining berries. Mix sugar, butter, and flour in saucepan. Add mashed berries. Cook, stirring constantly, over medium heat, until mixture thickens and boils 1 minute. Cool thoroughly. Pour over berries in pie shell. Chill 4-6 hours or until firm. Serve with sweetened whipped cream. Garnish with a few fresh berries. Serves 6-8.

Cook, Line & Sinker

 The Ohio State Fair is the largest state fair in the US. Eighty-seven of Ohio's 88 counties have an annual county fair.

Shaker Lemon Pie

2 lemons
1 1/4 cups sugar
1/4 cup cornstarch
1/4 cup cold water
1 3/4 cups boiling water
3 egg yolks, beaten lightly

1 baked pie shell
3 egg whites
1/8 teaspoon salt
1 1/2 teaspoons lemon juice
2 tablespoons sugar

Roll lemons on the work surface with the palms of your hands to soften. Grate yellow "zest" or rind and reserve. Squeeze out juice and reserve. In a double boiler, over hot water, mix sugar, cornstarch, and cold water. Add boiling water and cook until heated thoroughly and well thickened, stirring occasionally. To egg yolks in a bowl, pour a small amount of the hot, thickened mixture and stir to blend. Pour egg mixture gradually into the remaining thickened cornstarch mixture, stirring constantly. Return to double boiler bottom to cook for 5 minutes longer, or until egg yolk begins to thicken.

Remove from heat and add lemon zest and juice. Stir until smooth. Pour into a baked pie shell and chill. Beat egg whites with salt until soft peaks are formed. Beat in lemon juice gradually, and then sugar, a little at a time, until mixture stands in stiff, moist peaks, and forms a meringue. Top lemon custard filling with meringue and bake in a very hot oven 3-4 minutes to brown the meringue.

The Shaker Cookbook

Out-of-This-World Pie

1 large can cherry pie filling
1 large can crushed pineapple
    with juice
1 teaspoon red food coloring
3/4 cup sugar
1 tablespoon cornstarch

1 box raspberry Jello
6 bananas, sliced
1 cup chopped pecans
2 (10-inch) pie shells, baked
Whipped topping

In saucepan, combine first 5 ingredients. Cook until thick. Remove from heat and add Jello. Allow to cool. Add bananas and pecans. Pour into pie shells and top with whipped topping.

Heavenly Dishes

Di's Ohio Sour Cherry Pie

This is the recipe that won Diane Cordial of Powell the Grand Prize at Crisco's American Pie Celebration National Championship in 1991. A distinguished panel of food experts from across the country saluted Di and declared her Ohio pie the best pie in America, beating entries from the 49 other states. Crisco, of course, is a product of Ohio-based Procter & Gamble. Way to go, Bucks!

FILLING:

1 (20-ounce) bag frozen, unsweetened, pitted tart cherries, thawed (4 cups)
1 1/4 cups sugar
1/4 cup cornstarch
2 tablespoons butter or margarine
1/2 teaspoon almond extract
1/2 teaspoon vanilla extract
1-2 drops red food color

In medium saucepan, combine sugar and cornstarch; add cherries. Cook and stir on medium heat until mixture comes to a boil. Remove from heat; stir in butter, extracts and food color. Let stand for one hour at room temperature.

PASTRY:

3 cups flour
2 tablespoons sugar
1 teaspoon salt
1 cup Crisco solid vegetable shortening
1/2 cup water
1 egg, slightly beaten
1 tablespoon vinegar
1 tablespoon milk
1 tablespoon sugar

Preheat oven to 375°. In medium bowl, combine flour, sugar, and salt; cut in shortening until crumbly. Add egg and vinegar; stir until dough forms a ball. Divide into thirds. On floured surface, roll each third out to 1/8-inch thickness. Line pie plate; trim edges even with plate. Turn cherry filling into pastry lined plate. On second pastry circle, cut out the word "Ohio" and a shape of the state. Moisten edges of pastry in plate. Lift second pastry circle onto filling. Trim 1/2 inch beyond edge of pie plate; fold top edge under bottom crust, flute edges. Brush top of pie with milk; sprinkle with sugar. Bake 35-40 minutes or until golden brown.

With third pastry circle, cut out 3-inch shapes of the state of Ohio; cut small hole in center of each. Bake for 5-8 minutes or until golden brown; cool. To serve pie, place maraschino cherry piece in each hole. Place cutout on toothpick; insert in each piece of pie. Makes 1 (9-inch) pie.

Bountiful Ohio

Country Apple Pie with Lemon Glaze

Pastry for 2-crust pie	2 tablespoons flour
5-7 apples	1 tablespoon butter or
3/4 cup sugar	margarine
1 teaspoon cinnamon	

Line 9-inch plate with bottom crust. Pare, core and slice apples. Combine with mixture of sugar, cinnamon, and flour. Place in pastry-lined plate. Dot with butter. Place top crust over filling. Trim and seal. Prick or cut slots to allow steam to escape. Bake 400° for 30-40 minutes or until apples are cooked and crust is lightly browned. If crust gets too brown before pie is done, place a sheet of foil over pie and continue baking.

LEMON GLAZE:

1 tablespoon butter, melted	Powdered sugar (enough to
1 tablespoon lemon juice	thicken)

Wait about 10 minutes after pie is out of oven. Mix above ingredients in small bowl. Spread over pie.

A Matter of Taste

My Mom's Apple Crisp

The Best!

6 large apples	1 slightly beaten egg
1 cup flour	1/3 cup margarine
1/2 teaspoon salt	1 teaspoon cinnamon
1 cup granulated sugar	1 teaspoon vanilla
1 teaspoon baking powder	

Peel and slice apples and place in 13x9-inch pan. Mix together next 4 ingredients. Add egg and blend until mealy. Sprinkle on top of apples. Melt margarine and add cinnamon and vanilla. Pour over top of egg mixture. Bake at 350° for approximately 40 minutes or until golden brown.

Touches of the Hands & Heart

Apple Zucchini Pie

1 large zucchini	2 tablespoons lemon juice
2 tablespoons flour	Dash of salt
1 1/4 cups sugar	Dash of nutmeg
1 1/2 teaspoons cinnamon	1 (10-inch) unbaked pie shell
1 1/2 teaspoons cream of tartar	

Peel zucchini and cut lengthwise; scoop out seeds. Cut into slices to resemble apple slices. Cook 10 minutes in just enough water to keep from burning. Drain. Mix rest of ingredients and add zucchini. Pour into unbaked pie shell and cover with topping.

TOPPING:

1 stick margarine	1 cup flour
1/2 cup sugar	

Mix ingredients for topping in food processor and crumble over pie. Bake at 400° for 50 minutes. Makes 8-10 servings.

Per serving: Cal 362; Prot 3g; Fat 15g; Chol 54g.

Wadsworth-Rittman Hospital Cookbook

Easy Fruit Cobbler

1 cup sugar	3/4 cup milk
3/4 cup flour	1/2 cup margarine
Dash of salt	2 cups sweetened fruit
2 teaspoons baking powder	1/2 cup sugar

Combine dry ingredients with milk to make thin batter. Melt margarine in a deep bowl in oven while it is preheating to 350°. Pour batter into middle of melted margarine. Do not stir! Carefully pour fruit which has been sweetened with 1/2 cup sugar and seasoned as you wish over batter. (Any canned fruit pie filling may be used, too.) Do not stir! Bake at 350° for one hour or until crusted on top.

Czech Dancers Polka Club Cook Book

Fresh Peach Cobbler

1 tablespoon cornstarch	1 tablespoon lemon juice
1/2 cup cold water	1/4 cup brown sugar
1 tablespoon butter or margarine	4 cups sugared sliced fresh peaches

Cook all together till thickened. Pour into 8-inch pan.

CRUST:

1 cup flour	1/2 cup sugar
1 1/2 teaspoons baking powder	1/2 teaspoon salt
1/2 cup milk	1/4 cup soft butter or margarine

Mix crust batter and pour over fruit. Sprinkle with 2 tablespoons sugar, mixed with 1/2 teaspoon nutmeg. Bake at 350° for 30 minutes.

Note: Can use other fruits.

Cooking with Hope Ridge Families

Blackberry Crisp

BLACKBERRY FILLING:

3/4 cup sugar	5 cups fresh or frozen blackberries
2 tablespoons flour	

Preheat oven to 375°. Mix sugar and flour; then toss gently with blackberries to coat evenly. Transfer to a 9x9x2-inch baking dish that is well buttered.

CRUST TOPPING:

1 cup flour	1 egg, beaten
1 cup sugar	1 stick butter, melted
1 teaspoon baking powder	

Combine flour, sugar, and baking powder; blend. Make a well in center of dry ingredients and blend in beaten egg, mixing until topping is crumbly. Sprinkle over berry mixture. Drizzle melted butter evenly over crumbly topping. Place baking dish on a baking sheet or foil to prevent spillovers. Bake 45 minutes or until crisp.

Gardener's Delight

Sweet Potato Pie with Pecan Topping

1 pound (2 large) yams or sweet potatoes, cooked and peeled	1 teaspoon ground cinnamon
	1/2 teaspoon nutmeg
	2 teaspoons orange rind (optional)
1/2 cup margarine or butter, softened	2 eggs
1 (14-ounce) can sweetened condensed milk (not evaporated milk)	1 (9-inch) unbaked pastry shell

Preheat oven to 350°. Mash yams with margarine; add remaining pie ingredients, except pastry shell and eggs. Beat until smooth and well blended. Stir in eggs. Pour into prepared pastry shell. Bake 45-50 minutes or until knife inserted near center comes out clean. Cool. Refrigerate leftovers.

TOPPING:

1/4 cup margarine or butter	1/2 cup chopped pecans
1/2 cup brown sugar	

Melt margarine over medium heat. Stir in brown sugar and heat until melted and well blended. Remove from heat and stir in pecans. Spread on top of pie, once pie has cooled.

What's Cooking at Holden School

Apple Mystery Dessert

2 cups graham cracker crumbs	1 (14-ounce) can sweetened condensed milk
1/2 cup melted butter or margarine	1 cup thick applesauce
	1/3 cup lemon juice
1/4 cup sugar	1 tablespoon grated lemon rind
3 egg yolks, well beaten	3 egg whites, beaten stiff

Mix together crumbs, butter, and sugar; reserve 1/2 cup mixture. Press remaining crumbs in bottom and on sides of 8x12-inch pan. Combine yolks, milk, applesauce, lemon juice, and rind. Fold in egg whites. Pour into crumb crust. Top with remaining crumbs. Chill several hours or overnight. May also freeze for later use. Serve with whipped cream. Garnish with mint leaves if available. Makes 10-12 servings.

Appletizers

Pistachio Delight

CRUST:

1 cup flour
1 stick soft oleo

2 tablespoons sugar
1/2 cup nuts

Cut in as pie crust and pat in 9x13-inch pan. Bake at 350° for 15 minutes. Cool.

CREAM:

2/3 cup sugar
1 (8-ounce) package soft
  cream cheese
Cool Whip

2 packages instant pistachio
  pudding
2 1/2 cups cold milk

Cream sugar and cream cheese well and fold in 1/2 container of Cool Whip. Put on crust. Beat instant pudding and milk until thick; spread over cream cheese. Top with rest of Cool Whip. Sprinkle with nuts and cherries if desired.

Seasoned with Love

Strawberry Chiffon Squares

1/3 cup butter
1 1/2 cups crushed graham
  crackers
1 (3-ounce) package
  strawberry gelatin
3/4 cup boiling water
1 (14-ounce) can sweetened
  condensed milk

1 (10-ounce) package frozen
  sliced strawberries in syrup
  (thawed)
4 cups miniature
  marshmallows
1 cup whipping cream,
  whipped

Melt butter in pan. Stir in crumbs and mix well. Pat in 7x11-inch baking dish and chill. In a large bowl dissolve gelatin in boiling water. Add condensed milk and strawberries with juice; fold in marshmallows and whipped cream. Pour over crumbs and chill until set.

The Amish Way Cookbook

Ohio has the largest Amish population in the world; about 35,000 "plain people" live in the state. It is ironical that in their desire for a separate life, they make such an appealing picture, that the rest of us can scarcely leave them alone.

Pecan-Caramel Cream Squares

16 caramels
24 large marshmallows
1/2 cup milk
1 cup chopped pecans,
toasted

1 cup whipping cream
1 cup graham cracker crumbs
4 tablespoons butter, melted

Put caramels, marshmallows, and milk in top of double boiler. Place over boiling water. Cook, stirring occasionally, until mixture is melted and smooth, about 25 minutes. Remove from heat and cool. Stir in pecans. Whip cream and fold into caramel mixture. Combine crumbs and butter. Reserve 1/4 cup. Press remainder into bottom of 10x6-inch dish. Top with caramel mixture. Sprinkle with crumbs. Chill several hours or overnight. Cut into squares. Serves 6.

Note: May be doubled and put into 9x13-inch dish.

Favorite Recipes from Poland Women's Club

Fabulous Cream Cheese Squares

Simply elegant.

CRUST:

1 (8½-ounce) package
  chocolate wafer cookies
  (Nabisco only)
8 tablespoons unsalted butter,
  melted

1 tablespoon confectioners'
  sugar

Put package of cookies in food processor and pulse 6 times until cookies are all crushed. Put crushed wafer cookies in a bowl. Add melted butter and confectioners' sugar and mix well. Put in a 9x13 pyrex dish and press firmly until pan is covered to form crust. Bake at 350° for 10-15 minutes until firm. Cool.

CHEESE FILLING:

3 (8-ounce) packages cream
  cheese
2 eggs

1 teaspoon vanilla
2 teaspoons fresh lemon juice
¾ cup sugar

Cream well, until smooth, cream cheese, eggs, vanilla, lemon juice and sugar. Pour into shell; bake at 325° for 30 minutes. Remove from oven and cool one hour.

TOPPING:

1 pint sour cream (2 cups)
1 teaspoon fresh lemon juice

1 cup sugar

Combine all ingredients in a medium-size bowl and mix well. Pour on cheesecake. Bake at 350° for 15 minutes. Cool and refrigerate until serving time. Top square with Thank You Cherries, fresh strawberries, or crushed red raspberries with a little sugar to sweeten.

Angels and Friends Cookbook II

Chocolate Truffle Tart

CRUST:

6 tablespoons butter, softened
1/2 cup sugar
3/4 cup all-purpose flour

1/3 cup cocoa
1/2 teaspoon vanilla
1/8 teaspoon salt

Preheat oven to 350°. Grease 10-inch springform or tart pan. Cream butter and sugar until light and fluffy. At low speed, beat in flour, cocoa, vanilla, and salt until crumbly. Press dough into bottom and up sides of prepared pan. Bake at 350° for 8-10 minutes or until firm but not crisp. Cool completely on wire rack.

FILLING:

1 1/4 cups whipping cream
1 (12-ounce) package
  semi-sweet chocolate chips

White chocolate

Scald whipping cream. Remove from heat. Add chocolate, stir until melted and smooth. Cool until slightly thickened. Pour into prepared crust. Refrigerate tart 2 hours or until firm. Garnish with grated white chocolate or white chocolate curls. Serves 8-10.

A Cleveland Collection

Dirt

1 bag Oreos, crushed
1 (8-ounce) package cream
  cheese
1/2 stick softened margarine
1 cup confectioners sugar

2 packages instant chocolate
  pudding
3 1/2 cups milk
1 (12-ounce) container Cool
  Whip

Cream together cream cheese, margarine, and sugar. Mix together pudding, milk and Cool Whip. Combine chocolate mixture with creamed mixture. Stir well.

In flower pot, layer mixture with crushed Oreo cookies, ending with cookies on top. Add silk flowers and plastic shovel for serving.

The PTA Pantry

Harriet Beecher Stowe was living in Cincinnati when she heard the stories of escaped slaves that inspired her landmark novel, *Uncle Tom's Cabin*. The book became a catalyst in the anti-slavery movement.

Classic Tiramisu

8 ounces lady fingers*	8 ounces mascarpone cheese
1 1/2 cups sweet Marsala	at room temperature
wine**	1/4 cup espresso coffee
4 egg yolks	1 cup whipping cream
1/4 cup granulated sugar	2 tablespoons sugar (optional)
2 egg whites	Grated semi-sweet chocolate

Dip the biscuits or lady fingers into one cup of the Marsala. Line the bottom of a 2-quart bowl or casserole dish with half of them. Reserve the remainder. Make a zabaglione by beating the yolks and sugar in the top of a double boiler until very thick and very pale yellow; whisk in 1/2 cup of the Marsala. Whisk over gently, simmering water until mixture is thickened; cool by whisking over ice water. Beat the egg whites until stiff, but still shiny, and fold into the zabaglione.

Mix together the mascarpone and the coffee. Whip the cream until stiff, and sweeten with the remaining sugar. Cover the biscuits with half of the zabaglione and then half of the mascarpone and half of the whipped cream. Place another layer of the dipped biscuits and repeat with the remaining zabaglione and mascarpone. Finish with the cream. Sprinkle the chocolate over the top for garnish and chill for several hours. Serves 8-10.

Note: *A crisp cookie in a finger shape called "savoiardi" may be substituted. **Amaretto or a coffee liqueur may be substituted.

More Cooking with Marilyn Harris

Pearl Tapioca
(Frog Eyes)

This was always a family favorite. Today the nieces and nephews always say, "Aunt Helen, make the 'frog eyes' for the reunion."

1 cup large pearl tapioca	1 tablespoon vanilla
3 cups cold water	1 tablespoon butter
2 cups brown sugar	1 small carton Cool Whip or
Pinch of salt	¹/₂ pint whipping cream,
1 medium can crushed	whipped
pineapple	

Soak large tapioca in water overnight. Do not drain. To the water and tapioca, add brown sugar and salt. Stir well. Bake in a 350° oven about one hour, until tapioca is transparent. Stir once or twice. If too thick, add small amount of water. Take out of oven and add pineapple, juice and all, vanilla and butter. Stir well, let cool and top with whipped cream or Cool Whip.

TO WHIP CREAM:
Combine ¹/₂ pint whipping cream, 3 tablespoons sugar, 1 teaspoon vanilla, and beat until stiff.

Affolter-Heritage Reunion Cookbook & More

Quick Tortoni

¹/₂ gallon vanilla ice cream	1 cup sliced natural almonds,
2 cups almond macaroon	lightly toasted*
crumbs	
¹/₂ cup diced maraschino	
cherries	

Allow ice cream to soften slightly. Stir in the remaining ingredients. Pack into ramekins or other small dessert dishes. Cover with plastic wrap and store in freezer until ready to serve. Serves 12-15.

*Spread the almonds on a baking sheet. Place in a 350° oven for 5-6 minutes or until golden brown. If the almonds on the edge start to become too brown, remove from oven and stir.

Variation: If you are making this dessert strictly for adults, add a splash of almond liqueur, if desired.

More Cooking with Marilyn Harris

Shaker Spiced Apple Pudding

1 1/2 cups butter
3 cups granulated sugar
2 eggs
3 cups sifted all-purpose flour
3 teaspoons baking soda

2 teaspoons cinnamon
1 teaspoon allspice
1 teaspoon ground cloves
8 medium apples, peeled,
　cored, chopped

Preheat oven to 375°. Cream together butter and sugar until light and fluffy. Beat in eggs. Combine all the dry ingredients and stir into creamed mixture. Add apples and stir together. Turn into a greased 9x13-inch baking pan. Bake 45 minutes until set. Serve with vanilla ice cream or heavy cream flavored with maple syrup or vanilla. Serves 6-8.

Plain & Fancy Favorites

Best Ever Pineapple Noodle Pudding

1 pound wide noodles, cooked
　and well drained
6 eggs
1 cup sugar
1/2 pound melted butter or
　margarine

1 pint sour cream
1 teaspoon vanilla
1 (12-ounce) can crushed
　pineapple

Beat eggs and sugar until lemon yellow. Add butter, sour cream, vanilla. Mix thoroughly. Add pineapple including most of juice. Combine mixture with noodles. Pour into a well greased 9x13-inch baking dish. Mixture will be quite runny. Bake at 325° for one hour. Top should be lightly browned. Serves 8-12 (recipe can be cut in half).

Generation to Generation

Ohio has many art and history museums. There are also: The Rock and Roll Hall of Fame (Cleveland), the National Inventors Hall of Fame (Akron), the Pro Football Hall of Fame (Canton), the US Air Force Museum (Dayton), the Flint Ridge Museum (Brownsville), the Ohio River Museum (Marietta), Butch's Cola Museum (Marietta), the Degenhart Paperweight Museum and Glass Museum (Cambridge), the Goodyear World of Rubber (Akron), the Popcorn Museum (Marion), and Dr. John Harris' Dental Museum (Chillicothe), to name a few.

Homestead Inn Banana Pudding with Walnut Crust

CRUST:

½ cup margarine

1 cup flour

1 cup finely chopped walnuts

Blend margarine, flour, and walnuts. Press in bottom of 9x13-inch pan and bake at 350° until light brown. Cool.

FIRST LAYER:

1 (8-ounce) package cream cheese

1 cup powdered sugar

10 ounces whipped topping

Sliced bananas (4-6)

Beat first 3 ingredients together and spread on prepared crust. Top with sliced bananas, then pudding layer.

PUDDING LAYER:

3 egg yolks

1 cup sugar

3 tablespoons cornstarch

2 cups milk

Banana flavoring

In saucepan, blend ingredients and cook over medium heat until thick. Cool before spreading over cream cheese and banana layer, then top with whipped topping or sweetened whipped cream. Refrigerate, and cut into 12 squares to serve.

The Homestead Inn Restaurant, Milan, Ohio.

Dining in Historic Ohio

Tammi's Banana Pudding

2 (14-ounce) cans Eagle Brand Condensed Milk

3 cups cold water

2 (3½-ounce) packages instant French vanilla pudding

2 envelopes Dream Whip

1 cup milk

1 box vanilla wafers

6 bananas

Do not use mixer for this recipe. Mix sweetened condensed milk and water in large bowl. Add pudding and beat until thick. Chill 5 minutes. In separate bowl, mix by hand milk and Dream Whip until blended (not whipped). Take pudding from refrigerator and stir in Dream Whip. Layer wafers, bananas, and pudding until all are used. Refrigerate.

Oeder Family & Friends Cookbook

Pastry Tulip Cups
with Caramelized Apple Filling

Mastering the art of working with frozen phyllo pastry is a fun activity. (No need to tell your awed guests how easy it was!) Easily made hours ahead, this apple filling can be reheated in the microwave or in a heavy pan over gentle heat. If you don't have the apple brandy, Calvados, substitute some good Cognac.

6 large tart cooking apples,
  peeled, cored, and diced
6 tablespoons unsalted butter
6 tablespoons sugar
1/2 vanilla bean, split
  lengthwise

1/4 cup Calvados
1 tablespoon fresh lemon
  juice
1 cup whipping cream
2 tablespoons confectioners'
  sugar

In a large skillet, stir the apples with butter and sugar over medium heat until butter melts. Add the vanilla bean to the mixture. Increase heat to medium-high and cook, stirring frequently, until apples are brown and caramelized—about 30 minutes. Remove the vanilla bean. Pour off any excess butter and add the Calvados. Cook for one minute more over high heat, scraping up any caramel from bottom of the pan. Stir in the lemon juice.

Whip the cream until thickened; add the confectioners' sugar gradually and continue to whip until very stiff. While still warm, spoon the apple mixture into Pastry Tulip Cups and top each with a large dollop of the freshly whipped cream. Makes 6 servings.

PASTRY TULIP CUPS:
4 sheets phyllo   Melted unsalted butter

Stack phyllo with butter brushed between the sheets. Cut into 4-inch squares. Press each square into a buttered muffin tin, pressing the bottom flat and folding excess dough to create a petal effect on the sides. Bake in the bottom third of a 375° oven for 10 - 12 minutes or until golden. Remove from muffin tins and cool on a rack.

Cooking with Marilyn

With more wineries than any other Midwest state, Ohio is ranked fourth in the nation in number of wineries, and fifth in wine production.

Raspberry Peach Brulée

An easy, show-off dessert. Peaches and raspberry sauce under a blanket of whipped cream, topped with brown sugar, and caramelized under the broiler.

4 fresh peaches, peeled and thickly sliced	1 cup whipping cream
4 tablespoons Robert Rothschild Gourmet Red Raspberry Sauce	2 teaspoons vanilla 1 cup dark brown sugar

Place sliced peaches in a sieve to drain for a couple hours (they may darken, but that is all right). Place in a freezer-to-oven soufflé dish or deep pie dish. Drizzle raspberry sauce over peaches. Beat whipping cream, add vanilla and continue beating until cream is very stiff. Spread this over the fruit. Cover with plastic wrap and refrigerate. Two hours before serving, place the dish in the freezer to harden.

To serve, preheat broiler. Remove dessert from freezer and sprinkle top with a half-inch layer of brown sugar, covering the cream completely. Place 4-5 inches below source of heat. Broil 2-3 minutes or just until the top is hot and glistening. Serve at once. Yield: 6 servings.

Robert Rothschild Recipes

Puffs of Cream

1 cup water
1/4 teaspoon salt
1/2 cup butter

1 cup flour
4 large eggs
Vanilla Custard Filling

Heat water, butter, and salt in a saucepan and bring to full rolling boil. Reduce heat and quickly stir in flour, mixing vigorously with a wooden spoon until mixture leaves the sides of the pan in a ball. Remove from heat.

Put flour mixture into mixing bowl. Add eggs one at a time on low speed, beating approximately 30 seconds between eggs. Scrape bowl and beat on high for 15 seconds. Drop dough onto greased cookie sheet about 3 inches apart, any desired shape or size.

Bake at 400° for 10 minutes. Lower heat to 350° for 25 minutes. Puffs should be doubled in size and golden brown. Let them cool in turned-off oven for 10 minutes. Split and fill with Vanilla Custard Filling.

VANILLA CUSTARD FILLING:

1 small package vanilla
  instant pudding
1 1/2 cups milk

1 (8-ounce) container Cool
  Whip

Mix together pudding and milk and let set. Add Cool Whip. Fill puffs and refrigerate.

Hats Off to "Real Men Cook" Cookbook

The Grand Finale Grand Trifle

4 cups pound or yellow cake
  chunks
1 cup fresh or frozen, thawed
  strawberries in syrup
4 ounces port wine
4 ounces cream sherry
8 large scoops rich vanilla ice
  cream or custard

1 cup fresh or frozen, thawed
  raspberries in syrup
1 1/2 - 2 cups heavy cream,
  shipped
1/4 cup toasted slivered
  almonds
8 maraschino or chocolate
  covered cherries for garnish

In 8 large brandy sniffers or a 2-quart clear glass bowl, layer ingredients in order given and garnish with cherries. Chill about an hour to blend flavors. Serves 8.

Dining in Historic Ohio

Lorna Doone Dessert

1 box Lorna Doone Cookies	1 quart French vanilla ice
¹/₂ stick margarine, melted	cream
2 packages instant French	12 ounces Cool Whip
vanilla pudding	3 Heath bars
2 cups milk	

Crush cookies. Add margarine to cookie crumbs. Mix and pat in 9x13-inch pan. Combine pudding and milk. Mix until dissolved. Add ice cream. Stir until mixed. Pour over cookie crumb mixture. Spread Cool Whip over mixture. Crush candy bars and sprinkle over top. Refrigerate.

Cooking with TLC

Pretzel Dessert

CRUST:

2 cups crushed pretzels	3 tablespoons sugar
³/₄ cup melted oleo	

Mix together and press into a 9x13-inch pan. Bake at 400° for 8 minutes. Cool.

FILLING:

1 (8-ounce) package cream	1 cup sugar
cheese, softened	1 (8-ounce) carton Cool Whip

Cream together cream cheese and sugar. Fold in Cool Whip. Spread over crust.

TOPPING:

1 (6-ounce) box strawberry	2 (10-ounce) packages frozen
gelatin	strawberries
2 cups boiling water	

Dissolve gelatin in boiling water. Fold in frozen strawberries. Let set about 8 minutes, allowing strawberries to thaw. Pour over cream cheese mixture. Refrigerate.

Favorite Recipes from the Heart of Amish Country

Peanut Buster Dessert

CRUST:

1 cup flour
1 stick butter or oleo

²/₃ cup chopped peanuts, dry
  roasted (unsalted)

Mix flour and butter like pie crust. Add peanuts and spread in 9x13-inch greased pan. Bake at 350° for 15-20 minutes until golden brown. Set aside until cool.

FIRST TOPPING:

¹/₃ cup creamy peanut butter
1 (8-ounce) package cream
  cheese

1 cup powdered sugar
2 cups Cool Whip

Cream first 3 ingredients, then blend in Cool Whip. Spread on top of cooled baked dough.

SECOND TOPPING:

1 small box French instant
  vanilla pudding
3 cups cold milk

1 small box chocolate instant
  pudding

Mix all together with mixer until thick. Spread on top of cream cheese topping.

THIRD TOPPING:

1 (8-ounce) container Cool
  Whip
Chopped peanuts

1 large Hershey Chocolate
  Bar, crushed

Spread Cool Whip on top of pudding mixture. Sprinkle with chopped peanuts and chopped chocolate bar. Refrigerate.

Note: You can use one small box instant vanilla pudding and one chocolate pudding. Use 1¹/₂ cups cold milk for each box. Spread one on top of the other.

Cooking GRACEfully

Sport fish found in Lake Erie: Walleye, yellow perch, smallmouth bass, catfish, largemouth bass, freshwater drum, carp, white perch, white bass, crappie, steelhead trout, and more. Walleye, a nocturnal species, often stop biting once the sun reaches its midday high.

Death by Chocolate

1 chocolate cake, baked in
  9x13-inch pan
1/2 cup Kahlua
3 boxes chocolate mousse

6 Skor or Heath Bars,
  crunched up
1 (16-ounce) carton Cool
  Whip

Bake cake and cool. Poke large holes with fork; pour Kahlua over cake, cover and refrigerate 4-5 hours or overnight. Mix mousse according to directions. Freeze candy bars, crunch in package. In punch bowl, layer 1/3 crumbled cake, 1/3 mousse, and 1/3 Cool Whip, and 2 candy bars. Repeat for 2 more layers. Chill 3 hours or overnight. This is much better made the day before.

Gardener's Delight

Triple-Dipped Strawberries

A showstopper when served in a pedestal dish on a dessert buffet.

¾ pound white chocolate
2 tablespoons vegetable oil,
  divided
½ pound milk chocolate

¼ pound semisweet
  chocolate
1 quart strawberries

In 3 separate double boilers or bowls over hot water, melt white chocolate and 1 tablespoon oil, milk chocolate and 2 teaspoons oil, and semisweet chocolate and 1 teaspoon oil, stirring until well blended.

Dip berries in white chocolate to coat ¾ of the way up berry. Allow coating to harden, then dip into milk chocolate, about ½ of the way up berry, leaving a strip of white chocolate showing. Let harden, then dip tips of berries in semisweet chocolate. Store on a wax paper-lined plate in refrigerator. Yields about 20-25 berries.

The Heritage Tradition

Frozen Strawberries

Whole strawberries
2 quarts crushed berries
1 box Sure-Jell

³/₄ cup water
4 cups sugar

Fill 5 wide-mouth quart jars with berries within 2 inches to the top. Crush or blend 2 quarts berries. Mix Sure-Jell with water. Boil 2 minutes. Add sugar and crushed berries. Pour over berries in quart jars. Cap and freeze. Do not screw lid too tight to allow for expansion when frozen. Thaw to slush and serve for company breakfast. Tastes like fresh.

Tasty Recipes

Rosewater Ice Cream

1¹/₂ cups milk
3 egg yolks
³/₄ cup sugar

¹/₈ teaspoon salt
1¹/₂ teaspoons rosewater
1 pint heavy cream, whipped

Scald milk over low heat. Beat egg yolks with sugar and salt until thick and lemon-colored. Pour in the hot scalded milk, beating constantly. Return entire mixture to low heat and cook, very gently, until it is slightly thickened and coats a metal spoon. Remove from heat and chill thoroughly. Add rosewater and fold in the whipped cream. Place mixture in an ice cream freezer and process until frozen and thick. Remove dasher and pack. Let ripen for several hours. Makes about 4 servings.

The Shaker Cookbook

Barb Forman's Chocolate Sauce

3 tablespoons cocoa
3 tablespoons flour
1 cup sugar

1 cup hot water
1 stick oleo
Vanilla to taste

Combine ingredients in saucepan. Cook and stir until thickens. Delicious served immediately or cold. Makes 2 cups. Can microwave.

Heavenly Food II

Cranberry Ice

2 cups cranberries	1 package lemon Jello
2 cups water	Juice of 1 lemon ($1/4$ cup)
$1/2$ cup sugar	Juice of 2 oranges ($3/4$ cup)
$1/2$ cup light corn syrup	

Boil cranberries in water and strain. Add sugar and corn syrup and bring to a boil. Dissolve Jello in hot mixture and cool. Put in lemon and orange juice and freeze. Remove from tray and beat. Then freeze again. Serve in sherbet glasses.

Sharing Our Best (Elizabeth House)

Index

Marblehead Lighthouse has kept a lonely vigil on Lake Erie for more than 170 years.

INDEX

Catalog
of
Contributing
Cookbooks

Cincinnati's Museum Center at Union Terminal, a classic in art deco design.

CATALOG
of
CONTRIBUTING COOKBOOKS

All recipes in this book have been submitted from the cookbooks shown on the following pages. Individuals who wish to obtain a copy of a particular book can do so by sending a check or money order to the address listed. Prices are subject to change. Please note the postage and handling charges that may be required. State residents add applicable sales tax. Retailers are invited to call or write to same address for wholesale information. Some of these contributing cookbooks may have gone out of print since the original publication of this book. Quail Ridge Press is proud to preserve America's food heritage by keeping many of their recipes in print.

Affolter

AFFOLTER AE

Heritage Reunion Cookbook
and More....

Compiled by Mary Calendine

AFFOLTER HERITAGE REUNION COOKBOOK ANE MORE...
by Mary Calendine
Marsh Road Box 276
Hiddenite, NC 28636   828-632-6635

Originally from Ohio, Mary edited this cookbook because her family is now scattered over the United States. She wanted the old family recipes to be saved for the new generation. Although the young people may not cook quite as much as her generation, this book will be a heritage for them.

$ 14.95 Retail price
$ 2.00 Postage and handling
Make check payable to Mary Calendine

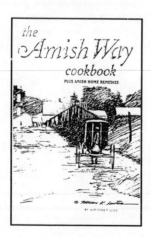

the
Amish Way
cookbook
PLUS AMISH HOME REMEDIES

THE AMISH WAY COOKBOOK
by Adrienne Lund
Jupiter Press
77 South Franklin Street   440-247-3616
Chagrin Falls, OH 44022   FAX 440-247-5431

Authentic Amish recipes collected from Amish homemakers in Ohio and Pennsylvania. The book was written-up in the *Cleveland Plain Dealer* magazine section as an outstanding Amish cookbook. 203 pages including Amish poems and hints, home remedy section, and illustrations. Sunset pink cover with black Amish buggy and white comb binding.

$ 12.95 Retail price
$ 2.00 Postage and handling
Make check payable to Jupiter Press
0-938400-06-1

ANGELS AND FRIENDS FAVORITE RECIPES I

Angels of Easter Seal
299 Edwards Street
Youngstown, OH 44512   330-743-1168

A collection of 840 easy-to-follow, favorite, tried and true recipes. This 436-page, illustrated cookbook has a durable plastic cover and features a triple cross index, chapters indexed with dividers, original family Old World recipes, and delightful area chef specialties. Featured in Family Circle and Good Housekeeping magazines. Proceeds benefit the Easter Seal Society, serving disabled children and adults.

$ 14.50 Retail price
$ 2.00 Postage and handling
Make check payable to *Angels and Friends Favorite Recipes*
ISBN 0-9613501-0-5

ANGELS AND FRIENDS FAVORITE RECIPES II

Angels of Easter Seal
299 Edwards Street
Youngstown, OH 44512   330-743-1168

This collection, beautifully illustrated in 19th-century prints, contains "all new," tried and tested recipes is designed for the 90's, but features the same winning qualities as Volume I. This 486-page cookbook features 435 recipes, has a durable, plastic cover, is triple cross indexed, chapters are indexed with dividers, special "On the Light Side" section, and an expanded Microwave section. Proceeds benefit the Easter Seal Society, serving disabled children and adults.

$ 14.50 Retail price
$ 2.00 Postage and handling
Make check payable to *Angels and Friends Favorite Recipes*
ISBN 0808150124

APPLETIZERS

Johnny Appleseed Metro Park District
2355 Ada Road
Lima, OH 45801   419-221-1232

All recipes contain apples, and a chart lists best uses for each variety of apple. Includes short history and information about legendary "Johnny Appleseed," and original line drawings by local artist Nancy Raver. Contains favorite apple recipes from famous Ohio celebrities. 340 recipes, 171 pages of apple cookery, including fact and folklore about apples.

$ 4.95 Retail price
$ 3.50 Postage and handling
Make check payable to Johnny Appleseed Park District

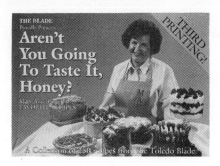

AREN'T YOU GOING TO TASTE IT, HONEY?
Mary Alice Powell's Favorite Recipes

The Blade Marketing Department
Attn: Mary Alice Powell Cookbook
P. O. Box 555
Toledo, OH 43697-0555   419-724-6275

Aren't You Going To Taste It, Honey? chronicles the cooking styles of Northwest Ohio as reported, pre-pared, and tasted by the *Toledo Blade* food editor for 41 years. The more than 250 recipes reflect the regional preference for honest, straight-forward foods, dependent on Ohio's indigenous ingredients, but it also shows an acceptance of foods of the '90s. 270 pages, 250 recipes.

$ 9.95   Retail price
$ 1.50   Postage and handling
Make check payable to The Blade
ISBN 0-9614554-2-X

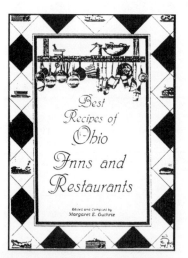

BEST RECIPES OF OHIO INNS AND RESTAURANTS

by Margaret E. Guthrie
Amherst Press
Amherst, WI

Satisfy your taste for travel! The variety and diversity of Ohio food and cooking extends far beyond its famous big cities. A certain sophistication has come to the small, out-of-the-way inns and restaurants, too. This collection proves it. High-quality, 4-color, laminated soft cover, 144 pages, illustrated. Part of a 5-state series. Currently out of print.

BOUNTIFUL OHIO: Good Food and Stories from Where the Heartland Begins

by James Hope and Susan Failor
Gabriel's Horn Publishing Co.
Bowling Green, OH

This handsomely illustrated volume is a celebration of the food and people of the state where America's Heartland begins. Written by two Ohioans who spent much time touring the state and meeting its people, this 224-page book offers 163 down-home recipes, plus heartwarming stories and fascinating lore. Currently out of print.

BY OUR COOKSTOVE

Shekinah Christian School Ladies Auxiliary
10040 Lafayette-Plain City Road
Plain City, OH 43064   614-873-3130

By Our Cookstove is filled with recipes from the Amish/Mennonite tradition. The food is simple, yet tasteful and attractive. Contents include every part of a meal from appetizers to desserts. Approximately 600 recipes. 300 pages. Has been printed four times due to its popularity.

$ 10.45 Retail price
$ 2.50 Postage and handling
Make check payable to Shekinah Ladies Auxiliary

CINCINNATI RECIPE TREASURY:
The Queen City's Culinary Heritage

by Mary Anna DuSablon
c/o Ohio University Press
Scott Quadrangle
Athens, OH 45701   740-593-1155

The distinctive flavors of Cincinnati's culinary traditions are recreated in this colorful collection of recipes from time-worn cookbooks, popular restaurants, family cooks, and celebrity chefs. Enlivened with nostalgic line drawings and historical anecdotes, every recipe is an authentic taste of the Queen City's cultural heritage.

$ 14.95 Retail price
$ 3.50 Postage and handling
Make check payable to Ohio University Press
ISBN 0-8214-0933-6

A CLEVELAND COLLECTION

The Junior League of Cleveland, Inc.
10819 Magnolia Drive
Cleveland, OH 44106   216-231-6300

A full-color, double-page photographic book featuring exquisite table settings and showcasing Cleveland landmarks. Over 250 triple-tested recipes in 9 very special chapters including a Gourmet Health Section and favorite recipes from Cleveland celebrities. Includes wine selections, special low-fat notations, and menu suggestions. Proceeds support the community projects of The Junior League of Cleveland, Inc.

$ 24.95 Retail price
$ 5.00 Postage and handling
Make check payable to The Junior League of Cleveland, Inc.
ISBN 0-9619027-0-1

COOK, LINE & SINKER

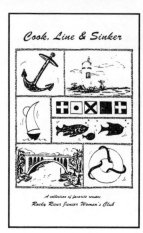

Rocky River Junior Women's Club
P. O. Box 16724
Rocky River, OH 44116   440-356-9860

From the shores of Lake Erie comes this treasured collection of over 600 twice taste-tested recipes. These diverse recipes range from easy family dinners and treats to elegant fare. Of special note are the herb and spice charts, area restaurant recipes, and terrific menu plans for various occasions.

$ 15.00 Retail price
$ 2.00 Postage and handling

Make check payable to Rocky River Junior Women's Club

COOKING GRACEFULLY

Grace Presbyterian Church
7 North 4th Street
Martins Ferry, OH 43935   740-633-2699

Cooking GRACEfully contains 130 pages of delicious recipes sure to delight your family and friends. Our community luncheon favorite, Wedding Soup, and our unique Sweet Potato Casserole are only two of the 350 recipes designed to tantalize your tastebuds and fill your home with mouth-watering aromas.

$ 6.50 Retail price
$ 1.50 Postage and handling

Make check payable to Grace Presbyterian Church

COOKING ON THE WILD SIDE
with the Cincinnati Zoo and Botanical Garden

Cincinnati, OH

Liven a party with House Warming Punch. Impress guests with Salmon Pasta. Receive rave reviews for freshly baked Cola Cake and Grape Pie. This 200-page hardbound book, filled with 250 superb recipes from Cincinnati Zoo volunteers, is also great reading. This cookbook is a must for collectors. Profits benefit the zoo. Currently out of print.

COOKING WITH CLASS

Garden Club of Apple Valley in Ohio
540 Baldwin Drive
Howard, OH 43028   740-393-0786

Need a gift for mom, daughter, sister-in-law, friend, or yourself? 458 proven recipes by Apple Valley's Finest Cooks with pages of helpful kitchen advice!

$ 6.00 Retail price
$ 2.00 Postage and handling

Make check payable to Apple Valley Garden Club

COOKING WITH HOPE RIDGE FAMILIES

Hope Ridge United Methodist Women
9870 Johnnycake Ridge Road
Mentor, OH 44060   440-352-2141

Hope Ridge Church's favorite meeting is a potluck supper. The 250 delicious recipes in 110 pages were contributed by more than 60 members of our congregation, as well as memories from previous cookbooks. We emphasize easy, healthy recipes for busy households.

$ 7.50 Retail price
$ 1.50 Postage and handling

Make check payable to Hope Ridge UMW

COOKING WITH MARILYN

by Marilyn Harris
Pelican Publishing Co
P. O. Box 3110
Gretna, LA 70054   800-843-1724

As you go through this book, pay special attention to the "steaming spoon" symbols. They flag tips and ideas as only Marilyn can offer them...from her years of teaching. This book proves that cooking is a creative art and fun to do. Marilyn writes in a conversational style, rich in culinary insight and stove-top wisdom.

$ 19.95 Retail price
$ 4.71 Postage and handling

Make check payable to Pelican Publishing Co.
ISBN 1-56554-075-1

COOKING WITH TLC

Trinity Lutheran Church
508 Center Street
Ashland, OH 44805   419-289-2126

Our cookbook collection is composed of two books: the large book has 325 pages containing 500 recipes of all kinds, and the smaller book has 140 holiday goodies in its 160 pages. Our recipes are all truly filled with tender loving care. Proceeds will go to our Reading Enrichment Program.

$ 12.00 Retail price (both books)
$ 3.20 Postage and handling
Make check payable to Trinity Lutheran Church

CZECH DANCERS POLKA CLUB COOK BOOK

Czech Dancers Polka Club, Inc.
1-15189 CR 4-1
Metamora, OH 43540   419-644-4271

Favorite Czech, American, and treasured old-family recipes collected throughout the years. The Czech Dancers Polka Club is proud of their heritage given to them by their ancestors who settled in a new land to seek a better life.

$ 10.00 Retail price, includes tax and postage
Make check payable to Czech Dancers Polka Club, Inc.

DINING IN HISTORIC OHIO

by Marty Godbey
McClanahan Publishing
Kuttawa, KY

Histories and valuable information on 47 restaurants throughout Ohio. From a fire house to a covered bridge, you'll find interesting and exciting places to dine as well as recipes for their most-asked-for dishes, all in *Dining in Historic Ohio.* 208 pages, paperback, illustrated, indexed. Currently out of print.

DOWN HOME COOKIN'
WITHOUT THE DOWN HOME FAT

by Dawn Hall
5425 S. Fulton-Lucas Road   FAX 419-826-2700
Swanton, OH 43558   419-826-COOK (2665)

This 200-page, hardcover cookbook for BUSY PEOPLE has over 250 delicious recipes and lies flat for easier reading. It takes ordinary foods to the limit, making them exceptionally scrumptious while reducing calories dramatically with mouth-watering recipes prepared quickly and effortlessly and all *EXTREMELY* low-fat! 36,000 copies sold in 27 weeks.

$ 15.95 Retail price
$ 3.00 Postage and handling

Make check payable to Cozy Homestead Publishing, Inc.
ISBN 0-9649950-0-X

DOWN HOME COOKING
FROM HOCKING COUNTY

Logan Hocking Chamber of Commerce
Logan, OH

This 74-page cookbook contains over 250 recipes in seven categories plus extra pages of helpful hints and even a calorie counter. All recipes were submitted from local residents of Hocking County. Currently out of print.

EASY COOKING WITH HERBS & SPICES

Triset De Fonseka
815 Elm Street
Cincinnati, OH 45202   513-723-1217

Easy Cooking with Herbs & Spices—250 exotic, palate pleasing recipes with less salt, and can be cooked in an economical way. Herbs and spices are blended with different sauces for aroma and flavor. In place of coconut milk stock, skim milk or water are substituted for a healthy lifestyle. 180 pages.

$ 14.95 Retail price
$ 2.50 Postage and handling

Make check payable to Triset De Fonseka
ISBN 0-9634997-7-7

THE FAT-FREE REAL FOOD COOKBOOK

by J. Kevin Wolfe
Im Press
Cincinnati, OH

Includes 130 fat free recipes for pasta, soups, meals, sidedishes, desserts and more. Each recipe has a nutrition label to see what you are getting (protein, sodium, calories, carbohydrates, fiber) and are not getting (fat and cholesterol) from your food. Comb-bound book lies flat for practical use. Laminated covers can be washed. Currently out of print.

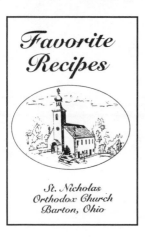

FAVORITE RECIPES

St. Nicholas Orthodox Church
P. O. Box 777
Barton, OH 43905   740-695-0707

Favorite Recipes was compiled to share our best Slovak (ethnic) recipes, customs, and foods to have at Easter and Christmas. Includes 400 delicious varieties of foods that have been prepared many times. This beautiful, hardcover cookbook has 166 pages which include grace at the table, household hints, cooking tips, herbs and spices, napkin folding, hints for bread making, and desserts.

$ 12.00 Retail price
$ 3.00 Postage and handling
Make check payable to St. Nicholas Orthodox Church

FAVORITE RECIPES
FROM POLAND WOMEN'S CLUB

Poland Women's Club
Poland, OH

Favorite Recipes from Poland Women's Club is a collection of 427 recipes, 152 pages, submitted by members of this service organization organized over 40 years ago. Poland, Ohio, known as Town One, Range One of the Connecticut Western Reserve, was founded in 1796 and is currently celebrating its Bicentennial. Currently out of print.

FAVORITE RECIPES
FROM THE HEART OF AMISH COUNTRY
by Rachel Miller
Sugarcreek, OH

Favorite Recipes from the Heart of Amish Country cookbook contains 219 pages and approximately 514 recipes that were contributed by Amish ladies. Recipes are simple and delicious. It also includes kitchen hints and a poem about the Amish, titled "Amish Lifestyle." Currently out of print.

THE FIFTH GENERATION COOKBOOK
Carol L. Wise
16099 Co. Rd. 172
Findlay, OH 45840   419-427-8608

The fifth generation of our family's favorite recipes is combined in 103 pages and 275 recipes, with contributors' ages ranging from 1 to 96! It contains bits of family traditions and history, pieces of humor, and "mouth-watering" German and Pennsylvania Dutch recipes dating back to the 1800s. Makes for wonderful evening reading.

$ 7.95 Retail price
$ 2.50 Postage and handling
Make check payable to Carol L. Wise

FIREBELLES COOKBOOK
New Philadelphia Fire Department Ladies Auxiliary
c/o Sue Caton
121 8th Street N.E.
New Philadelphia, OH 44663   330-343-8376

The Firebelles Cookbook is comprised of simple but good recipes from members and friends of our organization. It has 85 pages of around 300 recipes along with Kitchen Hints and a Calorie Counter. Proceeds from this book go to help fire victims in our city.

$ 6.00 Retail price
$ 1.25 Postage and handling
Make check payable to The Firebelles

500 RECIPES USING ZUCCHINI COOKBOOK

Southington Garden Club
Southington, OH

500 Recipes Using Zucchini is an unusual collection of zucchini recipes including: appetizers, soups, salads, main dishes, casseroles, breads, cakes, and even pies and cookies. Includes tips on herbs, spices, canning and freezing, plus a bit of trivia. The spiral bound 6½ x 9 cookbook has 268 pages, including basic kitchen information. Currently out of print.

FIVE STAR SENSATIONS

Auxiliary of University Hospitals of Cleveland
Department of Development
Cleveland, OH

Five Star Sensations joins America's finest chefs with Cleveland cooks to benefit the University Ireland Cancer Center of University Hospitals of Cleveland. Special foreword by Wolfgang Puck introduces 278 recipes with easy to follow directions. Award-winning design features a Plexiglas cover, die-cut tabs and spiral binding. Features 256 pages of truly sensational recipes. Currently out of print.

GARDENER'S DELIGHT

THE OHIO ASSOCIATION OF GARDEN CLUBS, INC.

"Knowing, Growing, Showing, and Sharing"

Gardener's Delight

The Ohio Association of Garden Clubs, Inc.
Green Springs, OH

Gardener's Delight is a collection of recipes from members of 398 clubs in Ohio. The Association grants two scholarships each year to students entering the horticulture or related field. Profit from the 320-page book, which includes many lowfat and diet recipes, food, household and gardening hints and poems, will be used to support this project. Currently out of print.

GENERATION TO GENERATION

Temple Israel Sisterhood
333 25th St. N.W.
Canton, OH 44709   330-455-5197

Our comb-bound cookbook contains 370 pages with convenient chapter tab dividers. It is practical and uncomplicated for beginners, as well as for experienced cooks. We suggest the section under Festivals as being unique and our favorite.

$ 10.00 Retail price
$ 2.00 Postage and handling
Make check payable to Temple Israel Sisterhood

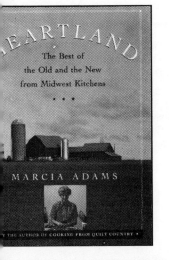

HATS OFF TO "REAL MEN COOK"

Women's Alliance for Recovery Services, Inc.
2012 West 25th Street Suite 620   216-575-9120
Cleveland, OH 44113   FAX 216-575-1933

Hats Off to "Real Men Cook" cookbook is a compilation of 103 recipes that come from the kitchens of "real men" that truly can cook. These distinguished chefs, from the occasional kitchen dabbler to the serious pro, have served their creations at Real Men Cook, a grazing GALA, one of Ohio's finest events, celebrated since 1989 to benefit Women's Alliance for Recovery Services (serving women and children affected with substance abuse).

$ 8.00 Retail price
$ 2.00 Postage and handling
Make check payable to Women's Alliance for Recovery Services

HEARTLAND: The Best of the Old and the New from Midwest Kitchens

by Marcia Adams
Random House
400 Hahn Road
Westminster, MD 21157   800-733-3000

Marcia Adams, respected PBS TV chef, has collected 200 recipes from 8 Midwestern states, including Ohio. Many are treasures from the oral tradition and all are carefully tested and placed in an informative historical manner. If you are looking for long lost and marvelous regional cuisine, this is your book. Hardcover, 258 pp.

$ 30.00 Retail price
$ 5.50 Postage and handling
Make check payable to Random House
ISBN 0-517-57533-7

HEARTLINE COOKBOOK

by Pat DiGiacomo
5723 McKee Road
Wooster, OH 44691   330-262-4375

Heartline Cookbook features 181 low fat, low cholesterol, low sodium recipes that have been family kitchen tested. It is especially designed for the busy cook, combining simplicity, easy preparation, and taste appeal derived from common herbs and spices. A 35-day main meal planner is the highlight of this 137-page cookbook.

$ 8.95 Retail price
$ 1.50 Postage and handling
Make check payable to Pat DiGiacomo

HEAVENLY DISHES

United Methodist Women of Union Pisgah Church
Attica, OH

Our cookbook contains 200 recipes in 74 pages and was compiled to celebrate the 150th anniversary of our little country church, Union Pisgah, better known as Swamp because when it was organized in 1844, it was located on swampy ground. Our membership is 55 and we have an average attendance of 40. Currently out of print.

HEAVENLY FOOD II

United Methodist Women
Sunbury United Methodist Church
Sunbury, OH

One hundred thirty-five pages of home-tested recipes (about 400) from the kitchens of our church ladies. You will find recipes from appetizers, breads, desserts to pickles and play dough. There is a recipe for roast loin, plus old-time favorites and many time-saving recipes as well. Currently out of print.

HEIRLOOM RECIPES AND BY GONE DAYS

Sherry Maurer
P. O. Box 626
Zoar, OH 44697   330-874-2873

Heirloom Recipes and By Gone Days is more than a cook-book. Rich in German heritage, this collection of recipes has been handed down for generations since 1817. The tasty recipes are easy to prepare, using common ingredi-ents. Four color cover, 185 recipes, 283 pages, and 42 photographs.

$ 14.95 Retail price
$ 2.50 Postage and handling

Make check payable to Heirloom Enterprises

HERBS: From Cultivation to Cooking

Herb Society of Greater Cincinnati
2715 Reading Road
Cincinnati, OH 45206   513-221-0983

This excellent, hardcover cookbook contains over 400 recipes in 240 pages plus advice on how to grow your own herbs—inside and out, preserving herbs, and herbal hints. Plus a month by month guide for what to do with herbs as well as an herbal description chart.

$ 13.00 Retail price
$ 3.00 Postage and handling

Make check payable to The Civic Garden Center
ISBN 0-88289-288-6

THE HERITAGE TRADITION

by Janet Melvin
Heritage Restaurant
7664 Wooster Pike
Cincinnati, OH 45227   513-561-9300

Howard and Janet Melvin have owned and operated Heritage Restaurant since 1959, continually incorporating their personal tastes into the business. Their restaurant and adjoining herb and flower gardens have become land-marks for those who love innovative and delicious cuisine. This cookbook is a collection of recipes that have con-tributed to their continued success.

$ 12.00 Retail price
$ 3.00 Postage and handling

Make check payable to Heritage Restaurant

HOME COOKIN' WITH 4-H

Jackson County 4-H Advisory Council
P. O. Box 110
Jackson, OH 45640   740-288-7192

4-H is a youth organization that boasts over five million members in the United States. The State of Ohio can claim over 200,000 members, 700 of those living in Jackson County. These excellent recipes were donated by 4-H Advisors, 4-H Members, Friends of 4-H, and Extension Homemakers. Proceeds help further the goals to strengthen a child's desire to learn, to participate, and to believe in themselves. 80 pages, ringbound.

$ 6.00 Retail price
$ 1.25 Postage and handling
Make check payable to 4-H Advisory Council

INCREDIBLE EDIBLES

Youngstown/Warren Dental Association
164 Winter Lane
Cortland, OH 44410   330-637-2873

Our cookbook is compiled by dental assistants, dentists, hygienists and dentists' wives in our area. All recipes have been tested and are guaranteed to be easy. Our book was the first book that was made available by the dental profession in the state of Ohio. Includes some fun recipes.

$ 7.50 Retail price
$ 2.00 Postage and handling
Make check payable to YWDAS

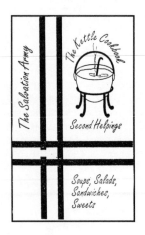

THE KETTLE COOKBOOK: Second Helpings

The Soup Sisters of the Salvation Army
Cleveland, OH

The focus of *The Kettle Cookbook* is its 97 delicious and carefully tested soup recipes that are suitable for any season or occasion. Also included within the 254 pages, are recipes for accompanying salads, sandwiches/breads and sweets. The cookbook was published in celebration of the 100th anniversary of the Salvation Army Christmas collection kettle. All proceeds are used to assist the Salvation Army with their programs to feed the hungry. Currently out of print.

Ms. Linda presents
kinderFun Kuisine
Shortcuts to Good Nutrition for Busy People

by Linda Leszynski

a National Public Television personality and career-long advocate for children's health enrichment

Healthy Young Children Enterprises, Inc.

KINDER KUISINE: Shortcuts to Good Nutrition for Busy People

Linda Leszynski   mslinda@healthyyoungchildren.com
173 Fredericksberg Drive   www.healthyyoungchildren.com
Avon Lake, OH 44012-1863   440-930-0573

Kinder Kuisine contains more than 300 recipes that are nutritious, easily prepared, and contain ingredients found on your grocer's shelves. Categories include snacks, appetizers, main dishes, muffins, breads, desserts, plus a section of "special occasion" desserts. The "idea pages" offer helpful hints for efficient meal preparation and clean-up. Spiral bound. This book has been re-released as *kinderFun Kuisine.*

$ 20.00   Retail price
$ 2.50   Postage and handling
Make check payable to Healthy Young Children Ent, Inc.
ISBN 0681634154

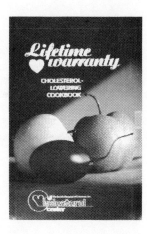

LIFETIME WARRANTY

Jewish Hospital Cholesterol Center Dietitians
Alliance Buuusiness Center
3200 Burnet Avenue   illigek@healthall.com
Cincinnati, OH 45229   513-569-3812

This 272-page, 365-recipe, spiral-bound cookbook contains information and family-oriented recipes designed to make low cholesterol cooking simple, creative and enjoyable. The recipes were developed, modified and extensively taste-tested by registered dietitians who specialize in cholesterol education.

$ 5.00   Retail price, includes postage and handling
Make check payable to The Jewish Hospital

LIGHT KITCHEN CHOREOGRAPHY

Cleveland Ballet Council
Cleveland, OH

A collection of low-fat recipes, *Light Kitchen Choreography* is filled with 200 recipes perfect for today's emphasis on healthy eating. Sections include appetizers, soups, salads, entrees, and desserts. Recipes have been analyzed by dietitians from nutritional data resources for calories, protein, carbohydrates, total fat, cholesterol, sodium and fiber content. Currently out of print.

MARY YODER'S AMISH KITCHEN COOKBOOK
Restaurant - Gift Shop
14743 North State Road   440-632-1939
Middlefield, OH 44066   or 440-673-5363

A warm welcome awaits you at Mary Yoder's Amish Kitchen. In this cookbook, you will find country home-cooking recipes of our staff and friends. These Amish favorites are mostly simple—and simply delicious. 168 pages. 227 recipes.

$ 10.99 Retail price
$ 3.50 Postage and handling
Make check payable to Mary Yoder's Amish Kitchen
ISBN 1-886645-04-3

A MATTER OF TASTE
PAULDING COUNTY REPUBLICAN WOMEN
18133 Rd 156
Paulding, OH 45879   419-399-5809

From Ohio's Great Black Swamp come 229 recipes of Paulding County Republican women, local and state elected and appointed officials. Reflecting robust pioneer settlers' simple taste, recipes range from apple dumplings to zucchini casserole, and include roast hog (used at the county Republican Party's fall rally) and roast bear.

$ 6.50 Retail price
$ 2.80 Postage and handling
Make check payable to Paulding County Republican Women

MDA FAVORITE RECIPES
Maple Dale Elementary School
10901 Windhaven Court   513/984-9339
Cincinnati, OH 45242-3113   FAX 513-984-9690

MDA Favorite Recipes is a collection of recipes from members of the Maple Dale Association of Maple Dale Elementary School. The MDA supports school activities and provides many extras for the students. This cookbook contains 154 pages with 385 delicious recipes, complete index and table of contents for each category.

$ 8.00 Retail price
$ 1.50 Postage and handling
Make check payable to Maple Dale Association

MORE COOKING WITH MARILYN
by Marilyn Harris
Paxton Press
Cincinnati, OH

From the kitchen of an acclaimed radio personality, columnist, food consultant, and cooking teacher: One faithful student describes her as "a marvelously creative cook with a charming personality, enthusiasm for good food and a never-ending repertoire of fresh ideas." This is her second collection of diverse and exciting recipes presented with humor and quick wit. Currently out of print.

NOW THAT MOM'S NOT AROUND COOKBOOK
Dawn DePew
7991 Winsome Court
Blacklick, OH 43004   614-866-7763

Now That Mom's Not Around Cookbook is an unusual combination of recipes that represent home cooking with an international flair. An all around cookbook that will delight both the novice and experienced cook. This cookbook will be the mainstay in anyone's kitchen.

$14.99 Retail price
$ .86 Tax for Ohio residents
$ 2.00 Postage and handling
Make check payable to Dawn DePew
ISBN 0-9628409-0-4

OEDER FAMILY & FRIENDS COOKBOOK
Dianna Browning
1980 Wilmington Road
Lebanon, OH 45036   513-932-2854

A delightful family cookbook spanning over five generations with nearly 600 recipes. Recipes for every "course" of meals including a "lite section" for the health conscious. Wirebound to lie flat and laminated covers to wipe clean. Includes 30 additional pages of household hints.

$10.99 Retail price
$ 2.35 Postage and handling
Make check payable to Dianna Browning

THE OHIO STATE GRANGE COOKBOOK

Ohio State Grange
1031 East Broad Street
Columbus, OH 43205-1398 614-258-9569

Submitted by Grange members from the state of Ohio—181 pages of outstanding recipes. The spiral bound cookbook was published to commemorate Ohio Grange's hosting the National Grange Convention in 1993. In addition to the many delicious recipes, there are quantity recipes, microwave recipes, equivalent chart and substitution chart.

$ 10.00 Retail price, includes tax
$ 3.00 Postage and handling
Make check payable to Ohio State Grange
ISBN 0-87197-339-1

175TH ANNIVERSARY QUILT COOKBOOK

Oak Grove Mennonite Church (WMSC)
7843 Smucker Road
Smithville, OH 44677 330-669-2697

Good recipes that call for common, inexpensive staples from a congregation nestled in the largest Amish-Mennonite community in the world. Plastic-coated cover, spiral binding, easy-to-read print. Also includes a cross-referenced index, 19 pages of homemaking hints, and 497 recipes.

$ 6.50 Retail price
$ 2.00 Postage and handling
Make check payable to Oak Grove Mennonite Church

ONE NATION UNDER SAUERKRAUT

Waynesville Area Chamber of Commerce
P. O. Box 281
Waynesville, OH 45068 513-897-8855

Whether gourmet, epicure, or feinschmecker, most every person has at some time plunged fingers or fork into a plate of sauerkraut and realized its culinary worthiness. In addition to the many recipes using sauerkraut, this Ohio Sauerkraut Festival Commemorative Edition (25 years) book tells the history of this ancient food, and gives several methods for making sauerkraut.

Please contact above for price and ordering information.

ONIONS, ONIONS, ONIONS

by Linda & Fred Griffith
Houghton Mifflin
181 Ballardvale Street
Wilmington, MA 01887   800-225-3362

Written by noted Ohio television personalities Linda and Fred Griffith, *Onions Onions Onions* is a 384-page, paperback book containing everything you could ever want to know about "the World's Favorite Secret Ingredient" including 207 delicious recipes. Winner of the James Beard Award. "A welcome addition to any food lover's library..." —Craig Claiborne, author of The New York Times Cookbook.

$ 14.95 Retail price
$ 1.50 Postage and handling
Money orders only.
ISBN 1-881527-54-9

OTTOVILLE SESQUICENTENNIAL COOKBOOK

Helen A. Devitt, Co-ordinator
Ottoville, OH

In 1995, Ottoville celebrated 150 years of the founding of this small rural community located on the Miami Erie Canal by Reverend Otto Bredick. Ottoville is identified by the 180 ft. twin steeples of the Immaculate Conception Church which was built in 1885. With predominately German ancestry, we present these 400 family recipes. Currently out of print.

OUR COLLECTION OF HEAVENLY RECIPES

Victory Christian School PTF
Cookbook Committee/Deb Williams
6759 State Route 5
Kinsman, OH 44428   330-924-2044

A smorgasbord of treasured family recipes that grace the tables of the families and friends of Victory Christian School. Ingredients used in all recipes are commonly found in stores. There are 431 recipes in 7 food sections that reflect the love of good cooking in northeast Ohio!

$ 7.00 Retail price
$ 2.00 Postage and handling
Make check payable to Victory Christian School

PLAIN & FANCY FAVORITES

Montgomery Woman's Club
P. O. Box 42114
Cincinnati, OH 45242   513-677-8568

This book is a collection of favorite recipes from the many fine cooks of the Montgomery Woman's Club. Published to coincide with the celebration of the Bicentennial of Montgomery, Ohio. In addition to 445 recipes, it contains drawings and descriptions of some of the historical buildings in the very attractive community. 356 pages, concealed wiro-binding.

$ 10.00 Retail price
$ 3.00 Postage and handling
Make check payable to Montgomery Woman's Club

THE PTA PANTRY:
Grade "A" Recipes from Fairlawn School

Fairlawn Elementary School PTA
65 North Meadowcroft Drive
Akron, OH 44313   330-873-3370

A collection of favorite recipes from Fairlawn Elementary School's multi-cultured members. Recipes traverse a broad range from easy to elegant. Illustrations are by Polly Keener, a former Fairlawn parent. She's an instructor in cartooning at the University of Akron. Our treasured recipes along with Polly's artwork make this a keepsake and a must have.

$ 10.00 Retail price
$ 1.75 Postage and handling
Make check payable to Fairlawn School PTA

RECIPE REHAB COOKBOOK

Cincinnati, OH

One hundred lower fat recipes "rehabbed" from reader-submitted high fat recipes, by registered dietitians Karen Weber, Pat Streicher and Ellen Illig, for Recipe Rehab column in *Cincinnati Enquirer*. Includes ingredient substitutions and healthy tips and hints. Convenient 3-ring binder makes it easy to add yearly recipe supplements. Currently out of print.

RECIPES AND REMEMBRANCES

Dotson Family
Lima, OH

From the Dotson Family Tree

Our 80 page cookbook is made up of tried and delicious recipes passed down from generation to generation. We trade so many recipes at our annual Thanksgiving Reunion (now numbering 92 years) that we felt it was time to make a collection in booklet form. Currently out of print.

RECIPES FROM "THE LITTLE SWITZERLAND OF OHIO"

Recipes
from
"The Little
Switzerland of Ohio"

First United Church of Christ
526 West Main Street
Sugarcreek, OH 44681   330-852-2632

Recipes from "The Little Switzerland of Ohio" contains 195 pages of Swiss/Amish family recipes. There are 12 pages of authentic Swiss recipes, including Appel Rosi, Bratzeli, and Swiss Soup. A great gift idea, with collectors especially liking the beautiful blue and white cover which features a Swiss Mural.

$ 6.00 Retail price, includes postage and handling
Make check payable to First United Church of Christ

ROBERT ROTHSCHILD RECIPES

Robert Rothschild Berry Farm, Inc.
P. O. Box 311
Urbana, OH 43078 800-356-8933

An elegant assortment of recipes utilizing gourmet food products from the Robert Rothschild product line. Robert Rothschild culinary collection features 132 recipes for appetizers, main dishes, salads, vegetables, and desserts. Recipes call for products such as preserves, mustards, vinegars, oil, salsas, dips, dressings and marinades.

$ 2.99 Retail price, includes postage and handling
Make check payable to Rothschild Berry Farm

Salem
Mennonite
Church

100th Anniversary
Cookbook
1891 - 1991

SALEM MENNONITE CHURCH 100TH ANNIVERSARY COOKBOOK
Salem W.M.S.C.
7012 Back Orrville Road
Wooster, OH 44691   330-682-8377

Comments we've heard, "Everything I've made from your cookbook is so delicious," and "the recipes usually take ingredients I already have on hand." I recommend everything in this cookbook! 190 pages of favorite recipes from past and present members of the Salem congregation.

$ 10.00 Retail price, includes postage and handling
Make check payable to Salem Mennonite W.M.S.C.

Saturday
Night
Suppers

Presented by the Women's Committee

The Cleveland Play House

SATURDAY NIGHT SUPPERS
Women's Committee Cleveland Play House
8500 Euclid Ave.
Cleveland, OH 44106   216-321-4873

These outstanding recipes, contained in a convenient three-ring binder, are used by members of the Women's Committee to prepare cast dinners at The Cleveland Play House on Saturday evenings between the afternoon and evening performances. The recipes chosen were the most popular with the actors and the easiest to prepare.

$ 15.00 Retail price
$ 3.00 Postage and handling
Make check payable to Cleveland Play House Gift Shop

SEASONED WITH LOVE
St. Joseph's Ladies Auxiliary
North Royalton, OH

Members of St. Joseph's Auxiliary and Parish shared their favorite recipes to bring together Seasoned With Love. The book consists of recipes, and the 164 pages are interspersed with engaging quotations. Other pages offer household hints which are a must for all cooks. Currently out of print.

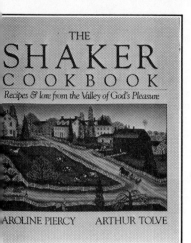

THE SHAKER COOKBOOK: Recipes & Lore from the Valley of God's Pleasure

Gabriel's Horn Publishing Co.
Bowling Green, OH

The latest revision of a classic, this 192-page book is filled with delicious, authentic recipes updated for modern convenience. In addition to the 200 recipes in this rare collection, there's abundant historical lore and many sketches from the vanished Shaker settlement where the Cleveland suburb of Shaker Heights now stands. Currently out of print.

SHARE WITH LOVE
SOMETHING OLDE AND SOMETHING NEW

Georgetown United Methodist Women
327 South Main Street
Georgetown, OH 45121   937-378-3353

The Georgetown United Methodist Women's cookbook, *Share with Love* is a history cookbook of 320 pages. It is spiral-bound allowing the book to lie flat. The cookbook contains historical sketches, photographs, interesting quips, and a time line history of Methodism since 1812 in addition to the treasured recipes of members back to 1954.

$ 9.75 Retail price
$ 3.00 Postage and handling
Make check payable to Georgetown United Methodist Women

SHARING OUR BEST

Ashland Church of God Ladies Ministries
1022 Masters Avenue
Ashland, OH 44805   419-289-9208

Our cookbook is an all-year round cookbook full of good recipes from our members and friends. The household hints are things your grandmother probably didn't know! From party foods to family-gathering fare, these recipes are sure to please, and we are pleased to share them with you.

$ 7.00 Retail price
$ 1.72 Postage and handling
Make check payable to Church of God

SHARING OUR BEST

The Elizabeth House for Assisted Living
2720 Albon Road
Maumee, OH 43537   419-865-5121

Sharing Our Best has recipes handed down for generations from some of Ohio's best cooks. All recipes are from residents of The Elizabeth House for Assisted Living and proceeds from sale of our cookbook will go towards enhancing the activities of our residents. Sharing Our Best contains 123 recipes in 69 pages.

$ 10.00 Retail price
$ 4.00 Postage and handling
Make check payable to The Elizabeth House

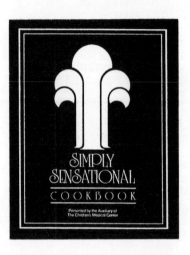

SIMPLY SENSATIONAL

TWIGS Auxiliary of the Children's Medical Center
Dayton, OH

Simply Sensational... 640 triple-tested recipes—the best of 3,000 tested... wine selection with each entré... children's section with special features on party planning... selections for every taste and occasion... tips for cooks... seven categories... 2-inch comb binding... durable 7¾ x 9½-inch beautiful hard cover in elegant black, red, and white. Currently out of print.

A SPRINKLING OF FAVORITE RECIPES

Ronald McDonald House
Youngstown, OH

This book includes favorite recipes that have been gathered by our volunteers, their families and friends, and guests of our "home." There are 164 pages and 230 recipes. Currently out of print.

ST. GERARD'S 75TH JUBILEE COOKBOOK

St. Gerard Church
240 West Robb Avenue
Lima, OH 45801   419-224-3080

A down to earth collection of recipes from the kitchens of northwest Ohio. Features 252 pages of family favorites that have been handed down for generations and some that are very contemporary. Most of the ingredients are already in your cupboards so you will be able to whip up a meal without any trouble. This is one cookbook that won't gather dust on the shelf!

$ 10.00 Retail price
$ 2.50 Postage and handling

Make check payable to St. Gerard Church

A TASTE OF COLUMBUS VOLUME III
A TASTE OF COLUMBUS VOLUME IV

by Beth and David Chilcoat
Corban Productions
P. O. Box 215
Worthington, OH 43085   614-888-1345

Each book is a compilation of "House Specialty" recipes of Central Ohio restaurants—special because of their blend of ingredients, not because of difficulty. They are, in fact, easy to prepare and to achieve elegance and excellence in every dish. Original pen and ink drawings of scenes and points of interest; recipes done in hand-printed calligraphy; 8½ x 11; comb binding.

$ 11.95 Retail price each book
$ 1.00 Postage and handling each book

Make check payable to Corban Productions
ISBN 0-9608710-2-0 / 0-9608710-3-9

A TASTE OF TORONTO—OHIO, THAT IS

The Toronto High School Alumni Association
P. O. Box 273
Toronto, OH 43964   740-537-9114

A Taste of Toronto—Ohio, That Is presents a taste of culinary history as well as a taste of current favorite recipes. The towns along the upper Ohio Valley are gold mines of ethnicity and some of that knowledge is preserved in the 360-page book filled with favorite recipes everyone can enjoy. It is truly a "Gem" of a cookbook!

$ 14.95 Retail price
$ 2.75 Postage and handling

Make check payable to Toronto High School Alumni Assn.
ISBN 0-9643221-1-0

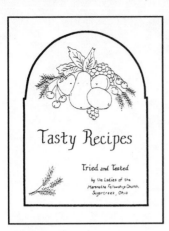

TASTY RECIPES

Maranatha Fellowship Church
641 Hickory Drive Southwest
Sugarcreek, OH 44681 330-852-4934

Tasty Recipes for good country cooking that have been tested and tried. Contains 11 different categories with 550 recipes in 227 pages. A section of "Large Quantity Recipes" are easy to prepare for large group cooking. Contents include recipes for canning and freezing. A taste of Holmes County hospitality and good cooking.

$ 12.50 Retail Price, including postage

Make check payable to Mrs. Clara Troyer

TOUCHES OF THE HANDS AND HEART

by Karen A. Maag
Columbus Grove, OH

A combination of the author's creations and recipes handed down from mothers and grandmothers of family and friends. The 200-page cookbook is mingled with quotes and stories about some of the 390 recipes. Whimsical angels begin each category, and on the last page, there is a caricature of the author. Currently out of print.

TREASURED RECIPES

Trinity United Methodist Church
Delphos, OH

This beautiful, laminated hard-cover cookbook features 800 recipes right from the "Heartland of Ohio," famous for its Buckeye trees. This spiral bound book opens easily and lies flat. It includes a special "Heart Smart" category. Concise directions are printed on heavy-duty paper. A great collection of our best recipes. 376 pages. Complete index. Currently out of print. Currently out of print.

TREASURED RECIPES FROM MASON, OHIO

Treasured Recipes
from
Mason, Ohio

Mason Historical Society

Mason Historical Society
P. O. Box 82
Mason, OH 45040   513-398-6583

We are very proud of our "delicious" cookbook. There are 87 pages, 288 recipes, seven different food sections, and 15 sketches of local buildings all drawn by local artists. The recipes are all favorites of our families around town. Getting the cookbook together was a fun time, getting a lot of people involved in a project so interesting to everyone.

$ 10.00 Retail price
$ 1.24 Postage and handling
Make check payable to Mason Historical Society

TREASURES & PLEASURES

Shawnee United Methodist Church
Lima, OH

A collection of talents, memories, inspirations, photographs, time-tasted recipes and award winning favorites all wrapped up within an award-winning cover. Imaginations are stretched to initiate chapters such as A Slice of Life, Children's Corner, etc. The index is a guide to culinary pleasure. More than a cookbook; it is a treasury book! Currently out of print.

TRIED & TRUE BY MOTHERS OF 2'S

Tried & True
by Mothers of 2's

Westshore Mothers Of Twins Club
1995-1996

Westshore Mothers of Twins Club
c/o Deby Konant
1802 Donna Drive
Westlake, OH 44145   440-835-4319

Westshore Mothers of Twins Club put together this collection of 400 recipes. *Tried and True by Mothers of 2's* has 177 pages of recipes within 14 categories. Most of the recipes in this book were selected with the thought of ease and kid accepted, although others were just too good to resist!

$ 8.00 Retail price
$ 3.00 Postage and handling
Make check payable to Westshore Mothers of Twins Club

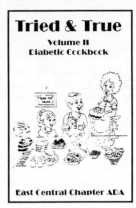

Tried & True
Volume II
Diabetic Cookbook

East Central Chapter ADA

TRIED & TRUE VOLUME II
Diabetic Cookbook
East Central Chapter-American Diabetes Association
Newark, OH

This book was written as a follow-up to Volume I. The need for a diabetic cookbook that was affordable was in demand in our area. It was also designed as a fund raiser for our chapter. We have had great success selling the book, as we have a statewide network. Not only for the person with diabetes, these 200 recipes are for the family looking for a healthier way of eating. Currently out of print.

TummYummies
1992
Supplement

TUMM YUMMIES
Y-Wives
180 Summit Street
Tiffin, OH 44883

Consists of 8 chapters plus an index. One hundred thirty-four pages filled with recipes from some of the best known cooks in the area. Buyers of the first book are constantly asking us to publish a second edition!

$ 7.00 Retail price
$ 3.00 Postage and handling
Make check payable to Y-Wives

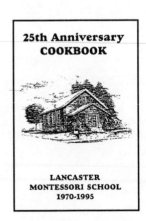

25th Anniversary
COOKBOOK

LANCASTER
MONTESSORI SCHOOL
1970-1995

25TH ANNIVERSARY COOKBOOK
Lancaster Montessori School
1111 West Fair Avenue
Lancaster, OH 43130   740-687-0592

This cookbook is a collection of over 200 favorite recipes of the many families who have been associated with Lancaster Montessori School since 1970. 94 pages.

$ 2.00 Retail price
$ 2.00 Postage and handling
Make check payable to Lancaster Montessori School

VIVA ITALIA

Maria Volpe Paganini
11340 Saddlewood Lane
Concord, OH 44077   440-352-8014

Viva Italia, was conceived by an instructor of Italian cooking after visiting Italy for many months. It covers food dishes and techniques drawn from all the provinces of Italy. In it the reader will find a full range of dishes from appetizers to desserts, sprinkled with art, history and folklore.

$ 19.95 Retail price
$ 3.00 Postage and handling
Make check payable to Viva Italia

WADSWORTH-RITTMAN HOSPITAL COOKBOOK: 75th Anniversary Edition

Wadsworth-Rittman Hospital
Wadsworth, OH

The Wadsworth-Rittman Hospital Cookbook (75th Anniversary Edition) contains 220 pages of recipes. Miscellaneous kitchen hints, caloric tables, alphabetic index, and free manufacturer coupons are also included. Each recipe is followed by a nutritional analysis including calories per serving, carbohydrates, fat, and protein content. The book is being sponsored thru the hospital auxiliary, and proceeds go to the hospital for equipment. Currently out of print.

WHAT'S COOKING AT HOLDEN SCHOOL

Holden School Association
132 West School Street
Kent, OH 44240   330-673-6737

Our cookbook was compiled of recipes from parents, teachers and friends of Holden Elementary School. Our recipes feature a culturally diverse background of individuals who are connected to the school. Holden School is in Kent, Ohio, home of Kent State University. Our cookbook has 85 pages with numerous, helpful cooking tables and kitchen hints. We also feature a kids' section by teachers.

$ 6.00 Retail price
$ 3.00 Postage and handling
Make check payable to Holden School Association

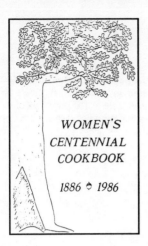

WOMEN'S
CENTENNIAL
COOKBOOK

1886 ◊ 1986

WOMEN'S CENTENNIAL COOKBOOK

Oak Chapel United Methodist Women
c/o Bernice S. Walters
143 N. Jefferson Road
Wooster, OH 44691-3209

Exciting recipes with just enough added zest of our church history to make our cookbook a must from the agricultural heartland of beautiful Ohio. 150 pages from appetizers to pickles, yes, candy too and everything in between we all love, from no cooking to microwave. Acorn denotes super recipes from our previous cookbooks.

$ 5.00 Retail price
$ 3.00 Postage and handling
Make check payable to Oak Chapel United Methodist Women

Special Discount Offers!

The Best of the Month Club

Experience the taste of our nation, one state at a time!

Individuals may purchase BEST OF THE BEST STATE COOKBOOKS on a monthly (or bi-monthly) basis by joining the **Best of the Month Club**. Best of the Month Club members enjoy a 20% discount off the list price of each book. Individuals who already own certain state cookbooks may specify which new states they wish to receive. No minimum purchase is required; individuals may cancel at any time. For more information on this purchasing option, call 1-800-343-1583.

Special Discount

The entire 41-volume BEST OF THE BEST STATE COOKBOOK SERIES can be purchased for $521.21, a 25% discount off the total individual price of $694.95.

Individual BEST cookbooks can be purchased for $16.95 per copy plus $4.00 shipping for any number of cookbooks ordered. See order form on next page.

Join today! 1-800-343-1583

Speak directly to one of our friendly customer service representatives, or visit our website at **www.quailridge.com** to order online.

Recipe Hall of Fame Collection

The extensive recipe database of Quail Ridge Press' acclaimed BEST OF THE BEST STATE COOKBOOK SERIES is the inspiration behind the RECIPE HALL OF FAME COLLECTION. These HALL OF FAME recipes have achieved extra distinction for consistently producing superb dishes. *The Recipe Hall of Fame Cookbook* features over 400 choice dishes for a variety of meals. The *Recipe Hall of Fame Dessert Cookbook* consists entirely of extraordinary desserts. The *Recipe Hall of Fame Quick & Easy Cookbook* contains over 500 recipes that require minimum effort but produce maximum enjoyment. *The Recipe Hall of Fame Cookbook II* brings you more of the family favorites you've come to expect with over 400 all-new, easy-to-follow recipes. Appetizers to desserts, quick dishes to masterpiece presentations, the RECIPE HALL OF FAME COLLECTION has it all.

All books: Paperbound • 7x10 • Illustrations • Index
The Recipe Hall of Fame Cookbook • 304 pages • $19.95
Recipe Hall of Fame Dessert Cookbook • 240 pages • $16.95
Recipe Hall of Fame Quick & Easy Cookbook • 304 pages • $19.95
The Recipe Hall of Fame Cookbook II • 304 pages • $19.95

NOTE: The four HALL OF FAME cookbooks can be ordered individually at the price noted above or can be purchased as a four-cookbook set for $40.00, almost a 50% discount off the total list price of $76.80. Over 1,600 incredible HALL OF FAME recipes for about three cents each—an amazing value!

Best of the Best State Cookbook Series

**Best of the Best from
ALABAMA**
288 pages, $16.95

**Best of the Best from
ALASKA**
288 pages, $16.95

**Best of the Best from
ARIZONA**
288 pages, $16.95

**Best of the Best from
ARKANSAS**
288 pages, $16.95

**Best of the Best from
BIG SKY**
Montana and Wyoming
288 pages, $16.95

**Best of the Best from
CALIFORNIA**
384 pages, $16.95

**Best of the Best from
COLORADO**
288 pages, $16.95

**Best of the Best from
FLORIDA**
288 pages, $16.95

**Best of the Best from
GEORGIA**
336 pages, $16.95

**Best of the Best from the
GREAT PLAINS**
North and South Dakota,
Nebraska, and Kansas
288 pages, $16.95

**Best of the Best from
HAWAI'I**
288 pages, $16.95

**Best of the Best from
IDAHO**
288 pages, $16.95

**Best of the Best from
ILLINOIS**
288 pages, $16.95

**Best of the Best from
INDIANA**
288 pages, $16.95

**Best of the Best from
IOWA**
288 pages, $16.95

**Best of the Best from
KENTUCKY**
288 pages, $16.95

**Best of the Best from
LOUISIANA**
288 pages, $16.95

**Best of the Best from
LOUISIANA II**
288 pages, $16.95

**Best of the Best from
MICHIGAN**
288 pages, $16.95

**Best of the Best from the
MID-ATLANTIC**
Maryland, Delaware, New
Jersey, and Washington, D.C.
288 pages, $16.95

**Best of the Best from
MINNESOTA**
288 pages, $16.95

**Best of the Best from
MISSISSIPPI**
288 pages, $16.95

**Best of the Best from
MISSOURI**
304 pages, $16.95

**Best of the Best from
NEVADA**
288 pages, $16.95

**Best of the Best from
NEW ENGLAND**
Rhode Island, Connecticut,
Massachusetts, Vermont,
New Hampshire, and Maine
368 pages, $16.95

**Best of the Best from
NEW MEXICO**
288 pages, $16.95

**Best of the Best from
NEW YORK**
288 pages, $16.95

**Best of the Best from
NO. CAROLINA**
288 pages, $16.95

**Best of the Best from
OHIO**
352 pages, $16.95

**Best of the Best from
OKLAHOMA**
288 pages, $16.95

**Best of the Best from
OREGON**
288 pages, $16.95

**Best of the Best from
PENNSYLVANIA**
320 pages, $16.95

**Best of the Best from
SO. CAROLINA**
288 pages, $16.95

**Best of the Best from
TENNESSEE**
288 pages, $16.95

**Best of the Best from
TEXAS**
352 pages, $16.95

**Best of the Best from
TEXAS II**
352 pages, $16.95

**Best of the Best from
UTAH**
288 pages, $16.95

**Best of the Best from
VIRGINIA**
320 pages, $16.95

**Best of the Best from
WASHINGTON**
288 pages, $16.95

**Best of the Best from
WEST VIRGINIA**
288 pages, $16.95

**Best of the Best from
WISCONSIN**
288 pages, $16.95

All cookbooks are 6x9 inches, ringbound, contain photographs, illustrations and index.

Special discount offers available! *(See previous page for details.)*

To order by credit card, call toll-free **1-800-343-1583** or visit our website at **www.quailridge.com.**
Use the form below to send check or money order.

Call 1-800-343-1583 or email info@quailridge.com *to request a free catalog of all of our publications.*

Order form

Use this form for sending check or money order to:
QUAIL RIDGE PRESS • P. O. Box 123 • Brandon, MS 39043

❑ Check enclosed

Charge to: ❑ Visa ❑ MC ❑ AmEx ❑ Disc

Card # _____

Expiration Date _____

Signature _____

Name _____

Address _____

City/State/Zip _____

Phone # _____

Email Address _____

Qty.	Title of Book (State) or Set	Total

Subtotal _____

7% Tax for MS residents _____

Postage ($4.00 any number of books) + 4.00

Total _____